A BIOGRAPHY IN NINE LIVES
MAYO

DECLAN VARLEY

HERO BOOKS

PUBLISHED BY HERO BOOKS
LUCAN
CO. DUBLIN
IRELAND

Hero Books is an imprint of Umbrella Publishing
First Published 2023

9781910827734

Cover design and formatting: jessica@viitaladesign.com
Photographs: Sportsfile

★ DEDICATION ★

This book is dedicated to the late Tony Finnerty of Ballinrobe,
and to all of the green and red supporters who have followed
the cause and kept the faith

★ CONTENTS ★

★ ACKNOWLEDGEMENTS ★

MAYO MUST HAVE per capita the highest number of talented sportswriters in the country – I have to acknowledge the work that they have done over the century and how grateful I am to have leaned on their words. How many hot days and cold nights they have scribbled on short-hand filled notebooks with complicated intricate score-keeping and wide-keeping statistics. They are too numerous to mention, but they know who they are. If I list them, I will surely omit.

To the local newspapers, who act as the heartbeat of their communities in Mayo; in particular the teams at *The Mayo News*, *The Connaught Telegraph*, the *Western People* and the *Mayo Advertiser*, I also enjoyed looking back at the pages of the now-demised *Western Journal*. Its arrival in my childhood was riveting. To the sportswriters at the *Irish Independent*, the *Examiner* and *The Irish Times*, thank you for the words that painted pictures.

I would like, in particular, to thank James Laffey, Terry Reilly, Ivan Neill and Keith Duggan for the context their books on Mayo have given to the Mayo century, and how they have each in a variety of works, encapsulated the emotion and excitement of the odyssey that is following Mayo. To my former colleague Tom Gilmore for his help in recreating that night in Lavally, when the Dubs were finally felled.

To Bernard O'Hara, my dear friend, whose lifelong affection for all things Mayo has kept alive a culture across the west.

To the Mayo players, and their families and friends, who spoke to me for this book and who gave me a sense of what it was like from their point of view, my heartfelt thanks.

To the Mayo supporters whose enthusiasm remains undimmed. Their curation of Ireland's most regarded sporting odyssey is to be admired.

And most of all, I would like to thank my wife, Bernadette Prendergast and my daughter, Giselle for the time I have stolen away to work on this project. Giselle had an early introduction to Mayo mania when she visited Santa Claus at Westport House a decade or so ago, and told Santa that her dad was from Ballinrobe.

'Huh, Ballinrobe. I see Donie Vaughan has gone to Castlebar… looking for a handy county medal no doubt,' he remarked.

Mayo football is obviously box office too at the North Pole.

Thanks for reading, folks.

Declan Varley
August 2023

Dublin captain, Stephen Cluxton lifts the Sam Maguire Cup in an empty Croke Park six days before Christmas 2020.

The Mayo team and management watch Cluxton receive Sam in the loneliest Croke Park of their lives. Cardboard supporters, drawn by Mayo and Dublin schoolchildren, watch from the Hogan Stand as one more agonising loss transpires.

★ INTRODUCTION ★

OUTLASTING A REIGN

NO SOONER HAD Queen Elizabeth II passed away at Balmoral but the memes commenced. With the world marking the longevity of her reign, the manner in which her empire had changed, and the world over which she governed had transformed, the slagging started on social media.

'Imagine being the longest reigning monarch ever, and never seeing Mayo win an All-Ireland,' the cynics jibed. While they may have been strictly correct that she never saw Mayo win an All-Ireland title, on the day when she became Queen, the team from the west were already All-Ireland champions, enjoying the second of their successive victories at the start of a barren period that has stretched past seven decades. When she ascended to the throne in February 1952, only six months had passed since that Mayo team had reigned supreme in Croke Park. On that day, with a world of possibilities in front of her, there was no way she could have foreseen the longevity of her reign and the momentous changes that would follow suit.

On that day too, there was little to suggest that an all-conquering Mayo team, who would soon be embarking on an historic quest for three in-a-row, would not taste success again, not just for that decade, but for at least six more after it, stretching well into the next century. To put it into context, imagine if you were told tomorrow that the Dublin team that won the All-Ireland final in 2023 would not win another until 2094. You would never believe it, but that is the span of barren-ness that Mayo fans have had to endure, so far.

THERE IS NO potential victory for any county that fascinates as much as a Mayo victory. A footballing superpower, the annual quest for glory is one that excites neutrals, and gives the fanatical fanbase a full summer. The affection for them, for the beauty of their play, has often stretched into sympathy, and perhaps there is nothing more irking to a Mayo fan than receiving the sympathy of a supporter from a county that never reaches the business end of the championship.

Much has been made of the famed curse, which is a complete nonsense as we shall see later in this book. But what is without doubt is the fact that Mayo's quest the fact that Mayo's quest for multiple All-Ireland wins has foundered on poor fortune, poor decision making, the issue of facing some of the greatest sides of their respective eras, and then on some occasions, when the only luck that they had was *bad* luck. What is also fascinating is that many of the issues that impacted on the great Mayo teams of the current era are the same that bothered them at many times over the last eventful century of competitive action. What would the fanatical Mayo fans be like if success had come along more frequently in that epoch? If the odd title was picked up one in every two decades even?

Right from when they faced off against a wonderful Wexford side in the aftermath of The Rising. In the 60s, when they reputedly went toe to toe with one of the greatest sides of all team, their old neighbours, Galway, who managed to achieve that elusive hat-trick of successive titles. In the 70s and 80s, there was hope, but also great tragedy that held them back, but if truth be told, that era belonged to the great Dublin and Kerry sides who swept all before them. The 80s brought some hope right at the end, when a victory was in sight, but as was Mayo's wont on more than one occasion, they managed to snatch defeat from the jaws of victory.

So, what has prompted me to pen this document of a journey? To paraphrase Linda Martin, why me? Why is there a need to remind myself of this century of misfortune? Surely, there are less frustrating aspects of life with which I could surround myself. But, no, it sort of found me.

There were a few symmetries that linked me to this – I had gone to the same school as the first man to lift Sam Maguire in a Mayo shirt; and those same shirts were stitched and weaved about four streets away from my own house in Ballinrobe.

But that's not enough.

Fast forward to the pandemic winter of 2020, to a time when everything changed. When nothing was immune to being moved around. A country that was in real fear. A death toll that was shocking. The news routine of a newspaper journalist mounted to little more than documenting the trauma of a world in shock. For the first time in my career, the whole world's media were covering the exact same story, every hour, every day. The news agenda focused around the search for immunity but in reality, the whole world was immune from being in control of its destiny. Nothing was too sacred to be cancelled or amended or reshaped unrecognisably. We lived in a state of flux, deprived of the routine of normal life as we had known it.

And such was the case with that year's All-Ireland series. The dry sod of summer pitches eschewed in favour of seeing out some sort of competition that winter. The national psyche needed the distraction, a cause to chase.

Something to keep people indoors, something to watch while a little watermark at the top right of the screen said **Stay Abhaile – Stay home**.

It was a time too when we were acutely conscious of the trauma Ireland had suffered a century before, and there was poignancy in the stunning coincidence that the last four teams in 2020 matched the quartet who fought out the 1920 semi-finals. The semi-finals held a century after Bloody Sunday saw Mayo defeat Tipperary in a foggy misty and silent Croke Park. The final, played in front of a record-small crowd in a stadium where every call reverberated across the vast empty stands, where every score was marked not by cacophonous crowds, but by the sharp blast of a whistle and the congratulatory remarks of teammates.

Mayo set records that evening too, conceding the earliest goal in an All-Ireland final… when Dublin scored direct from the opening throw-in. Mayo had form with early capitulation, but to be fair, they rallied in this game and with 20 minutes left were on equal terms; however, they failed to find the goals they needed to stop Dublin from registering a sixth All-Ireland on the trot.

Perhaps of all the finals, that was one of the most depressing; not just for the match and the result, but for the ambient atmosphere in which it was played. A foggy dark night, with every play-call and instruction audible throughout the vast emptiness of Croke Park. The place never felt more empty. The official attendance was zero, and apart from the players and backroom team (and three lads hidden in a Mayo kit van) there were fewer than 100 media in the ground.

Afterwards, shepherded from the stadium by dutiful stewards, I walked with colleagues to the car park behind the Canal End, and the realisation hit me that I had become a member of an elite club who had seen every All-Ireland final that Mayo had played in, and drawn or lost, since that day in 1951.

The surreal Saturday night drive through the empty streets of the city, which looked to have been cleared for some apocalyptic movie scene did nothing to change the mood. With every kilometre driven, there was a sense that this was a very new way of living and that life may never go back to how it was.

And yet, in the depth of such thoughts, one thought surfaced: would there be a chance now for a Mayo team to win Sam?

ALTHOUGH I WAS only born in the 1960s, I had been to every decider that Mayo had drawn or lost since, an honour shared by many diehard green and red supporters, but the 2020 final put me in an elite club. With just a handful of media allowed into the ground that evening because of Covid restrictions, I was one of maybe four or five Mayo people who had been granted the privilege.

Whatever joys and torments we Mayo fans had encountered seeing our team in person in those finals, one extra notch was added to mine. It was as if I was the carrier of a flame of hope. A member of a unique club who had the misfortune to witness at first hand each of Mayo's final disappointments. It felt almost obligatory for me to come forth and retell the feelings of that depressingly awful night.

It is a distinction that has no doubt affected me, as it has every Mayo fan. Every year, my summer plans are drawn up based on the dates of key matches involving the Green and Red. The wonder *If this will be the year?*

In each of the thrilling finals I had a clear idea of how I would feel after each near miss, every crushing disappointment. I had a mood for every result, bar one.

How would I cope if we won? Would I burst into tears? Is there a unique emotion that we have reserved for that day of glory? As a young man, in the 80s, I would have undoubtedly run onto the pitch and hugged every sweated shirt; as a working reporter, I would have had to restrain my emotions (or maybe John Healy-like, I would have yelped with delight), and in the last decade, as you fear that the chances of seeing success go past quickly every year, you leave all your options open.

I had known every sort of Mayo final result going, bar victory. Last minute points, own goals, balls bouncing over the bar… brawls, maulings… annihilation. Everything but victory. In each final with about 20 minutes left, I would think of that.

How I would compose myself or not?

But unfortunately, in all cases, the decision was made easier for me. I remember against Meath in the first game in 1996, I sat there thinking. *Is it going to happen? Are we on the verge of doing something unbelievable as time seemed to crawl?*

But then the ball bounced.

Such setbacks undoubtedly have an impact on your psyche. They send you out on the road a glass half-full type of lad. And then the agreeable, decent loser taking unnecessary and unwanted sympathies from well-wishers after every sad loss.

So, in this book, I want to bring you on a journey through the story of a county that just wants its day in the sun. I want all Mayo fans to know why it is that we are the way we are. Where did this pride and passion come from, and what would life be like if we had to exist without it? Are we defined by it?

There is no need to feel sorry for us, because what matters to us is that we matter when it comes to the big days, and more often than not, we matter. And now, as I reach an age where it is a distinct possibility that I may never see that day of glory, I want to understand why it matters so much to so many like myself.

This story of the Mayo pursuit for glory is wrapped around the lives and contributions of nine men who played a key role in passing on the batons of determination, pride and commitment. Around these stories, I wrap the tale of how our love affair with Mayo football has been shaped by time and circumstance. What is it about us Mayo people that we feel life will not be fulfilled unless one day we score more in a final than our opponents? Will it bring the happiness we expect or will life thereafter seem dull and pointless?

Will it bring to an end a dream that has walked with us for decades?

And so, as I left Croke Park on that cold foggy, frosty night in 2020, my mind went back to the exact same day, 104 years earlier when Mayo's first love affair with the pursuit of an All-Ireland title was ignited in that same patch of land in Dublin's Northside.

*The President of Ireland Michael D Higgins places a wreath in Croke Park in 2020
during the GAA Bloody Sunday Commemoration. One hundred years earlier, on Sunday
November 21, 1920, an attack by Britain's Crown Forces on the attendees at a football
match between Dublin and Tipperary during the Irish War of Independence resulted
in 14 people being murdered. Along with the 13 supporters that lost their lives that day
a Tipperary footballer, Michael Hogan, also died. The War of Independence and the
Civil War left the country, and the GAA as an organisation, in turmoil. Legendary actor,
Brendan Gleeson honoured the dead with his words.*

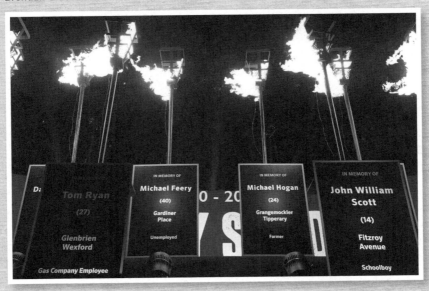

★ PROLOGUE ★

ICE COLD IN THE CAPITAL

A MISTY COLD haze hung over the capital. Straight lines of smoke rose from the chimneys, hanging there in the sharp cold air. The cobbled paths covered with ice were treacherous. It had been an eventful year, a sense of trauma hung like a cloud inside everyone's mind, but in the recent days, the conversation had changed from The Rising and fallen on the weather. Frost hung on the windows, and the bustling city was grinding to a standstill as people stayed indoors as much as they could. A year they wanted to see the end of was concluding with a bite and the coldest weather the city had seen for more than a generation.

The afternoon winter sun tried to burn its way through the haze and the smoke, and offered some respite from the gloom, but the melt was slow. More than a hundred people turned up at the infirmary with broken limbs and gashed heads suffered from falls on the unforgiving footpaths. Out in the west of the city, the patients of the Peamount Sanatorium put on heavy overjackets and ventured out for the fresh air.

Out here, away from the city centre, there was respite from the fumes and smog that attacked their lungs. If there was one thing that could be said for the big freeze, it was that the air seemed pure and cutting, and brought ease to them, as if its sharpness attacked the bug that drove it. The sanatorium had been established in 1912 by the Women's National Health Association as a place of convalescence for those with TB and other respiratory diseases which were prevalent and dangerous. It was occupied by patients who were not necessarily bed-ridden, but who needed care to recover from dreadful consumptive diseases.

SOME 300 METRES from the grounds of the sanatorium, in a place known as Burns' Quarry, a pond was frozen thick, the glistening ice strong; firm to the weight at the edges and as you moved further out. The patients slid on it, laughed like children at the wonder of it, inhaled the sheer white beauty of it. You could sense the sterility of it hacking away at their infections, the icy weather to kill a big myth in their brains. More and more of the men edged along it with a sense of unease and caution; three of them broke away and skated slowly in a different direction. It was a joyous scene, a rare moment of pleasure away from the confines of the dark depressing wards inside.

The three men, James Lynn, Michael Cannon and Johnny Flaherty revelled in the freedom, and moved towards each other with some renewed hope that perhaps there would be days like this again for them, days when they could run like children and not be burdened by illness. As they met mid-ice, they embraced initially for support and then latterly for camaraderie, but as they did, the combined weight in the one space fractured the ice.

In a scene of horrific beauty, cracks emerged from a centre. Like a lightning bolt, the lines shot along outwards. For a split second they realised what was happening, and almost instantly, the three men disappeared through the large hole that opened in the ice and plunged into 14 feet of freezing water.

They didn't have time to shout out, but the screams went out from the others who dashed over to try to help. However, as they approached, the cavernous hole opened further and five more plunged in. Pandemonium ensued, as needed coats were taken off and tied together and used as a rope to pull to safety whoever had not gone under the ice, but many had and those not killed instantly by the shock had the horrific experience of struggling to reach a surface in places where the ice had not splintered, their flailing hands visible through and pressed up against the unwielding ice.

News of the event went across the city like wildfire and those who could help made their way to the scene. Boatmen with sledge hammers and axes hacked at the ice to allow the pond to be dragged. By midnight, all the bodies were recovered.

The last of them was Johnny Flaherty whose watch was found in his pocket. It was stopped at 7pm.

The 24-year-old was the eldest of the three who had perished.

★ ★ ★ ★ ★

IT WAS INTO these conditions, with the city under siege to the weather, that Mayo were to play in the first of their many All-Ireland finals. Under normal circumstances, the weather and its casualties would have led to a cancellation of any planned events, but 1916 was not a year that could ever be classed as normal. A legacy of death and trauma hung in the air. The abnormal was the normal and there was still a fascination and legacy of the events of the previous Easter.

The staging of the game in such conditions came at the end of a traumatic year for the country and for sporting organisations. It did not help that the official Commission of Inquiry ordered by Dublin Castle into the April Rebellion identified the GAA as a contributory factor in its outbreak. This conclusion was one that the GAA leadership refuted, their cool-headed pragmatism leading them not only into a denial of any involvement in The Rising, but to openly enter into negotiations with the British authorities to fend off threats to their sporting operations and their ability to hold competitions and events such as the All-Ireland final.

Even for this game and before the impact of the weather, the legacy of The Rising was threatening the viability of the competition, with attendances tumbling and revenues slim.

What the GAA sought to secure as priorities was an exemption from a new entertainment tax to be levied on sporting and recreational bodies across Britain and Ireland, and an end to the curtailment of special train services to GAA matches.

If the actions of the GAA emphasised the primacy of play, those of the British authorities – in London and Dublin – laid stress on law and order, and on the monitoring and the suppression of anything, or anyone, who might undermine it. Towards that end, in the months after The Rising, police reports tumbled into Dublin Castle evaluating the political temperature in each county and detailing the strength of the social, cultural and political groupings within.

Reports from Mayo in the summer of 1916 revealed a county in a 'peaceable' condition and with, amongst other things, a thriving GAA community: the county was said to have boasted 18 clubs with just over 1,000 members. The strongest of these clubs was Ballina Stephenites. Founded in 1888, they had dominated the local Mayo scene since the turn of the 20th century, and spent years scorching all Connacht opposition at a time when champion clubs also served as county representatives in provincial and All-Ireland competitions. In 1908 they even secured national honours when defeating Kerry in a Croke Memorial Cup final.

It was into this traumatic environment that Mayo footballers got to play the first of their many All-Ireland finals, kick-starting a love affair with the competition that was as intense and strong over a century later.

And then, just as now, there was drama and distraction in the build up to their maiden All-Ireland final. Even en route to the match, there were issues that were less than ideal, given they were facing the strong and fancied Wexford team.

FOR MANY OF the players, this was their first experience of Dublin since the dramatic events of the previous Easter and there was a curiosity among the squad. Full-back Jack Waldron from Ballyhaunis, recalled years later that he was more interested in seeing the impact of the failed Rising than he was in the outcome of the game.

'I was more interested in seeing the GPO when we travelled to Dublin than in the game itself. When I got a chance, I crawled through the barbed wire entanglements and had a look at it,' he said.

His diversion was not the only unorthodox incident among his teammates. The aforementioned treacherous underfoot conditions in the city centre saw several of the team slip and slide en route to Croke Park. They togged out in Fleming's Hotel at Broadstone Station (now Busaras) and walked to Croke Park. However, as they navigated the banks of the canal at one end of the pitch, goalkeeper Padraig Loftus slipped into the water and had to be 'hauled out with a crooked stick'.

However, the Ballina man lost his signature 'hard hat', which he apparently wore both on and off the field, and insisted on it being fished out of the canal before the team members continued on their faltering way. 'Folk would use that route as a shortcut from Phibsborough where there were many Mayo folk in digs,' his nephew Paddy Loftus said a few years ago. Loftus had not conceded a goal in that year's championship, but it is said the quality of the three Wexford goals in the final were superb. A fine man with a chiselled visage, he had impressed all that year.

He may have featured for the team for many seasons, but within a year he was dead. Padraig was playing a rugby match when he was trip-tackled. The resultant fall onto the hard ball resulted in internal injuries to his liver from which he never recovered.

Inside Croke Park, conditions were equally treacherous. The pitch had frozen overnight and was rock hard on the morning of the match. However, both captains agreed that the match should be played. Across the channel, most of the English Football League programme had fallen foul to the cold snap which had left pitches unplayable right across the land.

In the end, only 3,000 turned up for the game, a tenth of the previous year's attendance; the worst attendance of any All-Ireland final in 15 years, partly because of the conditions, but also because special trains to and from the capital were curtailed due to the imposition of martial law after the Easter Rising. The eventual crowd gathered and huddled together in the cold expanse of the stadium, awaiting the throw-in.

The *Freeman's Journal* newspaper remarked that many were deterred from travelling to the game *'owing to the prevailing conditions'*. This was not a reference to the dramatic events of the previous Easter, but rather the horrendous weather in which the final was contested.

The *Irish Independent*, in clippings available in the GAA museum, reported that the final was notable, not for any drama, but for its tameness and the relative ease with which the Wexford side consigned Mayo to the first of many All-Ireland final defeats.

'The All-Ireland Championship football final was played in Croke Park yesterday before about 3,000 people and Wexford won easily over Mayo, who in their first final, gave a creditable display. It was a remarkable final in its tameness. Frost was everywhere around, and we doubt if any match has been played under such wintry conditions as

prevailed. It was this principally that was responsible for the lack of enthusiasm – which is the chief characteristic for a final. It seriously affected the attendance. Instead of 3,000 there should have been at least five times that number, and even then, it is doubtful if the struggle would have generated much enthusiasm.

'The players, who did their best, deserve credit for one and all, for turning out on such a pitch, for only in portions could they obtain firm foothold. The good football we saw was in rare patches and most of the work was necessarily fluky. The Wexford captain who criticised the decision to play the match on such a poor surface, gave every credit to Mayo and said that he would feel more satisfied when they met on a fitter ground as they were a fast-improving lot of footballers. Tribute was also paid to the Mayo team by the chair of the Wexford County Board who said that they were good footballers to play against and took their defeat like sportsmen.'

ALTHOUGH THAT WAS an era pre-hype, it can be said that the defeat did not register as calamitous by the Mayo players. Indeed, there was not any major post-mortem or gnashing of teeth within the county.

After all, the times that were in it, priorities would have been far removed from winning an All-Ireland, at a time when the rest of the country had a different sort of All-Ireland dream. On the night of the match, many of the players thawed out their chilled feet, washed and brylcreamed the hair and found surer underfoot conditions on the famed dance floor at Conarchy's Hotel in the heart of Parnell Square where they partied until dawn with the victorious Wexford players.

Captain Frank Courell, who had impressed in the defeat in the final said that their expectations were not dashed because they had come without any. 'We had never come to Dublin with any real idea of beating Wexford. We told ourselves that we would fight every inch of that ground and go down gamely. We Connacht men are proud of the fact that we entered the final for the first time and we are not a bit downhearted on our defeat by such a splendid side.'

It had already been a dramatic year for this Mayo side. Bolstered by members of the Ballina Stephenites side which had won the Croke Cup twice in the previous decade, they were not lacking in confidence. This bravado was to cost them in the 1916 Wolfe Tone final, one of two played that year. One in Croke Park, the other in Frongoch in Wales which was housing many of those who had been imprisoned for their activities in the failed Rising earlier that year.

Having qualified to play Louth in the home final, left half-back Joseph Lydon dismissed their north eastern opponents' hope saying 'We will have nawthing to bate in that final'. His words came back to haunt him, because the Louth men, obviously stung by his words, stormed to a comprehensive eight-point victory.

Undaunted, Mayo gathered their spirits and qualified for the All-Ireland semi-final by reasserting their superiority in the west, beating Roscommon by five points in the Connacht final, before facing Cork in the November All-Ireland semi-final. The Roscommon match though should have signalled some red flags about the harmony within the squad. Seven of those who were selected for the match failed to turn up – and two of those who did, refused to tog out.

That game was slated for Athlone, a sort of half-way house for both sides, as travel was extremely difficult in the conditions that prevailed that year. Mayo were clearly the better side, winning 1-2 to 0-2, but the result was overturned when it emerged that Mayo full-back Barney Durkan, a Bohola-native schoolteacher who worked in Cork, had turned out in the Cork club championship. There was outrage when Durkan, a member of Ballina Stephenites, was banned and Cork were offered a bye into the final. However, in an unusual degree of magnanimity, the Cork County Board was convinced that a replay would be a fairer outcome, and so the game was scheduled for Croke Park on November 19.

On that day too, weather hampered the conditions at Croke Park with gale force winds bringing down trees and causing floods across the country. Consequently, only 900 hardy souls made it to the match. The Dublin pitch resembled a quagmire and the areas in front of both goals had small ponds of water which made attractive football impossible. As a result, the match was a close fought affair with just five scores, with Mayo prevailing on a scoreline of 1-2 to 1-1.

In a sense, despite the inconvenience of having to play an additional match, it did not do them any harm. Indeed, it was the consensus that they needed all the minutes they could get, especially if they were to make any impact on the showpiece match of the year. Much as was the case a century later when Mayo sides faced the record-breaking all-conquering Dublin sides and pushed them all the way, the Wexford side that Mayo were to face in their first All-Ireland final was being hailed as the best ever proponents of the game. Even the chair of the Mayo County Board, Padraig McManus said he was impressed by them, labelling them one of the greatest sides in the history of the GAA. So, as you can imagine, expectation in the west was well and truly dampened.

If it was not enough that there was disparity in the playing resources, it was nothing compared to the funding difference between the two sides. A 'drive' in Wexford had seen them raise the princely sum of £100 and another £25 in a grant from the Leinster Council. Mayo could only look on in envy. Just 20 days before the final, the westerners launched their campaign to raise a war-chest for their assault on the title. They hoped the money would fund the cost of arranging trial and training matches so that they could enter the final without the fear of 'lacking the sinews of war,' as one local newspaper put it. Committees across Mayo were established to help bolster the fund. It was announced that those who put their hands in the pockets for this cause would be acknowledged in advertisements taken out in the local newspapers. The use of this technique was more about highlighting those who did not contribute than those who did. Not surprisingly, the bulk of the money came from Ballina and Crossmolina, while there was some ire towards the paltry amount donated in Foxford.

ON THE WEEKEND of the final, hardy volunteers had gathered hay from farms in North County Dublin and spread it over the turf in the hope that it might offer the ground some relief from the freezing conditions, but it was a forlorn hope. A dawn inspection drew no decision and it was to be left until early afternoon before a final inspection would take place.

Mayo has known finals such as their first. There have been games in the past two decades where an early mountain needed to be climbed. And so, it was in that first final.

The Kennedy brothers from Wexford were on fire that day. Sean hit two goals in the first-half, while his brother Gus got a third late on. All three goals were deemed unstoppable. Ballina man Tommy Boshell found the net late on to put a more respectable gloss on the scoreline, but there was no doubting who were the better side.

The *Leinster Leader* reported that *'None of us expected the West to be awake athletically to the extent of beating Wexford, but we were surprised how near they came to doing something like it. They are rattling fine footballers, are the Mayo men, and could teach even their champion conquerors some things. For one thing, four out of every five fouls seemed to be given against Wexford. For another thing, Mayo could kick the ball on the ground – a rather lost art under this much-mended Gaelic code of ours'.*

The Leader also bemoaned Mayo's misfortune at having to play big games in Croke Park in some of the worst weather conditions known to mankind. *'Three times recently they have been to Croke Park, and on the two previous occasions the rainfall was, I believe, a record to the then dates. I don't know how much the players (in the All-Ireland final) would have given for an inch or two of rain. One or two of them, who got occasion to fall, bled at the knees as an inevitable consequence, and I suppose other parts of their anatomies felt correspondingly sore. I pitied the brave fellows and wished them better luck than they experienced.'*

In truth, the game should never have taken place as it was unfair to both the eventual champions and the challengers, with ground too hard for any boot to stick into, too slippery for any sure footing to be secured. Full-back Jack Waldron told the *Western People's* Mick O'Connell a half century later that even though every contact with the hard ground resulted in injuries and wounds, there was no way they were going to succumb to the circumstances. To be taken off in those days would be to put your position at stake. So, they battled on, willing for the hour to pass.

'You would be ashamed of your life in those days to be (taken) off and your place taken. We would have had to be practically killed before we would go off. Otherwise, we would not think of leaving the field,' he said. Mayo were not immune from criticism though and the novelty of their maiden final appearance did not spare them from despair expressed about the shirts they wore for the final. After they had washed down their bloodied selves, several of the team trundled through the frozen streets to catch the late mail-train back to Ballyhaunis and to their jobs the following morning.

The others headed to the then Conarchy's Hotel where they partied until dawn with their opponents. The event was organised by the Wexfordmen's Association in Dublin and they were gracious hosts to the vanquished men from the west.

Over the door at the hallway were two banners…

Hard Luck Mayo; Better Luck next Time

And…

The Wexford Boys – Some Boys: Eh! What?

★ ★ ★ ★ ★

THE FINAL, IN a dramatic year for the country, was to be the first of many for Mayo sides whose travails would fascinate the country for the next century and more. However, given the nature of the pluckiness they displayed against a strong Wexford side, there was hope that a victory was imminent for the team for the west.

What was not known then though, was a further two decades would pass by before such a win was secured. The intervening 20 years would see the country strive for independence, and then be driven apart by a civil war that placed brother against brother, leaving fissures in Irish society that would last for generations.

However, in the midst of that turmoil, Mayo believed they were All-Ireland champions, only to have it dashed away by a cruel twist of fate.

★ ★ ★ ★ ★

IT WAS HEMINGWAY who wrote that there is no hunting like the hunting of man, and those who have hunted armed men long enough and liked it, never care for anything else thereafter. War, and even more so, Civil War takes its toll on the psyche of a nation. It robs a place of its core strength, its operating systems ripped asunder. Such was Ireland in the mid 1920s. Paranoia, distrust, fear and distraction were constants in the minds of our people.

Almost a decade had passed since The Rising, and a collective traumatic stress stalked the nation. Many families had been torn apart, many young men had fallen foul to the conflict and of those who had not, their priorities lay in interests other than sport.

Into this atmosphere fell the incidents that created the age-long rivalry between the neighbouring counties of Galway and Mayo. The fact that both share a jagged border that snakes along rivers, lakes and mountains, did not help. To this day, there is a great interchange of commerce and culture between the two; education and employment having attracted many south, to the City of the Tribes.

To this day, Mayo and Galway fans work or study or party side by side in the west. A myth persisted that all Mayo folk are walked to the tip of The Reek and have the faraway delights of Galway pointed out to us, with directions to go there in search of fortune. I have often opined that if Mayo are to win an All-

Ireland soon, there won't be a tap of work done in Galway that autumn. Even in my own family, there are cross-county connections. My grandfather married a Galwaywoman; I did likewise. I have worked all of my professional life in Galway to the point where I am now longer in Galway than I ever was in Mayo, yet my heart bleeds Red and Green.

The juxtaposition of Mayo and Galway led to banter and parochialism that has persisted to this day, but it is on the football field where a bitterness still exists. The events of 1925 perhaps offer some idea of why this is the case. Into this vacuum of war and dysfunction fell a role being played by people who had neither the experience nor the competence to take on the key organisational roles that an institution like the GAA required. It was inevitable that among all this disorder that the integrity of its top competition would be undermined and temporarily shattered.

THAT REACHED ITS zenith in 1925 when perhaps the most farcical ever All-Ireland Championship was held. Up to this point, no team from Connacht had ever won the title, and at different points in the process that year, two teams from the province were crowned champions.

However, just one was allowed to hold onto it, sparking off a rivalry that has remained constant to this day. Ironically, despite there being several All-Ireland champions named that year, no official All-Ireland final took place. To be fair to the GAA, it was operating under serious constraint. Having had to walk a delicate balancing act to stay transparently neutral during the conflict from the previous decade, they were now paying the price for that stance. Trying to be neutral in a state where being partisan was almost socially mandatory, saw the finances suffer.

The leadership of the association had in fact been supportive of the ruling Free State Cumann na nGaedheal government. Its continued financial weakness for much of the 1920s meant it operated at a significant loss throughout the first half of the decade. This shortage of income forced the association into an even closer relationship with WT Cosgrave's government, which bankrolled a large loan of £6,000 to help keep the GAA financially viable. Many of those who had administered the association at national and local level had departed the scene, victims to the conflict; either deceased, injured, mentally scarred or interned. This cohort had guided the association through its most demanding period and were well versed and flexible to handle whatever the situation threw at them.

Eventually this took its toll – and a poorer calibre of official was operating at all levels by the time hostilities had ceased. As such, by 1925, the association had a significant amount of new and inexperienced men in charge. Of those experienced veterans who remained, many now held local and national political offices, which began to divert their attention more and more. Many of these had taken opposing views and sides in the conflict, and harmony was rare.

With many of these having had a front row seat at the school of hostilities and negotiations in the previous years, a smooth transition was always going to be fanciful. The inexperience of its administrators and the continued tensions which simmered within the organisation between pro and anti-Treaty officials would lead to a range of objections and counter-objections within the national GAA in the first years after the Civil War. If there was any loophole or by-law or rule that could be invoked, it would not be left untouched. In terms of smooth operations or feeling aggrieved by whatever way a match went, it was the wild West.

Given the fractured state of life in the country, it was inevitable that a complacency to rules, regulations, and a distrust of authority would set in. This resulted in the farcical staging of the 1925 All-Ireland Championship.

The Connacht Championship had a staggering 11 games to decide its outcome, and that ultimate outcome resulted in the controversial crowning of the All-Ireland champions. Because of objection and appeals, Roscommon met Sligo an astonishing six times in the championship, while Galway played Leitrim twice, which meant that the competition ran well past its time. The Connacht draw for 1925 paired Roscommon with Sligo and the winners had a semi-final date with the provincial title-holders, Mayo. That left Galway and Leitrim to contest the other semi-final.

The Roscommon-Sligo series opened at Boyle on May 17. Roscommon won by a point, 2-3 to 2-2, but an objection by Sligo was upheld and a replay was ordered. This took place at Roscommon on July 5 when the game ended level at 1-5 each. Sligo on July 19 hosted the third meeting and again it ended level. Sligo 0-6, Roscommon 1-3.

These teams returned to Sligo on July 26 and once more failed to produce a winner. The next game was held in Roscommon and on August 2, Sligo beat Roscommon by 2-5 to 0-5. However, as very often happened in those days, yes, there was another objection, this time by Roscommon. The objection was upheld, and so on September 13, these two teams met each other for the sixth time, in Roscommon. This time Sligo won by 2-3 to 0-2 and were through to the semi-final against Mayo. This game took place in Tuam on October 4 in the old racecourse at Parkmore. Mayo won by two points, 1-6 to 1-4, and qualified to meet Galway in the final. Frustrated by this delay, Mayo were nominated to represent the province in the All-Ireland semi-final against Wexford before they played any Connacht Championship games.

It is now perceived that the decision to have Mayo nominated by Central Council was made in the belief that whatever team came from the west would provide little opposition for Wexford. Central Council chairman and Wexford native, Paddy Breen felt that the important matter of sorting out an All-Ireland Championship was not going to be held up by the prevarication and disorganisation of those out west who were unable to conclude their own provincial championship.

Mayo had been hampered by the non-resident rules for some years which had seen a flow of talent heading to the capital in search of work. This had boosted Dublin's profile in the game and there was no doubt this helped them to their three in-a-row in the 20s. An alteration of these rules enabled Mayo to nurture new talent that would otherwise have been unavailable to them. This served Mayo well in their semi-final against Wexford. The game had been expected to be a walk in the park for the Leinster champions, and this was reflected in their pre-game preparation.

They arrived in the capital on the morning of the match, two days after a hungry Mayo had headed east. Young Jackie Henry from Charlestown terrorised them from the off and goaled early on; a second ensued from George Williams and Mayo were flying at half-time, four clear. A stunned Wexford tried to respond in the second-half but try as they might, they could not prevent Mayo running out victors by six points.

The match surprised many and it seemed Mayo were on course to give the final a right effort, although they knew it would not be easy against Kerry or Cavan.

Having beaten Tipperary and then Cork in the Munster Championship of 1925, Kerry, the reigning All-Ireland champions, were nominated to represent Munster in the All-Ireland semi-final in August as their Munster final with Clare was delayed until September due to a backlog of fixtures. In Ulster, Cavan had continued their recent domination of the province and annexed their sixth title in eight seasons.

On August 23, the Kingdom welcomed Cavan to Tralee and after a close contest, Kerry emerged victorious, 1-7 to 2-3. Immediately after the game, however, the Cavan County Board sent an objection to Central Council stating that Kerry's captain, Phil O'Sullivan, had made himself ineligible to play for his county, having already played competitive matches with two separate clubs in Dublin in 1925, which was illegal. Cavan claimed Kerry's officials knew that they were prohibited from playing O'Sullivan, but had approached members of the Cavan board before the match and asked them not to protest if they played him. The Central Council upheld the objection and Cavan were duly awarded the match. Aggrieved, Kerry responded with a counter-objection of their own stating that a member of the Cavan team, JP Murphy, was guilty of a similar offence having played with the Keatings club in Dublin during the same year as he played with his own club in Cavan. As a consequence, Cavan were also disqualified.

It seemed unbelievable that the championship had been transformed into such a farce. However, as both Kerry and Cavan had now been thrown out of the competition, Central Council had stopped short of awarding the crown to Mayo, but by virtue of the fact they were the last team standing, it looked like the All-Ireland football title would be heading across the Shannon for the very first time, by default.

★ ★ ★ ★ ★

NINE YEARS AFTER their first final, Mayo would seemingly hold the title for the first time. Even newspapers in the west such as the Galway-based *Connacht Tribune* were referring to Mayo as the champions.

But, in Mayo, there was a feeling that the circumstances of the 'victory' had detracted from the achievement, that it was all too good to be true? What made it all the more frustrating was that there was a newfound belief in the team that the victory could have been secured anyway if they had been allowed to play either Kerry or Cavan in the decider. But that frustration was to be superseded by the feeling of being robbed.

The Sligo-Roscommon saga ended after six games and the Yeats County men qualified to meet Mayo in the Connacht semi-final. They would have probably gone one further to the final if former Mayo player Jim White had completed the game, after he had goaled before succumbing to injury. His departure inspired Mayo's comeback and they made it into the Connacht final against Galway. The game was fixed for Parkmore in Tuam and surprisingly, the referee appointed to it was Galway official Stephen Jordan. (Remember the name)

A crowd of more than 6,000 turned up at Tuam for the final which was nip and tuck with Galway ahead as the game entered the last 30 minutes. However, a superb strike from Jackie Henry fired Mayo in front, a lead they were holding as the game entered its death. The vociferous crowd hugged the sidelines as the contest grew in intensity, but it seemed if they could hold their heads for the remaining minutes then the Mayo team would show the value of their standing in what would be the last game of the season.

But then with minutes remaining, referee Jordan awarded a controversial penalty to his home county to the disbelief of the Mayo side, and Tommy Leetch fired the ball to the net to give Galway the victory that was to see them named All-Ireland champions within weeks.

James Laffey's remarkable book *The Road To '51* outlined in detail the chain of events that led to this proclamation. Stephen Jordan, yes, the Galway referee who referee-ed what was effectively the match that handed Galway their first All-Ireland by awarding them a late penalty, was also a member of Central Council. In addition, he was also a key Galway selector.

Despite not playing, there is no doubt he played the most important role in Galway's first All-Ireland, not just because of the above, but because it was he who proposed to Central Council that Galway be deemed champions because of their defeat of Mayo in the Connacht final.

Following his recommendation and a seconding by the famous chairman Paddy Breen, a set of medals was posted to the Galway team. Members of the Connacht Council were annoyed at this turn of events. At no stage had it been communicated to them that the Connacht final was a de facto All-Ireland final. If that had been the case, the game would surely have been played in front of tens of thousands at Croke Park, and not just in front of a smaller and less lucrative gate at Parkmore in Tuam.

Neither the Mayo nor Galway footballers who played in that final had any inkling what was on the line when they togged out at Tuam. On the mantra that 'When you're explaining, you're losing,' Breen tried to outline the basis for declaring Galway All-Ireland champions. He made the case that if the Connacht final had been played when it should, and had Galway beaten Mayo in that final, then it is they who would have been last men standing, as Mayo were.

But this was a baseless explanation and did little to dilute the notion that at top national level, Mayo were being short-changed and shafted by cute hoorism across the country, and most annoyingly, in their neighbouring county.

The Central Council's handling of the situation drew scorn from many. The popular newspaper Sport claimed the *'prestige and administration of gaelic games has been shaken grievously by these revelations and objections… that this should occur at the most crucial and popular stages of the games is the devastating aspect of the whole business.'* The Kerryman was similarly scathing about the decision made by the GAA's new president, Patrick Breen, who *'went one better than old King Solomon, for he allowed the All-Ireland infant to be cut in two, and he can now distribute the medals to Mayo at the wake. His actions have reduced the 1925 championship to a fiasco, and made the GAA a laughing stock.'*

The GAA tried to save face, by organising a substitute competition between the four provincial winners for a set of gold medals. The Kerry GAA Board unanimously decided not to enter it in protest at how the All-Ireland was handled. The GAA's substitute competition was a comparative failure that attracted poor attendance for its two games, with Galway beating Cavan in the final in January 1926.

The fallout from the 1925 championship was a serious, if temporary, setback to the prestige and image of the GAA; an episode which highlighted some of the animosities still rife within the organisation and the inexperience of many of its leading officials, such as Breen, who would only serve two years as the GAA's president. It was also to create an enmity between Galway and Mayo, creating a rivalry that stoked the fires of many in the west.

An Taoiseach and proud Mayo man, Enda Kenny, T.D., and GAA president, Liam O'Neill, present the match programme from the 1936 All-Ireland football final between Laois and Mayo, at the official unveiling of the newly-refurbished GAA Museum at Croke Park in 2013. And (below) the first Mayo man to lift the Sam Maguire Cup, team captain Seamus O'Malley.

PART ★ ONE

THE CUP ON THE BIKE

YOU COULD HEAR the silence on that September morning in 1936. The sun had risen and proud hearts beat with fresh blood across the west. Curlews sung up from across the lakes. The county was still awakening from what had happened the day before. Men and women stretched themselves in the Monday beds, squinted out at the sun peeking through from the east, and reminded themselves of what had just occurred. What was rare was wonderful and misunderstood.

On the roadways around Claremorris, farmers gathered the stock for the trek to the town fair. For most, it would be their first chance to digest what had happened, to look at another in the face and opine on the events of the day just passed. Some had been to Dublin and arrived back late in the night. Others, younger ones, had made the trip and might not be seen again until the middle of the week.

Later in the day, the men had planned to gather material for the bonfires to line the road to Castlebar, turf and hay and stout sticks. Some paraffin to ignite them. But that would be for later, after all the jobs were done. Just after eight o clock, on the road to Meelickmore, the only sound was that of a bike creaking along, its rider heavy-legged. Every push of the pedals a laboured one, because his calves ached, his body grimaced with the silent satisfying pain that athletes have after an exhorting run. That justifying strain of having achieved something physical and it having left a time-stamp, a sort of muscular FitBit before its time.

The sweet knowledge that despite his exertions in front of 40,000 the day before, he was well able for the cycle to work. There was something wholesome about it all, that the ear-shattering noise of that field in the capital would be replaced by just… *nothing*.

Just the dead sound of a beautiful Mayo autumn morning.

He pedalled again, remembering again just how demanding the gradient in the road was. Lots of thoughts went through his mind.

About what he was going to do, about where he was going to go and what the rest of the week, the rest of the year would bring.

Just six months earlier, he had stood up as county secretary of the GAA and fretted about the future of football in the area. After all, there were just two clubs in the county senior championship, a scenario that would allow standards to tumble if allowed to persist.

Just a year earlier, he could never have foreseen that his body would rise to such a challenge, that the powers of recovery would be such. Four years earlier, he had hobbled off a pitch, knowing that he might never cross that white line again, and that even if he did, it would probably only be as a fraction of the player he used to be.

But determination was in his DNA. He had come from a family of sportsmen – who all spoke football when they met. Not in a boastful way, but in a respectful manner. He looked forward to meeting them later and to having them shake his hand, and hearing him add his story of the final and the historic moment to the conversation repertoire.

And he pushed the pedals again.

In the rising sun, there was a reflection off something bright, silvery, shiny. It too was spending its first day in the county. He was not to know that a century on from then, just how prized that trophy would be. How revered it would become. How all-consuming the chase for it would be.

JUST 18 HOURS earlier, the rider of the bike had raised that cup above his shoulders in Croke Park. Now, as the rest of his teammates slept hard in a Dublin hotel, exhausted from their comprehensive victory and a night of celebrations, Mayo captain Seamus O'Malley was cycling to the school where he taught in his native Mayo.

Hanging off the bike was the Sam Maguire Cup. The county assumed it was still above in Dublin with the team and officials, but O'Malley had not been granted the day off work at Mellickmore National School – so he would teach, tell them a lesson that they would never forget, a story they passed on to their children and grandchildren. The cup would form the centrepiece of the celebrations in the coming weeks and months, but the first to get to see it would be the pupils.

'We came back to Barry's Hotel for tea and later had dinner at 10 o'clock that night,' he recalled later.

'I had to be back for work in Meelickmore school the next morning and John Smyth from Claremorris drove me home with the cup in the back of the car. Paddy Mullaney, who was a member of the county board, also came home with us that night.

'I was back at work teaching in Meelickmore the next morning. I remember there was a fair in Claremorris the same day,' he explained clearly. The car carrying the trio and the Sam Maguire did not arrive into Claremorris until the early hours and it was after 3am when Seamus got into bed, sleeping soundly with the cup not far from him.

How must that cup have felt, normally used to be feted on final nights, to having drink poured into it; to having fans hold it aloft and touch it and paw it, leaving broad fingerprints of top of others? Here, in a strange county for the very first time, it spent the night in the dark of a room, alongside the bed of a man who would go down in history as the first Mayoman to lift it aloft.

Four hours after his head first hit the pillow, Seamus was up and washed and shaved, picked up the bicycle clips to tuck in the trousers, and lifted the Sam Maguire and let it hang off the handlebars for the short journey to Meelickmore National School.

As he approached, the children could not believe their eyes.

Their school had opened in the same year as the foundation of the GAA, but in the 52 years since, nothing as exciting as this had ever happened in the humdrum of a September morning. They gathered around in wonder at the sight of this gleaming trophy. It was photographed on the sports page of every national newspaper that morning and yet here it was for them to see and touch. Photographs of the event were published far and wide, one with the headline **He is proud of the cup. They are proud of him.**

A day earlier they had been part of the excitement as they gathered around radio sets to hear the commentary from Croke Park. Never before had they heard their native country record a national victory that was so comprehensive, and never again, would they get to see Mayo record such a margin in the GAA's showpiece game.

LESSONS WERE SHORT that day because all the talk was of the final and of Maistir O Meallaigh's role in it. He took time to visit the classes and when word got around that it was in the school, a steady stream made their way to the schoolyard.

When the last bell rang, he brought it home again, freshened himself up and headed for Ballyhaunis to meet the rest of the squad, who had by now tumbled out of their beds and spent a day in Dublin basking in the glory of the victory.

Just as Seamus O'Malley was finishing class for the day in Meelickmore, above in Barry's Hotel, the team made their way to the now Connolly and then Broadstone Station to catch the train west. The area was thronged with hundreds of Mayo fans, many of whom had come straight from the hotel and from the city centre where they had been celebrating through the night.

They wondered where the vaunted trophy was?

For the many from the county working in Dublin, it was a rare moment of validation for all the trips to semi-finals and finals in the previous two decades. Especially in the mad year of 1925 when it seemed they would have been crowned if they had not been blackguarded and had been given the chance to win it in a properly-regimented final.

At last, now they were kings and they could bask in the reflected glory of the men from their own county. Many there spoke of their wish that they could be in Castlebar for the homecoming, but the need to work would not allow it, and so it was with swollen hearts of pride and sadness that they waved the train from the station and set about their day.

There was a strange giddyness as the train struck west.

The players had no idea what awaited them in their native county, but they got a sense of the excitement as the train edged over the Shannon at Athlone, and headed into the setting sun for the trip to Castlebar. Once they hit Ballyhaunis, bonfires, flags, banners adorned the way and musicians played jigs on the railside as the fans awaited the sight of the train.

Lit torches illuminated the night sky along the way and excitement grew when the horn of the train signalled it was approaching Claremorris. Seamus O'Malley had rejoined the team, reuniting it with Sam Maguire who had been back in Mayo almost a working day before they had.

They were welcomed by more music at Balla, a poignant stopping point, because it was there that the all-conquering team of 11 years previous had trained and had been denied a title by skullduggery and fraud. To carry Sam Maguire through the village as All-Ireland champions was a nod to all those denied the chance in 1925.

It seemed that nobody had been to sleep in Castlebar since the previous night either, and bonfires burned throughout the night. Shopkeepers and bars reported a brisk trade as people flocked to the town from all over Mayo. Groups made their way from South Mayo and Ballinrobe to marvel at the achievement. Fans knew how many times Mayo had knocked on the door in a period of great trauma, and they were not going to miss an opportunity to honour this greatness. If they only knew that night, just how rare that feeling would be over the next century, they would scarcely have believed it.

In the county town, the bonfires were needed because there was a great chill in the air, even though late September would normally have higher temperatures. Word spread through the crowd that the team were on the way, but this led to some disappointment and further waiting, as the train due into the station at 8.32pm arrived without them on it.

Well over a thousand flag-carriers and supporters had wrapped their way around the station to get a good view, but it was to no avail. The next train into Castlebar would be the late mail train, due to arrive in the early hours. The huge crowd then made its way back into the town centre to be entertained by the Castlebar Temperance Band who led the march back up to the station after midnight.

Sometime around 12.40, the mail train came into view, its light a beacon along the tracks, its whistle piercing the night air. It had been more than 30 hours since the final whistle had blown in Croke Park, and now, apart from a gathering of schoolchildren in Meelickmore, for the first time, Mayo people were going to see their captain carry the Sam Maguire aloft on native soil.

In the time since, we have all yearned for that Monday morning after an All-Ireland, that feeling after a victory. In Mayo, the celebration in 1936 was a beautiful

41

one, full of music and passion and meaning for a faithful whose hopes had been dashed on so many times. Around the county, music and dancing accompanied the cup as it made its way from town to village, from school to school.

After so much disappointment, Mayo fans had now woken to the morning when their team was mentioned as being among *'the greatest teams that have contested the championship'*, or read the report of a contemporary journalist after witnessing Mayo rout Laois in the 1936 All-Ireland football final.

SEAMUS WAS BORN in the same town as myself, at Cloonacashel, right next door to the current local golf club, considered by many such as Padraig Harrington to be among the best in Ireland. The estate dates back to 1238, a full 700 years before its young illustrious neighbour was to make his mark on the history of the county.

Seamus attended the Christian Brothers School in Ballinrobe, just like I did half a century later. Many of the desks when I attended in the 1970s and 80s contained the old inkwells and had hundreds of names scraped into the wood.

Seamus' initials were on one.

The hunger-striker, Frank Stagg had his name on another.

In 1976, when de Valera died, the teacher told us that we could use our compasses to carve DV into the desks to honour De Valera, an opportunity I availed of to carve my own matching initials. Perhaps decades later if it had still been open, Donie Vaughan might have become the third DV on those desks.

Just 200 yards from that school lay the mill for the Robe Knitting Industry whose promotional boast was that they 'make any style of garment in any colour or texture available'. Some boast, but their big moment came when they were asked to provide the jerseys for the Mayo team that contested that All-Ireland final against Laois. They did not waste any time capitalising on their association with the champions, and took out advertisements about this in the local newspapers just a week after the final.

So, a Ballinrobe man was the first to carry the Sam Maguire into the county; and a Ballinrobe jersey was the receptacle for the sweat and endeavour of that heroic first team. It is remarkable how little is celebrated about the contribution of the O'Malley family to sport in Mayo; but not just Mayo; to the west, and the region.

Seamus was one of five brothers born to Luke and Ann O'Malley, Lavally, Cloonacastle, Ballinrobe, all of whom played inter-county football for Mayo during the 1930s.

Seamus, Paddy, Luke, Jack and Tommy achieved the distinction during the period known as the 'Glorious Years' of Mayo football. Seamus, who captained Mayo to their first All-Ireland senior title in 1936, has been acknowledged as one of Mayo's greatest GAA players and administrators. Remarkably, he came out of retirement to captain that all conquering side, while at the same time being secretary of Mayo GAA Board.

His nephew Tommy told me of the childhood fascination there was for him to hear his father and four brothers discuss the intricacies of the game at parties when they would sit in one room, and with civility articulate their opinions on players they had all encountered from all over the country. For young Tommy, it was a PhD in the GAA that stood by him when he went on to excel for club, county, province and country in the decades ahead.

As I mentioned earlier, it was more difficult in that era to find people with the motivation, the time and the skills to take on roles of officialdom in the organisation, but Seamus did so, despite being still of able body to be considered fit enough to play for the county. As centre-back, he was a pillar of reliability, strong and astute, attributes that left no one in doubt about the wisdom of his decision to make a return, or about the significance of his contribution to the overall team performance.

He won every honour in the game with Mayo. He also won Sigerson Cup with UCG in 1932. Thirty years later, his son Michael was similarly honoured with Sigerson Cup success at the same university, and a further 30 years later, in 1992, his grandson and Galway star, Niall Finnegan repeated the achievement – a unique family record.

Seamus played club football for Cloonacastle, Castlebar Mitchels, and Claremorris who paid him the ultimate honour of naming their new stand on Fr James Gibbons football grounds after him. The roundabout entering Claremorris is also dedicated to the memory of Seamus O'Malley, so every time I enter the town from the motorway, my thoughts go to him and I say a little thanks for his efforts which enabled Mayo get off the mark in 1936.

The Ballinrobe native held every office on Mayo County Board as well as the

South Mayo GAA Board, and was similarly active with his club Claremorris. Seamus came from a strong Republican background, and played an active part in the War of Independence along with his brother, Michael. In fact, two of his sisters, Mary and Nora were members of Cumann Na mBan and carried despatches for the Republican movement. He had a kind word for everyone and his respect for those with different spiritual or political beliefs was undimmed.

His loyalty to GAA colleagues was such that at election times, he accompanied Henry Kenny, standing for Fine Gael, and Sean Flanagan, the Fianna Fail candidate, on the canvass. The name O'Malley is now synonymous with that memorable event of 1936, and Seamus is spoken of with reverence wherever great GAA feats are being discussed. Having retired, at the age of 32, he continued to promote the game, and Irish culture in general, right up to his death in 2002 at the ripe old age of 98.

Seamus' son, Michael captained the St Jarlath's team to win the Hogan Cup and played on the Mayo minor team in the All-Ireland final of 1962. Michael also featured on numerous occasions with the Mayo senior team. Another son, Luke starred with Claremorris and afterwards with the Swinford football team. Seamus' grandson, Niall Finnegan, won an All-Ireland senior medal in 1998 playing on John O'Mahony's star-studded Galway team.

THE 1930s WERE glorious years for Mayo football, with the county team garnering six National League titles in-a-row – a record that still stands – and that senior championship title in 1936. Paddy and Jack were members of that distinguished group of men. Paddy was an exceptional football talent who went on to play midfield during these years. He was also a member of the Cloonacastle team, alongside his brothers, Luke and Jack, which won the county title in 1929. Paddy also won a Connacht Junior Championship medal and two National League medals with Mayo in 1934 and '35. He played at centrefield and in the half-forward line and was instrumental in scoring the winning goal in the 1934 final. Paddy was also an accomplished cross-country athlete and was Mayo champion in that sport in the 1930s.

The family accomplishments continued with Luke who, like most of his siblings, was a consummate sportsman. He played for many years on the Cloonacastle team and went on to line out in goal for the Mayo junior team.

Luke was also a keen golfer and was captain of the Claremorris golf club in 1968. His daughter, Margaret won gold at Community Games in badminton and high jump at different levels. His son, Connor played on the St Colman's College team that won the Connacht Schools Championship in 1980. Luke junior was involved with the Claremorris club as part of the senior team management. Luke's grandson, Richard Fahey, played minor football for Galway in 2014.

Jack, like his brothers, Paddy, Luke, Seamus and Tommy, played football for Cloonacastle and his county, and was part of that very successful Mayo team in the 1930s winning two National League and Connacht Championship senior medals. He was known to be the most stylish footballer of the family and a forward of some repute for his county. After marrying his beloved Nell, Jack was transferred to Thurles and played inter-county football for Tipperary. He was a big GAA fan but when he moved to Waterford, he became interested in Waterford United soccer team with his next-door neighbour and Mayo-native, Tom Tuohy who was the team doctor. Jack's daughter Marian, won a gold medal in the Special Olympics in badminton held in Limerick in 2014. At that event, Míchael O'Muircheartaigh regaled Marian and her family with stories of Seamus bringing the Sam Maguire Cup on the back of a bike out to Meelickmore school on the morning after the all-Ireland final. Another daughter, Aileen, won huge standing as a top Munster tennis player.

Tommy, the youngest of the boys, was also part of that rich vein of talent. He played with Cloonacastle, Mayo minors and Cavan senior football teams. He captained the Arva senior club team in 1939 and '40 and later went on to coach and manage teams in the local Ballinrobe GAA club. He passed on the torch to his son, Tommy junior, who played minor, under-21, junior and senior football for Mayo with distinction, and who captained the Mayo senior side in 1975.

Tommy Jnr also won a Railway Cup medal in 1973 and a Connacht Championship in 1981. He played international schools' basketball, and was selected on the Combined University gaelic football and basketball teams while attending the then University College Galway. He represented Connacht in both codes throughout the 70s, travelling with the All Star team in 1976, and winning a B&I monthly award (presented to the star GAA performer for each month) for March 1978. In 1972, Ballinrobe representing Mayo, won the All-Ireland Junior Basketball title, beating Waterford in the final. Both Padraic and Tommy were members of that historic team. Gerard, Padraig, and Eugene also lined out with Ballinrobe, winning county junior and intermediate titles. Tommy's daughter, Maura played National League basketball with Galway Democrats for one year and won a Connacht football medal playing for Galway. She also founded the Claregalway Basketball Club after she retired from playing.

Tommy's grandson, Eugene junior, is carrying on the family football tradition in Ballinrobe as a past member of Mayo minor and under-21 panels. He also captained the Ballinrobe senior football team in 2015.

THESE FIVE REMARKABLE men, brought up on a farm in Levally, had qualities that would command respect in any generation – loyalty, kindness, dignity, dependability, and dedication. But it is their massive contributions to the sporting life of the county, for which they will be best remembered.

After leaving Ballinrobe CBS, Seamus O'Malley attended the then University College Galway where in 1934, he won that Sigerson Cup. After first playing competitive football with the local Ballinrobe club, he trained as a primary schoolteacher in St Patrick's College, Drumcondra. At that time, Ballinrobe CBS didn't take part in college championships, but while Seamus was in college, he had the opportunity to represent his native Ballinrobe when he was one of two past pupils who got permission to play with the school. The other was the late Martin Joe Murphy (uncle of Ballinrobe GAA referee, Martin Murphy).

After leaving college, he took up his first teaching post in Naas and worked there for four years in the 20s. He didn't make the great Kildare teams of 1927 and '28 but did play with such well known players as Jack Higgins, Gus Fitzpatrick, Joe Curtis and Tom Wheeler. Later, he moved to Carna in Galway and played with the local team and he had fond memories of the late Hugo Carney, who won an All-Ireland medal with Galway in 1934.

Club football wasn't as organised then as it is today. Club facilities were poor, with a hedge or ditch sufficing as a dressing-room. Sponsorship of any kind was unknown and the Mansfield Hotspur boots, which were popular then, cost a guinea, which was half a week's wages in those days.

Though living in Galway, he declared for Mayo and was at first selected for the county junior team. He came back to Mayo in 1930 to take up the post of principal at Meelickmore NS. Though living in Claremorris, he initially played club football with Castlebar as the parish rule did not apply. At the time Ballina had won the county championships and Castlebar were anxious to dethrone them.

'I was still living in Galway when Castlebar approached me and asked me to play for them. They knew I was coming to live in Mayo and they were determined to do everything they could to beat Ballina,' he said.

He was delighted to join them and even more so when they won the championship in 1930 and '31. Seamus played at centre half-back and the captain of Castlebar in those days was John Egan, also a retired teacher. In 1932, he later played with Claremorris, alongside such players as John Gilligan, Garda Wilkinson and the 'Nipper' Shanley, a native of Leitrim, who worked as railway clerk in the town.

There were only four senior teams in the county at the time… Westport, Castlebar, Ballaghaderreen and Ballina, and Claremorris joined them after winning a county junior title in 1931. There were no clubs in Hollymount or Garrymore in the 1930s. Seamus had the ironic experience of playing with the Claremorris side who beat the reigning champions Castlebar in the opening round of the 1932 championship.

He was on the Mayo team that was beaten by Kerry in the semi-final in 1931 and the All-Ireland in '32.

'I don't think there was the same hype about football then as there is today. There was only the Hogan Stand then. The Cusack wasn't built until 1938 but it was great to play for Mayo. They were great years,' he admitted.

Seamus was off football from 1933 until 1936, and it was Mayo's path to the All-Ireland final in 1936 that was his fondest memory. In that year, as well as playing with the county team, he also held the post of Mayo County Board secretary.

'One of my legs was giving me trouble and at the end of the 1933 season, I decided to retire. In 1935 I was asked to take over the secretaryship of the county board and I knew then that my playing days were really over, as the secretary of the board could not be a player on the county team,' he recalled. He added that when the team was selected for the final of the Connacht Championship – being the defending champions, Mayo had a bye into the final – a number of officials and himself visited St Coman's Park, Roscommon, on the eve of the game to check out the pitch.

'Nothing was leaked to me at that time that I might yet be playing, but one hour before the start of the final, I was informed by the chairman of the county board that Purty Kelly was unable to play, and that I was in on his place. The match against Galway ended in a draw. Some changes were made in the team for the replay the following Sunday and I was appointed captain.'

Even though he had retired from playing for almost two years, he always kept himself reasonably fit and that's what stood to him. Two weeks later, the old rivals played again. Purty Kelly was back, and Seamus was in his old position at centre half-back. 'We beat Galway in the replay after a really tough game and we were back again in Roscommon the following Sunday, where we beat Kerry in the semi-final.

'Then, of course, we went on to beat Laois in the final. It was great to win a final, especially as I was the team captain, but in reality, we won it very easily.

'We would have got a better kick out of it if it had been a hard game,' he resolved.

He received the Sam Maguire Cup from the then GAA President, Laois-man Bob O'Keeffe and minded it on its journey back to the team hotel and onwards to Mayo in that taxi… and to Meelickmore on the bars of his bike the following morning.

SEAMUS' GREATEST DISAPPOINTMENT though was to come the following year when Mayo once again won the Connacht title and went on to face Cavan in the All-Ireland semi-final. Leading by five points as the game entered its final minutes, they allowed Cavan to steal two late goals that gave them the game, and denied a wonderful Mayo side the opportunity to win back-to-back All-Irelands.

'That was a great loss for us. They were outstanding years for football in Connacht. The Connacht Championship was regarded as the best competition and people came from all over to watch the matches. I am disappointed that all that has changed,' he said years later.

Seamus' fitness which saw his regain his place for the 1936 final, stayed with him throughout his life, and he took great pride in watching his football prowess seep down through the family.

After his football career ended, Seamus turned to golf. He was captain of

Claremorris Golf Club in 1941, secretary (1970-1974) and president (1983-1984). He won the Captain's Prize in 1944 and the President's Prize in 1953. He enjoyed playing golf well into his nineties.

When he died aged 98 in 2002, Seamus O'Malley was Ireland's oldest-living All-Ireland medal winner. At his funeral Mass, just a few months after his beloved wife, Delia had passed away, the local priest paid tribute to him.

'The real gift of his life was that nothing was wasted. Every God given talent, ability, quality and character he brought to life and all the deeper human qualities of gentleness, compassion, understanding, humility.

'There is a lesson in his life for all of us and that is to make the most of whatever situation we find ourselves in, to meet success, and failure with equal modesty and to move on to the next challenge, always praising God with hope in our hearts.'

AMONGST THE GIFTS presented at the funeral Mass were a golf club, a school book, a candle, a rosary beads, a garden tool and, of course, that famous football from the final in 1936.

The ball is on display in Claremorris for people to see – its historical significance unrealised until recent years when the quest for a title became the obsession it now is.

There is no chance that the next time Sam comes to Mayo, that it will be concealed in a taxi or hanging off the bars of a bike. Its introduction to our county was a measure of the man who first held it over his head while wearing our colours.

Eamonn Mongey with his All-Ireland winners' medals from 1950 and 1951 at his home in Monkstown, Co. Dublin, in 2006. And (below) Sean Flanagan, who masterminded the double All-Ireland triumphs.

PART ★ TWO

MEN OF LETTERS

THE PAINT WAS gloopy and stuck to the brush which had hardened through, not being left for long enough in a jar of white spirits. But it softened enough to do the job. Up and down, methodical, no back and forth or splashing or half-doing it.

The timber was unforgivingly thirsty for the thick paint. It drank it in, the hardened bristles splashing specks back onto his face, little drops of red paint to match the drops of green which had splashed onto him for the other half. He stood back, the teenager, and looked at it.

Spotted the areas where the wood had absorbed the gloss and touched them up. Above, the dark clouds hung ominously, but if the rain held off for an hour, he'd be fine. He was proud of it. If a job was worth doing, it had to be done right.

A motto then and later; a work ethic that we would all see the benefits of. He stood back again, this time leaving down the brush… stepped out onto the road and admired his handiwork.

It was a gate to be proud of… half red, half green.

It would lift the spirits and maybe raise a cheer from everyone who passed by this house at Crossard, not far from Ballyhaunis. In years to come this would be serious hurling country, but for now, with just a week to go before the 1936 All-Ireland Final, it would encourage the supporters and create a swell that might reach the ears of the players. The painter was determined to do what he could to ensure Mayo would rise to the top of the football cream.

He wiped the paint off his hands, put the brush back into the jar of turps.

Fourteen-year-old Sean Flanagan was proud of his work. He stood back and looked at it. The passers-by remarked on it, tousled his hair, said fair play to him for bringing a bit of soothing colour to a country still smarting from the trauma of internal war, not knowing that another was in the offing a few years later.

At that moment, when he had done his piece for the Mayo cause, he, or those around him, could never have known just how much of a role he would play in the history of the game in our county, and how his name would forever ring out in the annals of Mayo football.

Indeed, we are where we are because of him.

PERHAPS WHAT CREATES some of the aura around Mayo football is that they are box office. Winning and losing are irrelevant, we still manage to create the headlines in a manner that is well out of sync on the table of column inches versus glory. No team that has won so few titles manages to fascinate as much as Mayo.

There are Kerry teams – a place counting their All-Irelands into the 30s – who have not received the column inches that the men from the west have received. Despite the great success in the National League enjoyed by Mayo in the 1930s, there is a still a strong belief that to return just one All-Ireland from such an era of dominance was a desperately poor reward for the talent of that generation. Six titles in-a-row still remains a record that is unlikely to be ever beaten, but it is often forgotten when year after year, the gap between the present and the last All-Ireland victory is the topic of the day.

It must be remembered too that the openness and transparency of team selection and squad inclusion, as we know it, is far removed from what passed then for consultation and agreement. Players, who after all were those entrusted with the strategic acumen to influence games as they evolved on the pitch, had little say in the tactical nous of those who should play alongside them, and often, major decisions in games were determined weeks beforehand in a smoke-filled room by men in suits and men in collars.

With the glory years of the 1930s, there was an instinct that of all the counties in Ireland, that Mayo must have been doing something right to have built up so much success. And there is validity in that point of view, but the fact that our standing as by far the best team in Ireland for the guts of a decade saw us return just one championship is equally damning.

GROWING UP IN the 70s, in south Mayo, the face of Sean Flanagan stared down at us from telegraph poles, the black and white photos juxtaposed with the green and orange of the Fianna Fail poster. As youngsters, we were not to know just what an iconic figure he had been on the sporting fields. But even then, there was something about him, the proud jaw, the determined face that had lived life.

Here in his sixties, was this man who had once been the boy who painted the gate. At one stage, he had been just like we were. Young and innocent. But Flanagan was born to lead. He had been to places and knew things. He carried a worldly-wiseness around with him that some others on the team did not, a trait that saw him through life, achieving a distinguished political career that brought him from Mayo to the European Parliament, with a long stint in Government in between.

He attended the renowned football nursery of St Jarlath's College in Tuam and made an immediate impact on the pitches of North Galway where he captained the school's junior team to their first provincial success. This gave the college great hope they could bring him through to star for the senior side, and his development progressed every year, with his wisdom beyond his years key to his evolution.

The inevitable triumph for the St Jarlath's senior side ensued and when he moved on to the next part of his education, success followed as well. Unusually for the man who is forever remembered as a left corner-back, whilst he was studying in University College Dublin, Flanagan won two Sigerson Cups in 1944 and '45 playing in the opposite corner. In 1945 he captained the victorious UCD side, but would suffer heartbreak the following year when, playing full back, they would succumb to University College Cork.

Any success on the college front is noted with interest in the home counties. Word floats through the county associations in the cities of Dublin, Galway, and Cork, so it was no surprise when Flanagan was elevated to the county senior set-up. Not that he or the other young players were too enamoured by it all. For a team that had dominated the 1930s, the decade from 1937 to '47 saw them win just one Connacht title.

By 1947, Flanagan had become disillusioned with the incompetence, as he had seen it, of the county board, and he sent a letter outlining his desire to resign from selection. After much persuasion though, he relented and took part in the first league game of the following season, in Kerry.

What followed was shambolic, though it did illustrate what could be achieved. In the game on November 9, Mayo arrived without a full team for the game against that season's finalists. The county secretary, Finn Mongey (brother of Eamonn Mongey) and the lad who drove the car were told to tog out. The players were incandescent with rage but they still managed to organise themselves to earn a share of the points with a 1-7 to 1-7 draw.

Afterwards, they determined that enough was enough, and that the general public had to be made aware of what was going on. Flanagan and some of the fellow senior players were moved to send another letter to the county board. In the letter the players riled against the inadequacies of the preparation and took it upon themselves to save Mayo football, before, as they elegantly and hauntingly put it, *'football disappears completely in Mayo – unwept, unhonoured and unsung'*.

For youngsters, such as the teenage Sean Flanagan and Padraig Carney and others, the calling of playing for the county was a strong one. But the knowledge among the squad that the team were being hamstrung each time they took to the field must have been frustrating. Like a boiling cauldron though, matters were coming to a head.

THE RUSTLE OF the crisp dry newsprint of the *Western People* was heard throughout the county that week, in the heart of the winter of 1947. There were utterances of 'Ssssh 'as someone was nominated to read aloud the missive that appeared on the sports pages. The Mayo players had had enough and had taken pen to paper.

'It has to be Flanagan who was behind this,' the faithful believed, but it was not, although there was no doubt but that the actions, standards and opinions of the Ballyhaunis man had strongly influenced the thinking that led them to take this action.

Up to this point, the public had never really heard from the players. They went along and supported them on the field, but the concept of them having a strong opinion that matched their playing ability was never considered. Flanagan

MEN OF LETTERS PART TWO ★

and others knew the capacity that existed in the Mayo squad if it was properly equipped, trained, and selected. If partisan nods and deal were eliminated… if some appreciation was given to the ability of the players to manage themselves… if given their head… if!

Their letter was a bombshell.

It read:

'A Chairde – It is some time since we decided that a letter in this strain should be written in an effort to remedy a state of affairs which, in our opinion, is detrimental to football in Mayo. Year after year we have seen the County Board bring to nought the hours of training which we have put in, but yet, believing it was outside our sphere as players, we have desisted from drawing your attention to the matter. Events in Tralee last Sunday have banished our indecision, however, and we feel the time has come when something must be done before football disappears completely in Mayo – unwept, unhonoured and unsung.

'Since 1939, Mayo football has struck a very lean patch and only now is it rounding the corner. The displays given by the team against Kildare, Antrim and Kerry show that with a little help and encouragement – along the right lines – the present batch of footballers is in the top line today. And, furthermore, we think we were in the same grade in 1946 when we played the disputed game with Roscommon. The collapse of the replay and the repetition of the debacle in this year's championship we blame on the total indifference of the County Board.

'For weeks before the championship, the Dublin-based players clamoured for matches with other counties, not for their own sake – they would have too much football in Dublin – but for the sake of the county and with the view of giving the members of the team an opportunity of playing together and of perfecting their combination. But the only matches were (1) against a makeshift Galway team and (2) against Longford when some of the players had prior engagements.

'Not only did these matches fail in their primary object, i.e. as a conclusive try-out for the team but they also failed in their secondary object. i.e. as an informative aid to the selectors in making their final choice, for the simple reason that there were very few selectors present at either game. It seems that when a Mayo team is selected, the selectors are permitted to depart home and never see the results of their work.

'They never go near an intercounty match, either at their own or the Co. Board's expense unless it is played in their own back garden. We ask you if this is the correct

attitude to adopt? Can such a selection committee be efficient and/or effective?

'Nor has that indifference vanished yet as can be seen from the fact that only one member of the County Board – and the most maligned member at that – travelled to Tralee for the recent League match. Where were the others? Did they think the result of the match a foregone conclusion, or are they solely a "victory" County Board?

'Perhaps if they had been present the result might have been a foregone conclusion! However, they weren't there, and the Secretary and four players selected, in approximately ten minutes, a team which was not afraid of Kerry, but which went out and justified their confidence in themselves as footballers. They may have missed the sermons and the fatherly advice and the old reminder that they had the confidence (?) of the Co. Board behind them! But the result of the match should answer that query. That the material is there has now been proved, but that it needs better management has likewise been proved.

'For instance, what lesson has the County Board learned from the Tralee game? Is it indicative of good management that one member is expected to bring back a full report on the prowess of each player, while the same member, while in Tralee, was meeting Kerry officials, making arrangements about hotel accommodation, meals etc., supplying bandages, elastoplast, and embrocation, presiding at a selection meeting, massaging the team before they went on the field, towelling and rubbing and supplying badly-needed refreshments at half-time, and even then at the team's request togging out as a sub? But more credit to the man in question – he did all that and something more when, in the first quarter he made two match-winning switches, a practice completely foreign to Mayo GAA officials. It is an unselfish efficiency and spirit such as this that a Co. Board wants, and not until this is forthcoming will football again flourish in Mayo.

'If we were asked to explain why recent Mayo selections have been unsuccessful we should say that, in the first place, the selection committee is too unwieldy to be effective. The present committee of from sixteen to twenty members should be slashed to approximately five, as big numbers tend to retard progress; secondly, the players don't get sufficient training as a team. Challenge games should (and can easily) be arranged with other counties so that (a) a team could be selected and (b) having been selected, that it could be trained as a unit. Thirdly, we feel that too much time and energy has been spent on petty squabbles existing among officials, but not among the players. We, as representatives of the four divisions within Mayo, ask you to put aside petty jealousies and favouritism, to get together, stay together and pull together, to pick a team, not of "historic" players, nor of "friendly" or "kindred" players, but a team made up of the best 15 players available.

'We know you can do it – we not only ask you but we demand you do this and do it here and now. If you do, 1948 will be our year. If you don't, then 1948 will echo the remarks heard from 1940 to 1947 – "Beaten again! Mayo, God help us!"'

THEIR HOPE THAT glory would be imminent did not transpire the following summer, or the summer after that, but the seeds had been sown.

In 1948 Mayo beat Galway after a replay and extra time, to win the Connacht title. They then shocked the country by decimating Kerry in the All-Ireland semi-final in Croke Park, 0-13 to 0-3. Flanagan excelled as the Mayo backs held the Kerry attack to what is still the lowest score ever recorded by the green and gold at the Jones' Road venue.

Could the Mayomen be on the verge of delivering glory at their first time of asking, as they had promised in their dramatic letter. Alas, the dream was shattered in September when All-Ireland champions Cavan edged a remarkable final 4-5 to 4-4, to retain the trophy they won the previous year in the Polo Grounds, New York. There was much controversy over the premature sounding of the final whistle in the 1948 final but the result stood.

The next year, they were also the best team in the province, beating Leitrim in the final, but in the semi-final against Meath, the concession of three second-half goals was just a bridge too far and they went tumbling out, but not without distinction. The plea to the selectors to do their job correctly and give places on merit and with structure fell on deaf ears and despite the belief that the Mayo team was superior to Meath, the disorganisation and the formation enabled inferior teams to make hay against the Mayomen.

Flanagan and the other senior players knew that this had to end and if the letter had not changed matters sufficiently, then they had to take it a step further. He was, of course, the logical choice to be captain of the team. Any other person would have been an imposter, but the rules stated that only the county champions could nominate a captain. Playing for Ballyhaunis, he knew that this route was one that might not be fulfilled in the remaining years of his career, so he lobbied for an alternative pathway to be drawn up.

Fortunately for him, it was the forward-thinking but diminutive club from The Neale who made the proposal to allow this rule to be changed. Their proposal that the captain should be selected by the selection committee was adopted, so one obstacle had been removed. Other obstacles in the pathway were disabled by the election of an ally as chairman of the county board. Dr Jimmy Laffey, a talented college footballer whose brother, Peter had starred with Mayo, become a link between the players and the board.

For the first time, there would be someone in local officialdom who would have an idea of the thinking of the players, who would be cognisant of their concerns and who would be well placed to make changes to enable Mayo to have the best chance possible to succeed. He was also a young man who knew of young men's concerns, of the issues that drove them as they matured. An educated man, he was intolerant of some of the buffoonery that existed in discussions at board level surrounding the county squad. He also felt that at last, the parochial nature of team selection would be wound down and that in the main, players would be picked on merit.

But old habits die hard.

In Flanagan, they had a bristly captain who was not going to take second best in terms of preparation. He ordered two dozen pairs of Blackthorn boots and had the bill sent to the county board.

For a team focused on glory, they were made to wait for their date in Connacht in 1950, as Galway, Roscommon, Sligo and Leitrim were all kept apart on the other side of the draw. Eventually, an experienced Roscommon team emerged as the other finalist. This was a Rossie team that were out for blood against Mayo, who had denied them a three in-a row five years earlier. In a physical game, Mick Mulderrig and Padraig Carney did the damage, getting the 1-7 which was enough to see them into the last four. Despite the lacklustre win, the team was still well out of sorts. A serious work in progress.

The team was readjusted for the All-Ireland semi-final against a tough Armagh side – the defence was turned into a garrison. They knew that the performance against Roscommon would not allow them to keep the ball kicked out to the Ulstermen. Peter Quinn and John McAndrew added to the wall that was Flanagan and Prendergast. Thou shalt not pass was the belief, and so it turned out. Mongey put in a star turn back in the middle of the pitch. Tom Langan was immense, tormenting the opposing defenders and scoring 2-3, and creating chances for as many again. Padraig Carney received a blow in the first-half that saw him treated for concussion and replaced at the break, but this Mayo side had serious endurance and they won by a dozen points.

At last, the team that said they wanted the help to get to a final, had done so. Now, it was just a matter of going out to win it.

UNDOUBTEDLY, SOME MEMBERS of the board resented being kept on the sidelines for an event such as this and did their best to get involved, to hop on the bandwagon on the road to glory. But Flanagan was not for turning, and he ran them all, including a priest who turned up one night at the camp in Ballina to get his tuppence worth in.

'Get out now, and I'll see you again when we have the Sam Maguire,' he said to the chastened cleric, who left the scene, smarting at the insolence of the Mayo captain.

Their sessions consisted of hard running, lots of sprints and dummies; of moving the ball through the lines with ease; of playing it to their running side. At night time, the players were given free use of the local cinema, and on other nights, they would sit down in groups and listen as captain Flanagan encouragingly outlined their respective strengths and weaknesses, listing stuff to work on the next day.

However, the county board, miffed at being omitted from the action, had a plan of their own, which they unveiled when they named the team for the final… listing a goalkeeper who had never played for the seniors before. Young Billy Durkin was a popular player who had been the star of the show when Mayo's juniors won earlier in the year, but he was not in the class of Sean Wynne or Tommy Byrne who had been the squad 'keepers for the semi-final. Indeed, Byrne was dropped from the final squad.

The squad were shocked, but there was little they could do. Flanagan in particular was very aggrieved that this stunt had been pulled at the last minute; a power-play by the Board to show they had still some relevance.

The team stayed in Barry's Hotel in Dublin but stopped for a much-needed meal in The Spa Hotel in Lucan, then out in the countryside. Mayo, going back to 1916, had had little luck with 'final day' weather and the Croke Park surface in previous finals, and this Sunday was no different.

Heavy showers around 11am left small puddles here and there on the pitch, creating a skiddy turf that mitigated a fast-running game that Mayo liked. James

Laffey in his excellent *The Road to '51* book tells of Flanagan's ability to break the tension. As they waited and shuffled nervously for Louth to leave their room and go onto the pitch, he asked a steward in a voice that could be heard down the corridor 'has that junior team gone out yet?'

To everyone who saw Flanagan that day, one thing was certain. He was not going to be leading a losing team back into that dressing-room that evening. He visibly took on the pride of being the captain, and it showed in his stance as he led his men, plus mascot Paddy Bluett who walked alongside Tom Langan despite having being ordered off by a Croke Park official.

Flanagan's desire even influenced the spin of the coin and Mayo elected to play against the mild wind that blew down the park, drying the disappearing puddles. Mayo have had many disastrous starts in finals, and this one was no different.

The Bishop of Killaloe threw in the ball, but Mongey and Carney, believing this to be merely ceremonial and to be followed by a real throw-in, did not even leap for it, and were stunned when the referee signalled play on.

Louth's McDonnell swept through to set up an opening score after just 11 seconds. Mayo were stunned and needed something or someone to settle them. Mayo conceding early in an All-Ireland final – how many more times would we read that in the 90 years afterwards?

Ball after ball was parachuted into the Mayo defence and, time after time, Flanagan rose to anticipate the challenge, clearing with aplomb. Padraig Carney spoke in later years of the importance of those early minutes and the role played by Flanagan in steadying the Mayo ship.

At that moment, few could see anything but another chastening defeat for the Mayomen. But settle they did. And when Quinn equalised and then Solan goaled, Mayo were on a roll. The lifting of the pressure and the changing of the momentum saw Carney and Mongey grow in stature, creating chance after chance, but wasted because of the slippery underfoot conditions. Billy Kenny was at the centre of everything, splaying passes around and creating the scoring opportunities.

The yielding turf though claimed a victim when Kenny slid into Louth's Frank Reid and let out a piercing roar. A compound fracture of his leg meant his day was over, but it also signalled the end of his competitive career. As he left the pitch in agony, he signalled to his teammates to find more within themselves to win the game.

The five-point advantage they held was soon overturned and Louth led at the interval.

At the break, Flanagan was insistent that Wynne replace the nervous Durkin in goal and the goalkeeper repaid this faith with a splendid full length save to palm a shot onto the post and deny Louth a goal that would surely have won them the match.

The clock was ticking down and changes had to be made as Louth moved two points clear. Langan was starved of ball inside, so a decision was made on the sideline to allow him to come out in search of better fortune. This he did to great effect, when his blockdown broke to Mick Flanagan who was flying through the middle, the momentum carrying him past the Louth 'keeper, his punch landing in the net to put Mayo ahead.

Louth were stunned as the Mayomen grew in stature, finding a second wind. When the two Mulderrigs combined, the result was a sharp point which turned out to be the last score of the game. But the last minute was not without drama.

Sean Flanagan replicated his early game form when he terminated a last ditch attack by Louth, winning back possession and sending Mayo away in search of an insurance point that they did not need.

They had done it.

What they had promised in that letter had come to fruition. For just the second time, Sam Maguire would be coming across the Shannon to Mayo. Twenty-six years after they were denied a title, 14 years after they had secured one, Flanagan's vision that this team was good enough was finally realised.

THE BOY WHO had painted the gate green and red had fulfilled his own dream. Forty-three years later, many of the men he had led around Croke Park that day attended to escort his coffin to Kilcolman Cemetery near Ballaghaderreen.

Following him in death, as they had in life.

Eamonn Mongey, who was one of those who carried his coffin on that sad day, said that Flanagan had been a missionary who had come along to lead Mayo football out of the darkness. 'We knew we had good players but what we needed was someone to come along and lead us. When he came out of defence, toe to hand, we knew that he was going to achieve something positive. He was a man who knew what were the important things in life.'

He played a great role in subsequent years in keeping the group together. Dr Mickey Loftus recalled that, when the 1958 Munich Air Disaster happened, he was unique in coming out and paying tribute to the Manchester United players and others who had died, saying that sport transcended all barriers.

John Prenty, another Mayoman who has served the sport well in the west, said that Flanagan wanted to get rid of one record.

'He wanted to rid himself of the tag of being the last Mayo captain to bring home the Sam Maguire. He made an immense contribution, and his deeds will last forever,' he added.

The search to succeed him as Mayo's last victorious captain continues.

On and on, it goes.

*Padraig Carney (top) in his
heyday and one of his many
visits home in latter years.
The 'Flying Doctor' (left)
rests up before one of his
big games after journeying
home from the US.*

PART ★ THREE

A TOUCH OF CLASS

THE BICYCLE SCREECHED to a halt outside the house, the boy upon it using his shoes to brake, because the brakes did more screeching than braking. He rested it down on its side of the pavement and lifted the knocker on MacConnell's door.

No answer after thirty seconds, so he rat-a-tat-tated again. This time, there was the shuffle of footsteps inside. The door opened... and the boy reached into the well-worn leather satchel he wore around his neck, the pocket sealed by a buckle holding its precious cargo. He knew the hard way that there was no sympathy for you if you lost a telegram halfway across town.

'Telegram for ya, Mr MacConnell...'

'Yeah, right thanks,' said the man holding the door with one arm, reaching out with the other. MacConnell had been expecting this, knew what it pertained to, but just didn't know which answer it would give. If it was a negative, it would disappoint tens of thousands. If it was a yes, it would lift a whole county, perhaps everyone else who enjoyed seeing excellence in action.

He unfolded the paper... and read the typed message.

Will travel 23rd. Awaiting instructions

Yes, he said to himself, clenching a fist. Now, there was work to be done, a trip to the travel agent to book the flight.

The boy was coming home... for the match.

A WEEK BEFOREHAND, the Mayo County Board had voted unanimously to allocate £200 to fly home Padraig Carney for the National League semi-final against Dublin on April 25. In those days of limited communications, it was a mammoth feat to do a weekend commute from New York to Ireland.

'I'd fly out of New York on a Friday evening,' Dr Carney recalled a few years ago. 'The first part of the trip took 12 hours... to Newfoundland. Then to Shannon... from there, I'd take a flight to Dublin, arriving on time to sleep in my father's house on Saturday night. Then on Sunday, after the game, I'd go straight to the airport and fly back... and be at work in the hospital in New York on Tuesday morning.'

Having sent the telegram to the county board, Carney got back to the rigours of the life of a medic in the world's most chaotic city. A place where he had made his home in his mid-twenties, knowing that opportunities to make a difference in medicine were better facilitated than in the austere Ireland of the early 1950s. Research in Irish hospitals was almost non-existent and the prospect of pushing to make the best contribution to the discipline were limited.

It was ironic that he was now communicating via telegram with the county board as one of the more recent correspondences he had with them was a few years earlier, when the medals from the All-Ireland success of 1951 were sent to the players through the mail, a move that did not sit well with any of the recipients.

When one looks back now and thinks of the perceived and emotional value of a Celtic Cross, to think that the county board did not deem the occasion worthy of a proper presentation says a lot about the administration of the game at that time.

In those circumstances, it is noteworthy that Mayo rose to the top of the pile in those years despite, rather than because, of the backing they got from the officials.

★ ★ ★ ★ ★

KILLASSER-MAN BERNARD O'Hara is a genial Mayoman, who has made his life in Galway. I first encountered him when I studied in Galway RTC in the mid-80s, just one of thousands of Mayo people who benefited from his encouragement and mentoring. The 80s were a bleak time and opportunity was scarce, so having someone like Bernard believe in you meant a lot. Respected in academic, historical and commercial circles, rising to become president of Galway Chamber of Commerce, he has been a constant drum-beater for the Red and Green in the neighbouring county.

Bernard was a close friend of the late Padraig Carney. Both hailed from Swinford, and both pushed the Mayo cause throughout their lives. It was through the magic of the pictures painted by radio that Bernard first became enthralled by the silken skills of Dr Carney.

'After listening to Michael O'Hehir's commentary on the Mayo v Dublin National League semi-final on April 25, 1954, Padraig Carney became my football hero with a 'Man of the Match' performance and where he was first given the sobriquet 'The Flying Doctor',' recalled Bernard.

'We first met in Galway in May 1978, when Padraig led a group of American doctors on a trip to Ireland. We really got to know each other when Padraig came to open the pitch and community centre in Swinford in May 1979.

'We then started to communicate with each other on a regular basis, and the Carneys stayed with my family on their yearly visits to the west of Ireland. From the early 80s, we had a ritual where we attended a Mayo football championship game together in summer and the All-Ireland football final in September.'

As a driving member of the Mayo Association Galway, Bernard was the chief organiser of the Golden Jubilee dinner in Westport to celebrate the Mayo All-Ireland winning teams of 1950 and 1951, in May 2000, and of another function in 2004 to honour the National League winning team of 1954.

'Padraig, in my opinion, was the greatest, and one of the all-time greats in the history of the game. He wore the green and red senior jersey of Mayo with distinction from the age of 17 in 1945 until his emigration at his prime in March 1954 at the age of 26.

'Mayo County Board brought him back from New York for the Mayo v Dublin National League semi-final on April 25, 1954 and he captained Mayo to a thrilling 0-11 to 0-7 victory. Michael O'Hehir, the wonderful GAA commentator, immortalised Padraig that day as 'The Flying Doctor'.

'He was brought back again for the league final, which they won,' recalled Bernard of his long-time friend.

IF PADRAIG CARNEY was a modern-era player, he would be a media superstar. Intelligent, articulate, measured, compassionate, a real poster-boy for the game.

To think that he played his last game for Mayo at the tender age of 26 is shocking, but what he had done for the cause up to that point, and for what he did for humanity afterwards, showed the measure of the man. Perhaps if he had played on, Mayo might have had more All-Irelands, and the long-stretch back to victory might not have hit 1951. However, the team that last won Sam Maguire was on the verge of breaking up, shattered by injury and emigration, so perhaps such thinking is just wishful in a lifetime of... 'What ifs'.

But Padraig Carney was different and knew that himself.

He told Keith Duggan in the terrific tome *House of Pain* that perhaps it was down to his 'one-child family' syndrome, this desire to be the best version of himself at everything he did.

'I guess I always had an in-born ambition to succeed in life. For better or worse, I went to the school where my mother taught and she made sure I was diligent. I was never forced to do anything. I was encouraged. My father always made it easy for me to play sports and from an early age, I realised that I wanted to excel at studies.

'Even then, I knew there was something after sports.'

Writing this reminds me of Tom Parsons and how he had several Mayo careers. One quite young, and another two during which he suffered his horrific knee injury. Tom equated his ability to recover from injury to the fact that there was so much more to his life at the time than football, whereas, as a young man, it was all-consuming.

Two Mayo men, decades apart, but of one mind with their thinking.

For Carney, the hardest decision was to make the choice between his sport and his career. He had won every honour in gaelic football: two All-Irelands back-to-back in 1950 and '51, four Connacht senior medals, two National League medals in 1949 and '54, and one Connacht minor in 1946. In addition, he won three Sigerson Cup medals with UCD in 1945/46, 1947/48 and 1949/50, and was captain in 1947/48.

After playing for the Combined Universities in 1948, 1949, 1950 and 1951, he was selected for the Rest of Ireland against the Combined Universities in 1952 and '53. He won a Railway Cup medal with Connacht in 1951, as well as two Mayo Senior Championship medals with Castlebar Mitchels in 1951 and '52 (while working in the County Hospital), and a Junior Championship medal with Charlestown Sarsfields in 1953 (while serving as a doctor in Charlestown).

Padraig was not selected on the Team of the Century, or the Team of the Millennium; in both cases he was nominated against Seán Purcell at centre-forward and because of the latter's long and distinguished record, there was only going to be one winner there. With all players on the millennium team included in the GAA Hall of Fame, Padraig Carney was nominated to the GAA Hall of Fame in 2001, the first year two new players were to be nominated each year (the other nominee was Jack O'Shea of Kerry).

This indicates how close he was to selection on the Team of the Millennium, and the result would be the same, regardless of who was nominated against Seán Purcell. A postage stamp (30p/38c) was issued in Padraig's honour on September 5 that year. His club is recorded as Swinford on the Hall of Fame plaque in Croke Park, the same as appeared on the 1950 All-Ireland final programme, an honour that brings pride to Bernard O'Hara, who to this day continues to honour his great friend at every opportunity that arises and who was delighted to help me pay tribute to him. When you consider all that Dr Carney achieved, it is remarkable to remember that these were secured in a football career that ended at such an early age.

THE IRELAND INTO which he was born shaped him for the contribution he went on to make in life. Padraig Carney was born on January 7, 1928 in the townland of Treenagleragh, near Kiltimagh, the only child of Thomas and Ellen Carney. Thomas Carney (1891-1971), a native of Treenagleragh, was a member of the Royal Irish Constabulary (RIC) from 1914 to 1919, when like other strong nationalists he resigned following the outbreak of the Irish War of Independence.

He married Ellen Groarke from Swinford in 1926, a primary schoolteacher and a member of Cumann na mBan. In 1932, the Carneys sold their home and farm in Treenagleragh and went to live in Swinford, where Padraig grew up. He went to Culmore National School, near Swinford, where his mother was one of his teachers.

In September 1940, he entered St Nathy's College, Ballaghaderreen, where in 1944 he came under the influence of a great football coach, Fr Patrick Towey, a, person for whom he had enormous respect, and who was quick to recognise him as a precocious football talent.

The Second World War badly affected football in St Nathy's, but Padraig played for the college in his junior and senior years. In his final year, 1945, St Jarlath's Tuam, defeated St Nathy's.

There was no minor team in Swinford at the time because of the war, and there were no All-Ireland Minor Football Championships in 1942, 1943, 1944 or 1945. He played minor football for Mayo in 1946 and won a Connacht Championship medal when they defeated Galway by 4-9 to 1-5 in the final. They were later narrowly defeated by Kerry in Tralee, but Padraig believed that Mayo would almost certainly have won that game if it had been played at a neutral venue.

He went to University College Dublin (UCD) in 1945 to study medicine and was chosen for their Sigerson Cup team in his first year, a rare achievement. He won three Sigerson Cup medals with UCD in 1945/46, 1947/48 and 1949/50. Sean Flanagan was captain of the winning team in 1945/46, and after captaining Mayo to All Ireland success in 1950 and '51 he became the first gaelic footballer to captain Sigerson Cup and Sam Maguire Cup-winning teams.

Padraig Carney was captain of the UCD Sigerson-winning team in 1947-48. His Sigerson career is well captured by Dónal McAnallen in his book *The Cups that Cheered: A History of the Sigerson, Fitzgibbon, and Higher Education Gaelic Games (2012)*, in which he states that *'Padraig Carney began the 1949/50 competition in stellar form, scoring 1-6 from centrefield against UCC in the semi-final'*.

Despite the efforts of Billy Durkin and Seamus McHugh, football was not well organised in Swinford in the late 40s and the club lost a great opportunity to avail of the talent of Carney. Even after several magnificent displays, his selection on the Mayo senior team was not assured, as the selectors considered him too young. But Fr Towey and many of Padraig's admirers knew his real ability, maturity and strength, recalled Bernard O'Hara.

'They finally prevailed on the senior selectors and Padraig was chosen to play for the Mayo senior football team in August 1945 at the age of 17 in a challenge game against Galway at Charlestown. He is said to have scored a point with his first kick of the ball.'

His consistent and brilliant performances over the following nine years far surpassed his great early promise, and all expectations. While still a minor, he was selected to play for Mayo at centrefield in the 1946 Connacht Senior Championship with Henry Kenny, an All-Ireland winner from 1936 who had come out of retirement.

On his championship debut on June 23, 1946, Padraig scored four points as Mayo defeated Sligo by 2-9 to 2-6. The 1946 Connacht final in Ballinasloe against Roscommon (All-Ireland champions in 1943 and '44) was a tough game, which Mayo could have won only for a controversial goal by Jimmy Murray. The ball was deflected around the post by the Mayo goalkeeper but it struck the umpire and the in-rushing Murray sent the ball to the net. While the referee was consulting his umpires, Murray raised the green flag.

After further consultation, the goal was allowed. Roscommon won by one point, 1-4 to 0-6 (with Padraig scoring two points). With an objection from Mayo and a counter objection, Roscommon agreed to a replay, which they won by 1-9 to 1-2. This great and strong Roscommon team, which was most unlucky to be defeated in the 1946 final by Kerry in a replay, also defeated Mayo in 1947.

After drawing 1-7 each with Kerry in the first round of the league in 1947, with Padraig scoring five points, he was one of five Dublin-based players who wrote that famous letter to the county board, dated November 5, 1947, demanding a new approach to team selection, training, and the provision of challenge games. The county board responded, as did the players and 1948 was very exciting for Mayo. After easy wins over Leitrim and Sligo in the Connacht Championship, Mayo defeated Galway in the final after extra-time in a replay by 2-10 to 2-7, the county's first Connacht title since 1939.

Carney was outstanding in both games at centrefield with Eamonn Mongey, but he really excelled in the reply, scoring nine points. James Laffey in his excellent book, *The Road to 51: The Making of Mayo Football*, stated: *'The Swinford man was still only 20 and knowledgeable football men in the county were already saying they had never seen anything like him.... the nine-point salvo in the Connacht final replay propelled Carney's burgeoning reputation through the stratosphere. The finest young footballer in the country had been revealed in all his splendour. And he was wearing a Mayo jersey. The famine of the Forties was officially over.'*

PADRAIG'S GREATEST DISAPPOINTMENT as a footballer was that 1948 All-Ireland final, in which Cavan defeated Mayo by 4-5 to 4-4, when a gale-force wind spoiled the game. The bizarre half-time score in that game was Cavan 3-2 Mayo 0-0.

Mayo, then aided by the gale, staged a magnificent second-half recovery and came within one point of Cavan (4-5 to 4-4) with approximately four minutes left to play. Mayo attacked and were awarded a close-in free. Carney took the free, but to the astonishment of the crowd, Mick Higgins, the Cavan centre-forward, whose father came from Kiltimagh, is said to have advanced within 14 yards and blocked down the free. The referee did not order the free to be retaken.

To make matters worse, seconds later, the referee blew the final whistle approximately three minutes before full time – not the last time Mayo had late free-drama in finals, as we were to experience in the years ahead.

It was a bitter disappointment for Mayo and especially for young Padraig Carney, who felt it was cruel to lose an All-Ireland final by one point in such circumstances.

'He sat down on the pitch, placed his hands over his face and cried and cried. He always accepted that the referee made a mistake,' recalled Bernard O'Hara

'However, he had the distinction of scoring the first goal ever scored from a penalty in an All-Ireland senior football final in that game. One of Padraig's great memories became the wonderful homecoming reception they received.'

MAYO WENT ON to win the National League title in 1949 with Padraig Carney excelling in all games. Mayo defeated Louth in the final by 1-8 to 1-6. In the 1949 championship, Mayo defeated Roscommon in the first round, then Sligo by 7-10 to 0-2 – the day Peter Solan scored 5-2 – and they overcame Leitrim in the Connacht final by 4-6 to 0-3.

Great things were expected of Mayo after the 1948 final and successful league campaign, but they were surprised by a good Meath team in the All-Ireland semi-final, 3-10 to 1-10. A number of players were played out of their usual positions in that game, especially in the half-back line where the recently-emigrated Pat McAndrew's absence was key.

In the 1950 Connacht Championship, Mayo defeated Roscommon by 1-7 to 0-4 in the decider at Tuam. Padraig Carney was brilliant at centrefield. Mayo defeated Armagh by 3-9 to 0-6 in the All-Ireland semi-final and went on to defeat Louth by 2-5 to 1-6 in the final, which, as we mentioned in the previous chapter, was not Padraig's or Mayo's best performance, but it was enough to take the Sam Maguire Cup to the county for just the second time.

Mayo had a very successful league campaign in 1950/51 but, without the injured Carney, lost to Meath in the final. However, he was back and was one of 10 Mayo players who won the 1951 Railway Cup with Connacht, the first since 1938.

In the 1951 championship, Mayo defeated Sligo by 3-7 to 1-5 in the first round, then Galway in the Connacht final by 4-13 to 2-3, and Kerry in the All-Ireland semi-final after a replay.

Mayo, with Carney at his brilliant best, retained the Sam Maguire Cup by defeating the 1949 champions and reigning league champions, Meath, by 2-8 to 0-9 in the final. He was 'Man of the Match' and 'Sports star of the Week' and only 23 years of age.

John D Hickey writing in the *Irish Independent* the following day said, *'It does not require any search to find the main reason for the Connacht side's easy passage – it was in the main due to the brilliance of Carney. The Swinford man did so well that it occasionally seemed that it must be the design of even his opponents to place the ball in his hands'.*

'Onlooker', writing on the All-Ireland final in the *Western People*, stated: *'Carney – The Inspiration – Padraig Carney made all the difference. This statement was in the mouth of every spectator leaving the field and I have no hesitation in naming him the best player on view'.*

Bernard told me that the victorious Mayo team became very disillusioned after receiving their 1951 All-Ireland medals at Christmas in the post; it was a terrible insult to the team, and many of them never forgave the county board for it.

By 1952, the team had lost a number of players to emigration... Pat McAndrew, Fr Peter Quinn, and the biggest loss of all, Peter Solan. Billy Kenny never played for the county again after breaking his leg in the 1950 final, and after graduation as a doctor, he also emigrated.

Mayo were in the doldrums for 1952 and '53. In 1952, they defeated Sligo in the first round but were beaten by Roscommon in the final at McHale Park by 3-5 to 0-6, a game they had taken too casually. In 1953, Roscommon again defeated Mayo – without the injured Paddy Prendergast – by 1-6 to 0-6 in the Connacht final at St Colman's Park, Roscommon.

Padraig Carney organised a football game in Swinford on Whit Sunday 1953 between a Mick Higgins (Cavan) selection of county stars from around the country and his own selection, chiefly Mayo players, to raise funds for Saint Patrick's College in the town, which opened in 1945. He had organised games between Mayo and Galway, and Mayo and Monaghan, to raise funds for the school in 1950. This exemplified the great community spirit of the man.

A BRILLIANT STUDENT as well as a sports person, Padraig had qualified as a doctor in 1951 and worked for four months in Cavan General Hospital, then for over a year and a half as a house surgeon in the County Hospital, Castlebar, before serving as the dispensary doctor in Charlestown. While in Castlebar, he made a huge contribution to the Mitchels club, winning two Mayo Championships with them in 1951 and '52. The following year, he played a leading role in Charlestown Sarsfields becoming Mayo junior football champions. It seemed he brought football success wherever he went.

Pádraig married Moira McCabe, from County Wexford, also a medical doctor and a member of his UCD class, in St Michael's Church, Dun Laoghaire on October 14, 1953. The groomsman was a member of the Mayo 1950 football panel, Liam Hastings from Westport, and the bridesmaid was Máire O'Caoimh, daughter of Padraig, the then General Secretary of the GAA (Moira had three brothers but no sister).

After their marriage, they lived in Charlestown. The 1950s was a most depressing decade in Irish economic history, with few opportunities and massive emigration. By 1954, emigration was exceeding 40,000 a year, a figure which can be compared with an annual birth rate of about 63,000 and an average death rate of 36,000.

There were then few employment opportunities in a depressed country for anyone, but there was consternation, shock and disbelief, when it was announced that Padraig and his wife were emigrating to the USA. Padraig and Moira had decided to base themselves in New York and went there in March 1954, a most difficult decision to make having regard to his achievements as a footballer and the adulation he enjoyed.

However, he was determined and ambitious to excel as much in medicine as he had on the football field, and saw that opportunity then in the US. They had intended to return to Ireland after a few years, but having raised a family Stateside, they never did.

He played his last game for Mayo before emigrating, in Castlebar against Cavan in the league on February 28, 1954, which they won by 1-11 to 1-3, with Padraig scoring six points. It has to be appreciated that he was then at his prime as a footballer and this factor has to be taken into account in any evaluation of his football career. One can only speculate as to what may have been the fate of Mayo football in the mid 50s had he not emigrated, but it was very possible that Mayo would have won All-Ireland titles in 1954 and '55.

PADRAIG SECURED A post-graduate junior doctor position in St Clare's Hospital in New York City, where one of his first patients was Rocky Marciano, then Heavyweight Champion of the World. It was shift-work, 24 hours on, 24 hours off.

Mayo qualified to meet Dublin in the 1954 National League semi-final in Croke Park on April 25, 1954. Dublin were league champions at the time and warm favourites. Mayo County Board, under the chairmanship of Fr Patrick Towey, decided to bring Carney home from New York for the game.

He had to leave Idlewild Airport in New York (now JFK) on the Friday evening, with a stop in Gander, Newfoundland for refuelling on the then almost 12-hour flight to Shannon, and then on to Dublin.

After the game, he had to fly back to New York for work on Tuesday morning. He was the first footballer to be flown from the US for a game, which generated huge national publicity resulting in him becoming known thereafter as 'The Flying Doctor'. Never has a county's faith in one man been so richly repaid, as Carney captained Mayo to a magnificent 0-11 to 0-7 victory over Dublin, scoring seven points of the total. It was his finest hour in the Green and Red. Supporters draped him in Mayo flags and carried him in triumph to the dressing-room.

Padraig Carney had reached the zenith of his distinguished football career and won an indelible place in the hearts of all Mayo supporters. He always said that the Dublin game was his greatest thrill as a footballer. He was again flown home for the 1954 league final in which he captained Mayo to defeat Carlow by 2-10 to 0-3. It was his last competitive game for Mayo on Irish soil. One can really reflect on his amazing achievements when it is appreciated that he played his last game for Mayo in the Polo Grounds, New York, in October 1954 at the age of 26.

MAYO OFFICIALS BELIEVED that they could win the 1954 Connacht Championship without Padraig Carney, and planned to bring him home for the All-Ireland semi-final and final (such faith). However, Galway and a brilliant Seán Purcell had other ideas and exploded the Mayo dream by defeating them in the championship.

Purcell was outstanding in that game, going to full-back to mark Tom Langan, and later two other Mayo footballers. That game proved that there was only one Mayo footballer who could handle Seán Purcell, and that was Padraig Carney. Padraig had been training hard in his spare time awaiting a call from the county board that never came, and the Galway victory was a big shock for him.

Padraig and Seán Purcell remained good friends and regularly met at Connacht Championship games and on other occasions. They met for the last time at the Mayo v Galway game in Pearse Stadium, Galway, on July 10, 2005, which was to be Seán's last game (he had an operation in mid-August and passed away suddenly on August 27, 2005 at the age of 74).

Padraig met up with his former colleagues living in Mayo on many occasions during his regular trips to the county – with Fr Peter Quinn, who retired to Enniscrone; with Fr Paddy Towey in Gurteen, County Sligo; and with Dr Jimmy Laffey in Kiltimagh, who was chairman of the Mayo County GAA Board in 1950 and '51.

He regularly met Paddy Prendergast from Tralee at Mayo games, Seán Flanagan on various occasions, John McAndrew from Birmingham before some All-Ireland finals where Mayo were involved, Frank Fleming from the 1954 Mayo National League-winning team every year in Dublin, as well as Dan O'Neill from that team, and the family of the late Liam Hastings in Galway.

All surviving members of Mayo teams from 1948 to 1954, their spouses, as well as two family members of deceased players, met at the Golden Jubilee function in May 2000 in Westport for the Mayo All-Ireland winning teams of 1950 and '51, organised by the Mayo Association Galway – and was a memorable night for everyone.

PADRAIG CARNEY EXCELLED in all the skills of gaelic football and perfected them assiduously, almost on a daily basis. He played most of his football as a midfielder or centre-forward, and regularly moved between both positions as the occasion demanded, adopting a simple direct style. He assisted all his colleagues and used his foresight to advantage, frequently gaining crucial and opportunistic possession. A great strategist and team man, he was always superbly fit and, in all games, exploited his speed, side-step and body swerve.

Bernard O'Hara stresses that Carney's physique and stamina were his calling cards.

'He was undoubtedly one of the strongest players of his time, fourteen stone plus, but never used his strength to unfair advantage. Neither did he shirk a challenge. His remarkable stamina was evidenced by the fact that he could, and did, play three competitive representative senior football games on the same day, without apparently tiring or reducing his work rate.

'His fielding was perfect and rarely did he lose possession. He perfected the pick-up, the chip and the solo run, all of which he used intelligently for team advantage in defence and attack. In kicking, the essential art, he spent numerous hours on his own practising and following kicks through to achieve accuracy, and was equally good with each foot from play, but placed balls were taken with his right. He was consistently Mayo's leading scorer, with a total of 11-185 in 55 league and championship games for Mayo, an incredible figure for a player at centrefield or who spent periods there in almost all games

'About two-thirds of that figure came from frees, in many cases when himself was fouled, and the balance from play.'

Following the advice of his great mentor, Fr Towey, he believed that the first 10 yards were the most important in the race for possession, and was alert for every opportunity, especially quick frees for and against his team. He believed strongly that a pass should be given to a player running to it at speed, and never to a player standing in a stationary position. Features of his performances were his consistency and enormous work-rate. For him, every game was unique, and he always adapted to and mastered the conditions and circumstances.

Padraig Carney was a non-drinker, a non-smoker, a superb athlete and golfer, as well as a gaelic footballer. He was a member of the Swinford Golf Club's team that won the Connacht Shield in 1953.

In New York, Padraig played football for Mayo and for New York against visiting Irish teams, including Galway in 1957.

AFTER SPENDING ALMOST a year in New York, Padraig and Moira Carney went out for dinner one night to discuss whether they should return to Ireland. The lives of Padraig and Moira were about to take a new turn.

That evening, they met a Killasser-born priest, Fr John Conlon, a pastor in the diocese of Los Angeles, who advised them to forget New York and go west to California, where there were great opportunities for good doctors.

They took his advice and went to Long Beach, California, where Padraig obtained work in a local hospital, and they both fell in love with the place. Always ambitious and focused, Padraig saw a big opportunity to specialise in gynaecology. He and his family moved to Detroit, where he undertook four further years of study and training from 1956 to 1959, qualifying as a gynaecologist and obstetrician.

While studying in Detroit, he played for the Mayo team there and won the US Mid-West Championship (which included teams from Delaware, Pittsburgh, Cleveland, Chicago, Toronto and Buffalo). In 1959, the Carney family (by then there were three children, together with his mother and father, who had moved out to the US in 1955 to be with them) packed into a Chevrolet car and drove to Long Beach, California, an amazing adventure covering about 600 miles a day.

In Long Beach, Padraig developed a very successful private practice, and quickly established a national reputation in his field. He was attached to the Memorial Medical Hospital, Long Beach, a training hospital for the Medical Faculty of the University of California at Irvine. During his working life, he delivered about 10,000 babies and performed 2,000 surgeries, before spending the last five years of his career as Chief of Staff of both Long Beach Memorial Hospital and Long Beach Memorial Women's Hospital.

Over the final years of his career, he served on a national review committee responsible for hospital accreditation and compliance.

His daughter-in-law, Mary Beth Carney said that during his four-decade medical career as an obstetrician and gynaecologist, he was an exceptional, dedicated doctor. 'No matter what time or where he was, when he got the call, he stopped what was doing to care for his patients.

'He was instrumental in establishing the Long Beach Memorial Preferred

Provider Organization in recognition of the changing practice in medicine and health care insurance in the United States. He was also a leader in treating pregnant women with RH-Negative blood for babies, factors which can cause severe problems,' she said.

PADRAIG CARNEY PERFORMED the official opening of the new pitch and community centre in Swinford in May 1979, when he travelled specially from California for the occasion. He was there again on May 6, 2012 to dedicate the pitch in honour of Garda Robert McCallion, the young Swinford and Mayo footballer who died after being knocked down on March 26, 2009 by the driver of a stolen car, while on duty as a guard in Letterkenny, County Donegal.

Padraig and Moira had a holiday home at Fethard-on-Sea in Wexford (Moira's native county). Pádraig brought several groups of tourists, especially medical people, from California to Ireland over the years, including to Mayo and Galway. In 1996, he attended six All-Ireland finals during a three-week vacation in September of that year and he believed in being early for all games.

Padraig holds a special place in the hearts of Mayo football supporters, and his name and deeds are still remembered with affection. Sean Flanagan, captain of the Mayo 1950/51 team, in a tribute in 1979 said Padraig Carney was gifted, fearless and at his best, majestic. *'He combined great strength with the most delicate touch and gained more possession than any of his contemporaries. Of his greatness, there is not and never will be any doubt, and he is deservedly a legend.'*

One, indeed, can only speak of Padraig Carney in superlative terms as a footballer and as a person. He was a great Mayo man, a great Irishman, a great Irish-American, a loyal son, a devoted husband, and an exemplary father. His wife, Moira died in late 2017, and in June 2019, Padraig also passed away.

Is it possible to read of his achievements and not to marvel at his life?

He made red blood flow with pride through the veins of Mayo fans for a decade; and in life, he gave life to thousands of young Americans who might never know that they were delivered by the safest pair of hands possible.

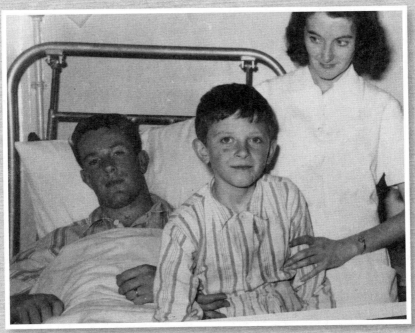

John Morley photographed in hospital before the 1967 All-Ireland semi-final, with the author's brother, Michael, for company.

PART ★ FOUR

THE MAN IN THE STRIPED PYJAMAS

ALL THROUGH MY early childhood, the photograph fascinated me.

There it was in among the dusty pictures of my parents in their courtship – the wonderful Hyannisport-esque Kodachrome of the American relations who came home every few years to Irish salads of scallions and ham and eggs, and tea served in willow blue teacups.

It didn't belong to those groupings in the albums. Nor to the sturdy formal poses of the early 20th century. Nor was it of the vintage of the sepia studies of long dead grandparents at which you'd stare to see if that's where you got your ears, your noble jaw or the big forehead.

No, this picture was different.

Indeed, it could have been described as an imposter in the family photo album, were it not for the fact that it featured my big brother, Michael. It was obviously taken in a hospital, which in itself was a strange setting for a photograph, and it showed a fine man in striped pyjamas, sitting in a bed, with a nurse standing alongside, her arms around the shoulder of a young lad, aged no more than 10 at the time.

The boy, also in striped pyjamas, was Michael who was hospitalised for a few weeks in 1967 to have his appendix removed. The nurse, her name not recorded, guarding over them... and the man, one of the iconic footballers in Mayo's history – the outstanding John Morley.

Morley's illness was in the news, and the photograph in the newspaper because his bout of appendicitis in the weeks before that year's All-Ireland semi-final could not have happened at a worse time for the county's footballing fortunes, at the end of a decade in which to that point, they had failed to play in an All-Ireland semi-final.

'He was a total gentleman,' said Michael Varley recently. 'They say that perhaps you should never meet your heroes, but in this case, that old maxim was not true, because John was the epitome of the iconic sporting star. There was a constant stream of visitors in to see him, and none of them came empty-handed, and whatever goodies were among his haul, he passed onto me,' he recalled.

Squared jawed and athletic, Morley was the epitome of a footballer of that age. How supporters must have wished he served in a different era when his undoubted talent would have surely brought a Celtic Cross for his mantelpiece.

The Mayo team of which John Morley had been the star for the guts of a decade had been starved of success, denied glory by the supremacy of a Galway team who had their best decade ever, winning three Sam Maguires in succession and setting the bar for the rest of the country in terms of style and set-up.

But in the summer of 1967, just weeks before this photograph was taken in the County Hospital in Castlebar, Mayo had finally beaten the Tribesmen, and because of this feat, could look forward to their first All-Ireland semi-final in the 60s, with hopes high that they could defeat a talented Meath team and proceed to a final against Cork. But disaster struck when Morley was diagnosed with appendicitis and was hospitalised for surgery with just three weeks left to the Croke Park showdown with The Royals. The photograph was taken and published in the *Connaught Telegraph*, such was the massive interest generated by Morley's illness and the nurse and his ward-colleague, my brother, Michael were brought on board by the snapper to add context.

Without Morley, Mayo's chances would be diminished considerably. Remarkably, but perhaps unwisely, the recuperating Morley was thrown into the fray in Croke Park, coming on in the second-half. But, understandably, constrained by the impact of the surgery and the stitches, he was a shadow of himself and Mayo lost heavily.

The headline in the *Telegraph* two days afterwards was **DEMORLEY-ISED** after a Mayo loss that summed up the 1960s for the men in green and red.

WHEN I DISCOVERED the photo in my scrapbooks in the attic at home a few years ago, I tweeted it, tagging @MayoGAA. The response was enormous and the comments generous, as the image was shared far and wide, with compliments and messages about the man who looked every inch the hero in the picture. Morley was a massive man, with legs like tree trunks and an understanding of the game that enabled him to play in the demanding role of centre half-back, where he never let his county down.

The photo is all the more iconic because just 13 years later, and just six summers after he hung up his Mayo boots, John Morley would be dead, struck down by the guns of heartless killers as they struggled to escape the pursuit of the former legend, following a bank raid in Ballaghadereen. Mayo has had a sad legacy of losing gardai who were killed in the service of the state. Even in these times when terrorism is no longer the scourge it was in the 1980s, the county has suffered immeasurably.

Swinford's Robbie McCallion was killed after being hit by a vehicle driven by a fleeing suspect he and colleagues were attempting to apprehend while stealing another vehicle in 2009. Ballina Garda Tony Golden was shot and killed while attending a domestic dispute in Omeath, Co Louth in 2015… and more recently, Charlestown's Colm Horkan was shot and killed after being disarmed during an incident on a mobile anti-crime patrol in Castlerea. These deaths, all heart-breaking and tragic like Morley's, cut short fine young lives of men who would have gone on to continue the strong role they played in their communities.

Morley's death came at the start of a depressing decade in Irish history.

The morning news bulletins were still peppered with details of the latest atrocity in the north of the country. In the west, we were spared the worst of it. Or so we thought. It was just an ordinary summer Monday – the Connacht football final between Mayo and Roscommon was just six days away, and to be honest, nobody gave Mayo much hope of causing an upset. Roscommon were strong and battle-hardened, and Mayo were being Mayo. To towns like Ballaghaderreen, the cross-county rivalry is intense but in the main good-humoured, just surfacing every so often when the occasion demands.

The talk on the streets of the town that day was dominated by the match. Mondays were slow days in provincial towns. Back then, Sundays were even slower, and it took time for towns to re-awaken to the pace they lived at. Like the old radios and TV with the valves, they needed to be switched on for a while before they got to full speed. The lead up to the tragedy began shortly after 2.30 on that July Monday, when a gang of armed and masked men entered the Bank of Ireland in Ballaghaderreen.

They threatened to shoot a female customer and warned the other people in the bank to lie on the floor. The gunmen were armed with Armalite rifles and pistols and they discharged one shot in the bank, which went through the window. Local man Gabriel Casey, who lived right across the street, was in the bank at the time and refused to comply with the order. When he threw an ashtray at the window to warn people outside, a bullet was fired over his head.

A pregnant woman, a Mrs Grennan, who was also doing business at one of counters, was later treated for shock. Outside on the street, Garda Brendan Walsh, who was on bank duty in his patrol car, was ordered out of his car at gunpoint and was forced to lie on the street by one of the gunmen who proceeded to smash his car radio. The robbers escaped with around £35,000, in a blue Cortina and drove through the town brandishing the guns, with their heads out of the windows.

Locals who saw the scene could not believe their eyes. If it had not been a Monday, they looked for all the world like boys celebrating a match victory, such was the brazenness of their behaviour. Bernard McDonnell was painting the inside of a pub window a few yards away when the raiders passed by.

'I saw this car with three or four men and they were leaning out the window. My impression was that it was a wedding, or something like coming from a match. They were more or less cheering, as if they were after a football victory. They had what I know now to be guns, but as far as I was concerned, they could have been sticks or hurleys. People were running up and down: it is one of the things you don't expect in a town like this,' he said.

The raiders left town on the Aughalusheen Road and abandoned the car, setting it alight two miles from the town. They then entered a white Cortina car and were about to come out of a by-road onto the main Ballaghaderreen/Loughglynn Road, at a point known as Shannon Cross, when they met a garda patrol car speeding from Castlerea.

Stunned by the collision, the four gardai had little time to react to the sight of the raiders with their guns cocked. A volley of shots rang out. John Morley was sitting in the back with Henry Byrne as the shots shattered the windscreen, killing Byrne instantly and missing Morley. Both Sgt Michael O'Malley and Garda Derek Kelly who were in the front seats miraculously escaped injury, despite being in the direct line of fire.

The gunmen then took to the fields to try to make their way to another country road from where they could escape or disappear into the undergrowth. Morley showed his strength and bravery in pursuing them, opening fire on the men who had killed his colleague. However, one of them turned and returned shots at Morley, hitting him in the chest and leg – the latter proving fatal as it ruptured an artery. The gunmen then made their way to the main road where they hijacked a car belonging to a 70-year-old farmer, Michael Kneafsey, which contained a passenger, and his son, Thomas, who was driving.

They brandished guns at both men and Michael, a former garda, struggled with one of them and knocked the gun to the ground before being overpowered and ordered to lie on the ground.

'We were returning from a mart in Castlerea when the two men with guns stopped us and said they wanted the car,' said the elderly man. 'When I got out, I struggled with one of them and knocked the gun out of his hand, but they overpowered us and after they unhooked the trailer… they drove off at high speed.

'About 20 yards back the road, I found Garda Morley lying on the roadside with gunshot wounds in his chest,' said Mr Kneafsey. By now, word was spreading of the raid and the injuries inflicted. By tea-time, the word was out, and the country shocked. The Justice Minister flew to the scene as the search continued. On a black evening for the Morley family, for the country, the force and for Mayo, a hero had passed.

THE WORLD WAS in the midst of war in 1942 when John Morley was born in Kiltimagh. As a youngster following football, his first decade culminated with Mayo's two in-a-row; performances broadcast on the wireless bringing wonder to the young lad's mind. It was no surprise that this wonder continued when he went on to the football nursery of St Jarlath's College in Tuam, the bastion of schools' football in the region.

The school was a magnet for young players, mingling with students from across the region, and even from the offshore islands where secondary education was unavailable and from where the brightest and the best were sent to school in

Galway City or in Tuam. Morley was one such star. The talk in Mayo in the days after his death were of his Herculean feats on the football field, how he strove to bring Mayo to greatness... and nearly succeeded, having come from the stern stuff that he was taught in the famous St Jarlath's nursery.

With them, he won two All-Ireland Colleges' medals in a row. He told respected local journalist Sean Rice once that beating St Mel's of Longford in 1961 to win his second medal was among his most satisfying moments in football.

In 1960 he played minor football with Mayo. The following year, in September, he was chosen for the Mayo senior side which played Galway in the Gael Linn Cup tournament. He played junior in 1962 and was a regular on the senior team until he retired in 1974. During that period, he won every honour in the game... except an All-Ireland senior medal. It was the one football wish he never realised.

Sean Rice recalls that John Morley was one of the old-style catch-and-kick players. 'Fielding was his forte, and the grace with which he could rise for the ball and bend backwards in an arc is one of my abiding memories. No single display stands out in my memory. He had attained such a high standard that it became news only when he failed to reach it.

'Nothing less than a good game was expected of him. He typified the granite in the Mayo team of the 60s and you felt secure when he took up position.'

Writing in the days after the shocking incident that claimed the Mayo man's life, Rice said that Morley's football attitude typified the spirit that saw him do his duty to the State to the utmost of his ability.

'Ray Prendergast, who played behind him at full-back in those years, recalls a picture of John Morley and Roscommon's Eamon Curley in a duel. All 14 stones of Curley were sprawled on the pitch after the two had clashed shoulder to shoulder. Morley was on one knee, his teeth gritted and the ball firmly clutched in one arm. That one picture summed up the grit and courage of the man; that same unbending courage with which, although wounded, he pursued those evildoers on Monday and died in a hail of bullets.'

He was still playing club football in Castlerea and only a couple of weeks earlier watched, fascinated, as his 10-year-old son, Shane, showed all the signs of another Morley at midfield in a local under-12 match. Another son, Gordon, went on to play for Mayo for some time, although he was tempted to play for Galway, to where the family relocated in the years after the shooting. In recent years, a grandson, Cathal Sweeney has gone on to star impressively for Galway seniors under the management of Padraig Joyce.

John Morley thought agonisingly before he decided to retire from inter-county football in 1974. He was still county standard, but had seen, one-by-one, his colleagues of the 60s call it a day. Although he felt he had something left to offer, he was always conscious that Mayo needed a younger man with a long-term future. So, he left the scene in body, but not in spirit. He monitored every Mayo performance closely and indeed it was Mayo's prospects in the 1980 Connacht final the Sunday after his death, that he was discussing when the call arrived that took him on his fatal journey.

He had laid a lawn at their new home in the month before his death, and that summer, it grew and flourished, a natural reminder of his being. His wife, Frances recalled that last afternoon as just being one like any other. He had come home for his dinner, as he used to, and then once he had finished, he wandered out the door... 'See ye later'. She told Keith Duggan in *House of Pain* that 'that was at two o'clock, and by a quarter to three, he was probably dead. That was the hardest thing to get my head around'.

IF THERE WAS hope that a sad week might be lifted, just a little, by a strong performance in the Connacht final, it was not to be. Tommy O'Malley who played that day in Hyde Park said that there was a deep sense of shock throughout the team.

'There was such a massive outpouring of grief all that week. Many of us had played with John and knew him well. A colossus of a man, so we were all broken by sadness and we just were not able to get going for the match at all. Mayo scored just eight points, while Roscommon got 3-13.'

Eleven years had passed since Mayo had last won a Connacht title – the 1969 replay win over Galway in which John Morley had played and starred. The loss to Roscommon came and went without much mention.

Nobody had the heart for it.

IN THE GRAND tradition of the GAA, there was always the element of what I call the 'brother at home' scenario. No matter how talented any individual was, how skilled he might have been, how dedicated he was to the cause of his team, there was often a case of how he had a 'brother at home' who was twice as talented and twice as skilled and twice as fast, but who had never bothered to train.

The brother had unfulfilled potential that would never be realised because of some mad reason, like he was building a house, or never showed for training and who had a falling out with a selector or was heading for Boston. How Mayo were perceived during large tranches of the 1960s was as the 'brother at home'.

Only brilliant, if given the opportunity to shine on the greater stage.

Champions, if only there wasn't another team so obviously in our way. No matter how impatient current Mayo fans might feel about the drought since 1951, back in the 60s, Mayo football fans felt that it was surely time for them to bring home at least one if not two All-Irelands in that decade.

What a team we had in that time! Sean Rice writes about the granite of the men who played in it. Giants of men. Think of the tallest men in our current side and apply to them the natural muscle, not the type accumulated through modern strength and conditioning. Just big men, talented footballers. Tommy O'Malley recalls the traffic traffic through Ballinrobe on match day Sunday when Mayo played Galway in Castlebar, and thousands travelled to see these heroes in action.

Unfortunately for Mayo, Galway had similar dreams of success. They had won an All-Ireland in 1956 when, inspired by Seán Purcell and Frank Stockwell, they struck glory. It was universally accepted that without the 'Terrible Twins', Galway would not have come close to a title that year, but even the most optimistic of their own fans were unaware of the deep pool of talent that was rising within the county and which would make the coming decade the most successful that they would ever enjoy.

All of which was bad news for Mayo. Lore has dictated that the closeness to which Mayo ran Galway would suggest that they would lay serious claims to being the second-best team in the country... the best of the rest. Indeed, it has been used as some consolation that, while our neighbours were ruling the roost, it was only ourselves that would keep the ball kicked out to them. In the great hindsight rear-view mirror that we Mayo fans use when casting an eye back to the years since 1951, rewriting the 60s becomes a convenient crutch. In reality, perhaps too much is made of this and the reliance on this cold comfort to ourselves resulted in not one, but two decades of irrelevance at the top table in national football.

At the time it was all fun… wrapped in deadly seriousness.

Annually, the scenario of the two best sides in the country slogging it out in Castlebar or Tuam, each believing they had the edge over the other. The lasting result was a tight connection between both squads that stayed with them for life. The decade got off to a disappointing start when Mayo exited the 1960 championship in the preliminary round, losing to Galway by two points, 1-6 to 2-5, in Castlebar. A year later in Tuam, they went down by four points to the same opposition, so you would think they would be glad to avoid Galway in 1962.

On this occasion, just their third championship match of the decade, they were to face Sligo at Fr O'Hara Park, Charlestown. Sligo were on a bit of a roll at the time and were no pushovers, but it was still a surprise when the game ended in a draw, 1-13 to 3-7. A fortnight later, Sligo finished the job with a one-point win in Markiewicz Park. In 1963, the picture was no rosier and Galway triumphed in Mayo's first championship outing, winning 2-8 to 1-6 in Castlebar. After a healthy win over Roscommon in Castlebar, Mayo were blitzed by Galway, 2-12 to 1-5, in the 1964 final, the foundation to *their* three in-a-row, but the Tribesmen went into the game after a narrow escape against a Mickey Kerins-inspired Sligo.

So much for Mayo being the second-best team in Ireland; in 1965, they fell to Sligo again, losing by three points in the semi-final in Charlestown. The 1966 Connacht final, however, was the game that sparked a controversy that has survived to this day.

With Mayo leading 1-8 to 0-10 at the end of normal time, astonishingly, an extra four minutes was played. In that time, Galway struck an equaliser, before Liam Sammon fisted over a dramatic winner. Mayo hearts sank again.

Ace Mayo forward from that era 'Jinking' Joe Corcoran from Ardnaree Sarsfields had memories of the game. 'We were ahead at full-time but the referee played four minutes extra and they won it. Patsy Devlin, the referee from Tyrone, was nearly lynched,' he recalled

'There was never an explanation why he did it because people never questioned things like that back then. Yet people talk about those added minutes everywhere I go. It's amazing how far people can go back.'

Joe missed the '64 final in protest at not being brought to America for a tour in 1963, but was back for the later games. 'There was a very good bond between the two teams. We had good time for one another… once you left the field,' he recalled some years ago. 'We always had a healthy respect for them because they had won three All-Irelands in-a-row.

They had some of the best backs in the country in Noel Tierney, Enda Colleran, Bosco McDermott... at midfield Jimmy Duggan, and in attack the legendary Mattie McDonagh... a great team.'

In 1967, Mayo had their revenge, destroying Galway in the Connacht semi-final on a scoreline of 3-13 to 1-8 and satisfyingly ending the Tribemen's hopes of a four in-a-row. However, while Mayo fans will take the win and mark it down in the history books as the victory that brought a stop to Galway's gallop, the context in which the game was played had to have a factor in the one-sided scoreline.

Galway had won the 'home' league that year and had to play New York in New York. Exhausted by the trip and all they had to do during it, they lost to the home side, but then, instead of coming home to prepare for the Mayo game, they had to play the Whitby Tournament at Wembley, which added to their exhaustion.

NEVERTHELESS, MAYO HAD made it into the All-Ireland semi-final for the first time in that decade and hopes were high that a breakthrough could be made; a testing of the 'second best team in Ireland' theory. However, news of John Morley's appendicitis put a dampener on the preparations. When he was first diagnosed, few thought he had little chance of recovery, never mind be back in time for the sort of rehabilitative rest and training he would need.

One man who remembered very clearly the events of that match was Seamus O'Connor, who played at left full-back for Mayo on the team that lost to Meath. 'Morley's loss was a big blow. Our main aim that year was to beat the three in-a-row winning Galway team. They always used to beat us by a point or two, and then go on to win the All-Ireland final. We were lucky that year, in so far as we had a good team. We met Galway in the Connacht semi-final in Pearse Stadium and beat them by eight or nine points. Then we met Leitrim in the final and had an easy win.'

Missing Morley though meant a major change.

'Morley's loss was a big blow because it meant a team reshuffle. Luck went against us. On these occasions you need a bit of luck and Meath had it all. They scored a soft goal just before half-time due to a mix-up in defence. Johnny

Farragher was forced to move into Morley's position at centre half-back; then he was forced to go off with cramp.

'When Morley came on it was a surprise. I think the selectors hoped to boost morale because Meath were going strong at that stage.

'Before the game, we had high hopes of beating Meath, though we weren't overconfident. I can't remember a longer train journey home than the one we made that night. There had been great euphoria before the game and, suddenly… it had all gone down the drain. Though you're disappointed for yourself, you feel for the supporters who come all that way to cheer you on. We were all glad that Meath went on to win the All-Ireland final by beating Cork that year because it meant something that it took the winners to beat us,' he said. Indeed, over the past decade or so, that has been a sort of cold comfort to Mayo, having being beaten by the eventual winners from 2012 to 2023 (apart from 2018 when we lost to Kildare).

AS I WAS writing this chapter in the summer of 2023, the books in my bookshelf behind me, which I had been moving around that evening, suddenly crashed to the floor alongside my desk. Some were books I had forgotten I left there, but the one that I had been looking for, entitled *We Are Mayo* and penned by the aforementioned Sean Rice and Tom Brett, lay splayed on the floor.

Sean had sent me a copy a few years earlier, but I had put it away so carefully, I had forgotten where it was. When I picked up the book, I saw that it had fallen open on page 142, and I gasped at what I saw…

On the page, in front of me, appeared a lovely photograph of John Morley, his wife, Frances, and Joe Langan.

How ironic that this should happen on a chapter that opened about one photograph of the iconic Mayo star and was now closing on this note about another.

Tommy O'Malley fetches the ball against Sligo in the 1975 Connacht final, when he had the honour of captaining Mayo.

PART ★ FIVE

THE SILKEN TOUCH

IN CALIFORNIA IN 1976, Tommy O'Malley was in a dilemma. A serious dilemma. In a county still coming to terms with the shock death of Ted Webb that Spring, the significance of the 1976 Connacht Championship had renewed importance. With the anger vented at the manner of the capitulation of the side in the previous summer's loss to Sligo being toned down in the aftermath of the tragedy, it was expected that the team would give that summer's campaign a good run. The first chance to redeem themselves would come against Leitrim, a game they were expected to win. However, surprisingly, Mayo failed to beat them and the game went to a replay.

'The game was scheduled at the same time as I was on the All Stars trip to Los Angeles,' recalls Tommy. 'Mayo surprisingly only drew the first game and it went to a replay. I was in California with the All Stars and I got a phone call from the Mayo County Board saying, "Come back, come back, there's a ticket out for ya at the airport. Get out there, don't say anything to them out there… get on the plane as we need you back."

'Billy Fitzpatrick, the regular free-taker had gotten injured, so Johnny Carey wanted me back. I went to Seán Ó Síocháin and I said that Mayo had drawn with Leitrim and had a replay and wanted me back.

'He said to me, "You can't go back… you're contracted to the All Stars trip." Then he added, "And even if you do go back to play the game, you won't be halfway across the Atlantic before the Central Council will have you suspended for leaving the trip."'

Without Billy Fitz, and without Tommy, Mayo lost the replay.

'So that was 1976, after the disappointment of '75... and all those young lads again had lost twice and some careers were cut very short.'

WHEN I MET Tommy for this book, he arrived laden down with scrapbooks of the type I used to keep myself. Full of newspaper clippings collected and stuck in by his late mother and by his proud sister, Maura, in whose house we met.

'I was born lucky,' he tells me, as we recall the many highlights of his career. His voice trails off when he says that, and thinks of Ted Webb and John Morley... both of whom he played with. Both taken far too early from this life.

When I was a teenager in Ballinrobe, Tommy was already a superstar to us all. Tanned and super fit, always ready for sport. In Ballinrobe, that meant football or basketball. The hurlers had been revitalised and had many battles with Tooreen. The town's soccer team which reached the quarter-final of the FAI Junior Cup in the early 70s, had gone by the wayside. Rugby was for lads from Cong or for merchant sportsmen.

Basketball was played in the court constructed inside that old goods' shed made vacant by the closure of the town's railway station. The placed we called 'The Basketball', with the stone walls level with the court lines, you had to be nimble to play tight attacking sport. You had to move fast, have quick feet and even quicker hands. The shed had no natural light, and was lit high up by a dozen wattage bulbs which would shatter if hit by a ball, as often happened. In here, in the darkness, were conceived the basketball moves that created Jimmy Maughan's famous flick-goal in the 1978 All-Ireland minor final win over Dublin. Here too were honed the tight moves and skills of Tommy O'Malley; also created here was the screening basketball tactic that selector Peter Forde introduced to the Mayo forwards on their way to the All-Ireland final of 1996.

On the other side of the town, out the Castlebar Road, Ballinrobe Races used to bring the area to a standstill several times a year. We always got a half-day at school and, if lucky, would get a job selling racecards or admission tickets at the entrance. Afterwards, we spent the time scouring the floor of the bar area for any discarded tote tickets that were lost in the dragging from pockets of pound notes to pay for pints. There were always discarded tickets and that, plus whatever you would have earned during the day, would generate the pocket money for the week. For the other 360 days of the year, the racecourse would lie silent. Except for the dogged running of the few lone runners in the early morning. Cross-country runners like my brother, PJ, a talented athlete; and fitness afficionados such as Tommy O'Malley.

'Back then, Ballinrobe didn't wake up until 10 o'clock,' Tommy jokes. 'So, I did all my training in the morning.' It was fitting that Tommy trained at the racecourse because he was as lean and well-turned out as the fittest racehorse, strong tanned legs made muscular by the hilly climbs of the track. His enthusiasm for the game and for Mayo has remained undimmed, which is not surprising given how spectacular his first months with the senior team were.

'My first game was in 1967 when I played minor football… we lost to Sligo. Mayo had won the title the year before. I had three years with the Mayo under-21 team and then I played with the Mayo junior team in 1970. I joined the Mayo senior panel then and I played from 1970 to 1982.

'It was amazing that the first real game I played for Mayo was out in New York. The team had just won the National League and the prize for that was a three-week trip to America, all along the East Coast. I only found out the Monday before the Thursday we were due to leave, as senior player John Gibbons had to pull out because his dad was ill. I got a phone call saying, "You're going". Three days before they were due to leave…

'I will never forget the call. They said get down here quick and get an injection from Dr Mickey Loftus. Then I had to go up to Dublin to get a passport… and then I was on the plane. I looked around me and I found that I was going off with all my heroes. These were all lads that I had admired so much in the 60s. The likes of Ray Prendergast, Eugene Mooney, John Morley, Joe Langan, JJ Cribben, Willie Magee and Sean Kilbride. Sean and I were great friends because our careers ran parallel, we played basketball together on the Irish schoolboys' team. So that was my first time with the seniors.

'It was also my first time leaving Ireland and going overseas, and here I was flying with all my heroes. Remember, I was only 19, so it was exhilarating. We played in New York and we played in Cleveland, and back down to Chicago, then up to Toronto and then back to New York.

'It was like going to heaven or going on the Lions Tour.

'My parents were away at the time in Cavan, so I didn't tell them because they'd only interrupt their stay in Cavan and come back to see me off, but the entire Glebe Street came out and clapped me off when I left town that week. Sally Gibbons and others were all packing my bags and getting me ready for America.

'It was a massive thing to go to America back then for such a short time. For a 19-year-old from Ballinrobe, it was eye-opening. That Mayo team I travelled with were a great team in the 60s and had some iconic games against Galway in 1966 and '67 and the Galway three in-a row team.

'Joe Corcoran was an absolutely brilliant footballer and people would come in their thousands just to see him playing. Himself and Johnny Donnellan used to have terrible battles altogether. They became my best friends.

'Confidence wasn't my biggest thing. I was shy enough, but I wasn't nervous. I played in all the games and in all the matches, and I played well. I had played a challenge in Sligo in Crossmolina a while before that. I was reading the paper back home with Dad and, in those days, the Mayo team was announced in the paper on a Monday. I remember seeing T O'Malley on a team-sheet and I said to Dad, "Is there any other T O'Malley?", because at that stage I wouldn't have been all that confident.

'Dad said, "I don't think so, so it must be you". Then Johnny Mulvey wrote to me to say that it was me, and I think that was two weeks before I went on that trip, so everything happened pretty quickly.'

TOMMY BEGAN A long association with America with the reaction he received from that first trip. 'When you saw what it meant to Mayo people out there, to see their reaction to witnessing Mayo doing well. Remember, this was at a time when people from Mayo had been out there for 40 or 50 years, some left after the War of Independence and were never coming back.

'There was a dance in the ballroom in Queens the Friday night after we arrived and Ray Prendergast sang *The West's Awake* and he was carried shoulder high around the hall by Mayo people. It was a very emotional scene, and even talking about it now, I get emotional. To meet them and to see how proud they were after Mayo had won the National League. It was something that stayed with me for all these years afterwards, just how much Mayo doing well means to people far from home.

'To wear the county jersey was huge. I remember in the 60s when Mayo and Galway were playing in Castlebar, I'd go up to the Main Street there and watch all the traffic going down to the match. It was a huge honour to play, to put a Mayo jersey on your back. It had to rank as one of the most important things in my life. My most important ambition was to help Mayo win an All-Ireland. It was all I ever wanted.

'I played football with Ballinrobe from 1966 to 1982, then I played with Ballintubber and Castlebar, so I had a long club career and the club memories, and affiliations, stay with you emotionally all through life. People know you because you live there. It gave me a fascinating life.'

As a nephew of Seamus O'Malley and the carrier of the football gene in a sport-mad family, his influences were obvious.

'What would have influenced me would be parties in our house when they would all come together and all they'd be talking about was football. We were reared on football and politics. The family was very proud of Seamus and all that he had achieved. The brothers were all very upstanding men and wouldn't be going around boasting. And we, as the generation coming behind them, we all knew what they had achieved too.

'Seamus had retired when he won that All-Ireland. He was county secretary and he came on for the championship and he played in the Connacht final at centre-back, and held his place for the semi-final and final as captain. His is a remarkable story, and the tale of him going with the cup out to Meelickmore is one for the ages.'

Was there extra pressure being the nephew of the man who first carried Sam home to Mayo?

'No, because at home in Ballinrobe, we never talked county football. We talked local football. Dad became manager of the Ballinrobe team in 1970, and sacked all the older players and put all his sons in,' he laughs. 'It caused mayhem.

'Once, we were playing in Shrule in a tournament and my brother, Padraic got hit near the sideline, so Dad went in and hit your man who hit his son, and then Dad went home with a black eye.

'Seamus would ring me for chats but we always avoided the personal, because I wanted to make my own way in the game, and I did. In fact, a lot of people at the time didn't realise I was Seamus' nephew because I never made much of it. I wanted to leave my own mark on it.

'Indeed, the biggest welcome I ever got because of the name was in Cavan, when I went back to play a game there because my father had played there from 1939 to 1945 and there was great excitement that Tom O'Malley's son was playing that day.'

Right from the start of his career, Tommy O'Malley has believed that there is an All-Ireland in Mayo. 'In the 70s, when I came on the team, I was one hundred percent convinced that we were going to win the All-Ireland. We had players the likes of Morley, Rooney, Prendergast, Joe Langan, Peter Loftus, John Gibbons, JJ Cribbin.

'But in 1974, there were 13 of the panel dropped and, in my opinion, that buried Mayo football for 10 years. There were players who were in their prime who were let go. It was a shock. All of a sudden, I went from being one of the youngest on the team to being one of the oldest. This happened out of nowhere.

'I was captain for the '75 Connacht final. We had drawn the first match in Sligo and the replay was set for Castlebar. I don't want to take away from Sligo's win because they deserved it, but a few things went against us refereeing-wise. It was a huge disappointment for me because I was captain, but I knew I played well that day and I hadn't let Mayo down. It was disappointing, but you had to move on and not dwell on it.

'The 70s were disappointing, but there is a perception that we never got to Croke Park. We were getting to Croke Park for league finals and semi-finals, but just never there for the championship. We did well but could have had more success.'

Before the backdoor came in, Tommy, with his 14-157, was second highest scorer for Mayo behind Joe Corcoran. 'But now, others have passed us out, but I am hoping that about a hundred more pass us out," said Tommy, who you just know would love to tog out again.

"I was totally at home out on the football pitch, more than anywhere else. That was my natural habitat.' Tommy also represented Connacht in the Railway Cup on many occasions and played in a Rest of Ireland selection against The Dubs the same year, on a night when he ended up sharing a bed with a Kerry legend.

'That game was on in Croke Park and there were about six Kerry players on that team, and Dermot Earley was the captain, but there was no accommodation arranged for us. The night beforehand Ger Feeney and I met Páidí Ó Sé inside in McGoverns in Dublin. We had no place to stay, but Ger had arranged some place for us to get our heads down. Páidi had no place either so we invited Paidi back and, when we got there, we saw there were only two single beds.

'So, I said to Páidi, you'd better sleep with me. But in the middle of the night when we were asleep, Paidi hops up and he starts punching me and saying, "Hickey, I hate ya… I hate ya, I hate ya Hickey". And he hit me three whacks in the jaw. He had been dreaming about David Hickey. Himself and Hickey used to have some fierce battles in the Dublin-Kerry matches and here we were sleeping and me beside him, and I got three thumps into the jaw. I was black and blue.'

'It was an honour for me to have been picked for that game, and an honour to get the B&I Award for scoring 1-5 against Leinster up in Navan and for scoring against Roscommon in the league.'

But it is the impact on the fans that Tommy is most proud of.

'I remember playing for Mayo in New York in Gaelic Park, and Johnny Mulvey came to me after the match and said "Tommy, your jersey is missing". I had just left it down. "The No 10 jersey is gone, Tommy," he said. Then someone said, "There's a guy wearing a jersey out in the bar" and the bar now was nearly as big as the pitch and it was packed and wedged. Then I saw my old classmate from school in Ballinrobe, George O'Malley was there, and he had the Mayo jersey on him. Back in those days, none of the supporters wore Mayo jerseys, unlike now when everyone has one.

'And George was having a ball and didn't want to the give the jersey back to me. "I'm keeping this jersey," he said. He was as proud as punch that someone from Ballinrobe was playing for Mayo out in New York.'

TOMMY'S VOICE DIPS when he recalls the sudden deaths that shattered Mayo football in those years. That iconic photo of Ted Webb and himself playing in the sunshine in 1975, and then just seven months later Ted was dead.

'It was an awful tragedy. It was the freakiest thing to have happened, but it was so sad. The fact is Ted was the loveliest guy you could have met. He was really genuine and I have no doubt that he would have been one of the all-time greats. He was a huge man and he had a huge stride, and a quick turn of pace. He was born to be a hero. He was an awful loss to Mayo.'

Tommy believes that if the 1975 team had won the Connacht title, it would have represented a major boost to the Mayo team of the time and more Mayo careers would have been prolonged. As it was, there was a lot riding on success the following year, but understandably the shock of Ted Webb's death left a deep emotional imprint on the side.

The contacts he made Stateside in that inaugural trip were to stand to Tommy and he became a regular player on the US scene.

'I made big contacts and I wrote to them and offered to play, and I was invited back to play in New York every year. For three years I went to New York, for three or four years I went to Chicago, and then Boston. I would get a phone call saying, "There's a ticket at Shannon Airport".

'As a young man, it was a magical experience, getting a telephone call from the US during the week to tell you that plane tickets would be left at the airport on a Friday evening to travel out to New York for a match at the weekend.

'I regarded it as a huge honour and, to be honest, I rarely missed a game. Other Mayo stars of that era, including Ray Prendergast, John Morley, Sean Kilbride and Frank Burns and others would be with me on those journeys.

'We'd arrive out there, get a mighty welcome, spend Saturday taking it easy and, on Sunday, there were matches taking place all day at Gaelic Park. It was the place where all Irish exiles gathered and people setting out on a new life in the US found their first jobs by meeting the right people there. We played our matches and, I can tell you, there was no quarter asked or given. As soon as we finished, it was back to JFK and we were back home for work on Monday.'

He witnessed the appetite the exiles had for anything from home at first hand when the 1972 All-Ireland final was screened live in New York for the first time via Eurovision at Lowe's Paradise Theatre in The Bronx, thanks to a brave business initiative by some great Mayo GAA men in New York. John Fitzgerald (Irishtown), Mattie Forde (Kiltimagh), Michael Glynn (Claremorris), Mickey Morley (Ballyhaunis) and Michael McDonnell (Balla).

'It is still one of my greatest memories. Going to the theatre to see the match between Kerry and Offaly that morning was like walking up Jones' Road in Dublin, such was the crowd, colour and excitement. There were 3,000 inside the venue and when the pictures first started coming through, the Artane Boys Band was playing in Croke Park. The place lit up with the emotion... that moment will always live with me.

'The moment the Eurovision sound came up, the link went down… and everyone thought, *Arragh, that's it gone now*! But then the screen burst alive with the colour of the band in the parade. It was magical.'

Tommy admits that he was fortunate to have escaped serious injury and not have his inter-county time curtailed. 'I was born lucky. When I started playing for Mayo, I just wanted to have a long career. I did not want to be in for one year and then out again. Fitness was very important to me. I took over the Ballinrobe team in 1979/80 and my cousin, Michael Flannery became the captain. Michael was a Mayo under-21 star from 1974. We came back from Spain and took over the team. We trained Monday, Wednesday and Friday, and the county team trained Tuesday and Thursday. We did savage training and we won the Intermediate League, the Intermediate Championship, Senior League, and we should have won the Senior Championship. But we had two goals disallowed against Knockmore and they were definitely good goals, and we lost by one point.

'If we had won that, we'd have beaten Castlebar Mitchels in the county final, without a doubt in the world. But it was not to be. I was player-manager in 1979. I ended up as player-manager in Ballintubber by default. I went to a meeting to see how the club was getting on. I was well past my best and when I left the meeting, I was player-manager and I did that for three years. I moved house to Castlebar then and I became coach of the Castlebar team, and we won two county titles with Mitchels.'

When the end came to him, he was pragmatic about it.

'I decided in 1982 that I was losing pace. I was losing my speed and when that happens it's time to go.' As the end neared, he had started kicking with his right foot, having used his left all his career up to that point. 'When I had good pace, I could go around anybody, but all of a sudden, you were coming back a bit, and when you can't go around them as good as you could, you need something else. That's why I started kicking with my right.'

HE HAD ANOTHER shot at an All-Ireland when he came in as a selector in the John Maughan team of 1996, '97 and '98.

'I was instrumental in the appointment of John Maughan in 1996. I knew of his skill-set. I was manager of the Mitchels' team and John had joined and we went to the All-Ireland final with that team. He was the right man at the right time. I came in as selector with Peter Forde and Mayo went from Division 3 to an All-Ireland final. The training was so savage and so serious.' Tommy believes that Peter Forde should have taken over the reins from Maughan.

'When John Maughan retired, the incumbent should have been Peter Forde. Peter was a marvellous tactician and very far-sighted in his thinking. After Peter and I studied the Kerry team for our All-Ireland semi-final clash, we introduced a basketball tactic called "screening" into the forward line. Peter amazed me with his ability to apply that basketball tactic on to the football pitch.

'Our forwards were not blessed with blinding speed and we were always under pressure shooting. It basically meant that before the ball was kicked into the full-forward line, one of the forwards screened one of the opposition backs to get a forward completely free to receive a pass and get a free shot at the goals.

'By using that tactic, we beat Kerry in the semi-final, and should have beaten Meath in the final. No one knew what our forwards were doing, including referees.

'It was a very simple Ballinrobe-conceived basketball tactic that I'm proud to say we introduced into the Mayo game plan for the very first time in Croke Park. It was a game-changer for our team, with David Nestor getting Ray Dempsey free and vice versa.

'Nowadays, every back is being screened or hampered to enable a forward to get free and have a free shot. It is easier when you have 28 players playing in a condensed area, but back then it was more difficult to apply.'

IN HIS RETIREMENT, Tommy O'Malley set a new record as perhaps one of only a few Mayo men to play in Connacht finals more than 50 years apart. While he might have been orchestrating things out on the field in the 70s, in the last few years, Tommy has been playing the trombone in the Castlebar Concert Band, bringing the big band sounds to the crowds.

One wonders how many of the new era Mayo fans realise that out there among the trumpets and the drums and trombones, was a former star who really was one of the best in the country.

A lifelong musical fan and performer, Tommy was instrumental in bringing the Artane Boys Band to Ballinrobe in the 1970s for a concert.

A few years later, as he warmed up for a league semi-final in Croke Park, he was amazed to see them calling out his name and wishing him well in a game against their own team.

A star and a gentleman all his life.

A man you don't meet every day... Tommy O'Malley.

John Finn in action in the Connacht Championship in 1985, but after breaking his jaw he did not get to line out against Dublin in the 1985 All-Ireland semi-final replay.

Willie Joe Padden at the end of the battle against Tyrone in the 1989 All-Ireland semi-final, and the Mayo team that just failed to Cork in the final.

★ INTERMISSION ★

THE LAST OF THE CHOC ICES

★ ★ ★ ★ ★

THE SUN SHONE, so we were all freckled from the unexpected heat. Back then, all the summers seemed to be warm, proper summers, where you could laze around all week, maybe get to the cinema and then on a Sunday, get to a match. For some in the group, it was our first summer holidays from secondary school, so the months seemed to stretch ahead.

The car we had travelled in was parked on the Ballinrobe Road on the outskirts of Castlebar. 'We'll be turned for home,' said Willie Jennings, the local butcher, car owner and father of about half of the six lads squeezed into the front and back for the 30-minute journey to the county town. The car was reversed into position, wheels jammed into the sod to allow others to get by. Already there was traffic.

Everyone wanted to see this game, so there was going to be pandemonium. To the right, across the Partry Mountains, stood the triangular majesty of Croagh Patrick. To the left, scorched ferns and bogland stretching all the way over towards Lough Carra and Moorehall. If you were on top of The Reek that fine day, you would have seen out across Clew Bay, and from there onwards to the tip at Achill and from there, further up that rock-torn coast, stood Sligo, today's opponents, seeking their first title in almost five decades.

There were five of us in the back, one lad stretched across the other. Fifty pence coins in the pockets. There was kicking and punching and horseplay, and then there was the walk... two miles or more. We were all in shorts and t-shirts paled from being overwashed and handed down. Our runners were flat with no heel, the cheap sort in the days before Converse, so each step on the hot road reverberated up through us, the way the sting from a Wavin hurley travelled up the arm.

It is July 20, 1975, smack in the middle of the school holidays.

For many of us, it is our first ever Connacht final.

'ANYONE FOR THE CHOC ICES?'

'THE LAST OF THE CHOC ICES... NOW'

The vendors badly wanted rid of their choc ices.

Flared trousers, shirts open to the naval are the order of the day. To us all, it was as if the entire province had turned out to see the showpiece game of the Connacht Championship.

A fortnight earlier, the teams had battled in a thrilling draw at Markewiecz Park, when Mayo were fortunate to get the replay. But, there in the clear blue skies above MacHale Park with the grass never looking greener, and the county colours never looking richer, we were watching as close to the business end of the championship as we would see for the rest of the decade. Maybe that is why it is so imprinted on my mind; the juxtaposition of hope and colour. It should have felt like the beginning of something, but instead, it represented an ending.

By the time a Spring would come around again, there would be tragedy and set-back for the Mayo dream. But on that day, there was sunshine, and hope, and there was the Mayo captain Tommy O'Malley, our local man, nephew of Seamus who had lifted the Sam Maguire for Mayo, and brought it on the handlebars of his bike to school the morning after.

In the days before mass media, not much was made of the fact that with this Connacht final, Tommy was just two games away from repeating the feat of his uncle.

★ ★ ★ ★ ★

IN A COUNTY that is so consumed by the performance of its senior football team, it is hard for current generations of Mayo fans to imagine the competitive wasteland that was the 1970s. Although, it should have represented so much more.

When people from places that have only ever seen the inside of Croke Park when Garth Brooks was at one end of it, come up to me and sympathise on my disappointment as a Mayo fan, I snort and say, 'Disappointment? Disappointment was the 70s when we never got out of Connacht'.

A dozen years of semi-finals and finals is not a disappointment. I remember the 70s and what it could and should have delivered. There was a league victory in 1970 and we were runners up in 1971, '72 and '78. Minor titles in 1971 and '78, and an unlucky defeat in 1974. An under-21 title in 1974, following a close loss to a strong Kerry outfit in '73. With so much promise of success, why then did the decade deliver so little?

Granted the era was dominated by the fantastic Dublin and Kerry teams who played thrillers in front of packed audiences at Croke Park. To look at that level of performance, we could only marvel at the elite athleticism and accuracy that marked the clashes of those giants. The smoky foggy look of a crowded Croke Park on All-Ireland final day seemed a world away for supporters of Connacht teams in those years.

Granted, the dying sting of a wonderful Galway generation was fading, but they had enough in the tank to have made the 1973 and '74 deciders, but without success. And so, in 1975, opportunity knocked for whatever Western team felt up to the challenge.

★ ★ ★ ★ ★

IT WAS AN era of colour.

The red and green of the Mayo jerseys in these years seemed a blood red, a rich green. Players were tanned and strong; hair was long and luscious. In the 70s, two decades had passed since Mayo had won an All-Ireland title, and even back then, the images of the triumph seemed confined to a world of black and white. In the 70s, we had colour flooding from the Munich Olympics, and the 1974 and '78 World Cups. It was into this setting that the 1975 Connacht final entered my brain... and has stayed there ever since.

This was also the era of the sports superstar. The fashionable chaos of

George Best had reached its nadir. But just 12 months beforehand, the world had marvelled at the silken skills of Johann Cruyff, playing the liberated and demanding total football, where every player had a multi-purpose role in the team, enabling them to change shape and formation with ease and precision. It was the era of the individual as part of a team structure. Cruyff was individualistic and stylish and had transformed the football fortunes of a nation that only a few years beforehand was receiving regular drubbings from the Republic of Ireland. The Mayo team, that season, also had a sense of fashion about it. They were a mix of clean shaven and long-haired; they were proud of jaw and fashion. Beards, manes of hair and generous sideburns that framed the sides of the head. There was a swarthiness about them.

The omens were good.

In the league, they ran to five straight wins to give some inkling that the sap was rising was in the west. That run brought them to a league semi-final against a Meath team but there, a reality set in, when the Royal County hit them for four goals in a 19-point win at Croke Park. It was a defeat that stunned Mayo, and ought to have sounded as a warning ahead of the forthcoming Connacht Championship campaign. But there was tremendous potential in this squad, so nobody knew what to expect. With talent, there is always hope.

London made their debut in the senior championship on May 25, putting up a creditable show against Mayo before going down by 4-12 to 1-12. This set up a semi-final meeting with Roscommon. On the other side of the draw, ominously, we should have noticed that a Mickey Kearins-inspired Sligo were motoring along nicely under the radar, finally putting an end to Galway's long run of success. But this was not just a lucky win for the Yeats men. They hammered Galway on a scoreline of 1-13 to 0-6. Unbelievably, Galway hit a dozen wides in the first-half that day, and still led by a point at the break. But nobody bargained for what happened in the second-half, as Kearins tormented the Tribesmen, finishing with a total of 0-12 as Sligo emerged victors on a staggering 1-13 to 0-6 scoreline. Admittedly, Galway lacked the services of John Tobin and Jimmy Duggan, but there should have been a warning within for Mayo if they thought Sligo were going to be a pushover in the final. There was disbelief in some quarters that the final was fixed for Sligo on July 6, with Leitrim's Tommy Moran the referee. Sligo led by 1-6 to 1-4 at half-time and might have been further ahead if they had not been as wasteful in front of goal, including one chance that went begging from just a few yards out. Indeed, either side could have snatched victory but the nail-biting finish saw a scoreline of Sligo 2-10 Mayo 1-13.

The replay was set for MacHale Park on July 20 and the Sligo fans travelled in numbers, confident that having nearly achieved a win in the drawn game, that they would end a 47-year wait for a provincial title. It was an action-packed game throughout, the searing heat taking its toll on both sets of players as supporters watched on in excitement, faces pressed up against the wire mesh. Mayo had a goal controversially disallowed early in the second-half. If that had gone in, it might have been a different story. Des McGrath also crashed a shot against the crossbar with nine minutes left on the clock. For true football fans, seeing Mickey Kearins win that elusive Connacht medal was some reward, but there was great disappointment at Mayo's defeat, with the year having started so well.

Kearins' total of 1-4 included a bullet penalty that 'keeper Ivan Heffernan did well to get his fingers to. Fine margins that saw Sligo edge the game by the minimum score, 2-10 to 0-15.

All credit to Sligo for their win, but once ahead, they pulled every trick in the book to break up play in a free-ridden, niggledy game that boiled over on one or two occasions. At one stage, when the referee asked for the ball from a Sligo defender, he refused to hand it over, feigning misunderstanding and counting down almost three minutes on the clock. Bang on the 30 minutes, the referee blew it up. A few more minutes, and Mayo might have staged the late comeback and gotten the point they needed for parity.

Small margins here and there, but Sligo had controlled the key areas. The fall of midfield put pressure on the Mayo backs, while there were frees that failed to be raised; a mad solo across the face of our own goal that gave a pointed free, and the wasting of a great goal chance that came with just minutes left.

Tom Rowley's report in the *Connaught Telegraph* was headlined **Oh Mayo, You've Done It Again**. Terry Reilly in the *Western* lashed into the selectors for picking a team that had serious deficit in quality. Without begrudging Sligo their title, the fact remained that Mayo had blown a great chance to win a Connacht title; not alone in the drawn game, but in their decision-making in the replay. *'Unless we get down to the fundamentals and employ good old common sense, the full potential of Mayo football will never be realised,'* he wrote. *'That the selectors could* *not visualise the limitations after something like 10 months contains the threads of the tragedy which had to come sooner rather than later.*

It was a frustrating loss for the success-starved faithful. The Mayo senior team that contested the 1975 Connacht final against Sligo was an amalgam in the main of the minor and under-21 teams of 1971 and '74 and should have been able to do better. In contrast, Sligo was a team that had heavy mileage, with the likes of Kearins coming to the end of his playing career.

John Cuffe writing decades later in the *Western People* recalled that a year earlier a beast known as The Dub arrived and meeting it was a young Kerry team which also made up of 10 of the county's All-Ireland under-21 winning team from 1973 against Mayo. *'Whereas the transplant worked for Kerry, with O'Dwyer's babes winning their first of eight senior All-Irelands in 1975 and spreading over the next 10 years, the Mayo experiment fell at the Connacht final.*

'Recalling that 1975 Mayo team we see Ivan Heffernan in goal and a full-back line of John O'Mahony, JJ Farragher and Seamus O'Reilly. Ger Feeney Con Moynihan and Mick Higgins made up the half-back line and at midfield were Frank Burns and Eamon Brett.

'A half-forward line of Tommy O'Malley, JP Kean and Ted Webb was augmented with a full-forward line of Willie McGee, Sean Kilbride and Ger Farragher. Ardnaree's Johnny Culkin came on as sub over the two games.

'On paper it's one of the finest Mayo line-ups I ever saw,' wrote Cuffe. 'Ten were All-Ireland minor winners, including Sean Kilbride who won his in 1966, aged 16. Throw in the experience of Tommy O'Malley, Frank Burns, Mick Higgins and TJ Farragher, along with the aforementioned Kilbride and McGee, and this was a team primed for bigger stages.'

'In 1976, and this time meeting Leitrim in the first round of the Connacht Championship, Mayo sought change from the scarring defeat 12 months earlier with a raft of new faces. In came Dan O'Mahony, Jim Timoney, John Gallagher, Paddy Corrigan, Anthony Egan, Richie Bell, Micheal Sweeney, Billy Fitzpatrick and Dixon. Game one was Leitrim 0-11 Mayo 0-11, the replay Leitrim 2-8 Mayo 0-10. The team were without Tommy O'Malley who was away with the All Stars in America.

'It was a momentous win for Leitrim.'

However, what cannot be understated is the impact of the trauma that the squad suffered within seven months of that loss to Sligo in Castlebar.

★ ★ ★ ★ ★

TED WEBB SEEMED to have been made for the 70s; a fine build of a man with a massive leap. The butcher's son who had sculpted an impressive frame through lugging sides of meat around was the star everyone was talking about. Already two of his goals in underage competition had gone down in history, with Michael O'Hehir breathlessly proclaiming one as the best that he had ever seen in Croke Park. In the early 70s, when there were just quiet rumblings of the volcanic coming of Kerry and Dublin, out west the feeling was that Ted Webb would ultimately be the rock around which Mayo's successful title chances would be built. His thunderous goal against Antrim in the 1974 All Ireland under-21 final is still available to see on YouTube. He was on the Mayo team that day in Castlebar in 1975, notching two points, just as he had in the drawn game in Sligo a week earlier, but he was also criticised for a free that failed to rise.

Webb's iconic photo is of him rising high in midfield on that sunny day in MacHale Park. As we pressed our faces to the fence, tried to guard ourselves from the relentless sun, we watched the glare of a star in the making. He wore his hair long in the style of the times, a Mario Kempes or John Travolta; he was an immense hulk of a man, with dashing good looks, and a swarthiness that brought him renown in his native Ballyhaunis. A teetotaller, he was fantastic company, always willing to lend a hand, to do someone a good turn, but apart from being a good person, he was a great footballer. Some players have a moment of glory that illustrates their potential, a golden shot, a high field.

He was the future of Mayo football. However, on February 19, 1976, seven months after Webb starred in those warm Connacht final games against Sligo, he was dead, killed in an accident comprising a good deed, a freak chance and a forewarning, all on one tragic Spring night that stunned Mayo football for perhaps the rest of that decade.

At the time, the county was already the centre of national media attention for another reason, as the body of Hollymount-native, hunger striker Frank Stagg was returned to the county, having been flown there in a military helicopter from Shannon. A Republican prisoner, Stagg had died in Wakefield Prison on February

12, 1976, after 62 days on hunger strike, so tensions were high that week. Like myself, Stagg had attended Ballinrobe CBS. His burial caused considerable controversy in Ireland.

Republicans and two of his brothers sought to have Stagg buried in the Republican plot in Ballina, beside the grave of Michael Gaughan, in accordance with his wishes which he had added to his will in prison during his hunger strike. His widow, his brother, Emmet Stagg and the Irish government wished to have him buried in the family plot in the same cemetery and to avoid Republican involvement in the funeral. As the Republicans, journalists and his family separately waited at Dublin Airport for the body, the government ordered the flight to be diverted to Shannon Airport. His body was then taken to the parish church in Hollymount by helicopter and buried near the family plot.

On the night the eyes of national and British TV channels were covering the arrival of Mr Stagg's body in Hollymount, the Mayo squad were training in Castlebar. A challenge match against Clare had been arranged for Kiltimagh the following Sunday.

THE SAME NIGHT, Ted wasn't long in from returning home from the session. After the disappointment of the Sligo defeat the previous summer, he and his fellow squad members were determined to bring Mayo back in 1976. Sligo might have been Connacht champions, but their ability to regroup after a chastening All-Ireland semi-final, coupled with Galway's demise, opened the possibility that this year might see Mayo realise the great potential that was emerging in their team. Ted and his brother, Mike got a seat home with their good friend John O'Mahony. Keith Duggan's book *House of Pain* recalls how the car had a minor skid en route from Castlebar, but that nothing came of it. Indeed, ironically, if something had, and if the car had lodged in a ditch without seriousness, then perhaps the timeline of the night might have been altered and we might not ever have been writing these words.

Ireland was a different place back then. There was just one TV channel, just one radio station, the country operated at a slower pace. The roads were quieter, people could leave their doors unlocked and calling out to do someone a favour or strolling up the path for a chat was commonplace. It was a world removed from the country of today. Always keen to do a good turn, Ted volunteered to pick up his bachelor uncle, Pat Lyons and drop him home to Scahard, even eschewing the bowl of warming Ambrosia rice that he was eating to restore some energy after the county session earlier that evening. Kojak was on the telly, but Telly Savalas, Stavros and Cracker and the rice would have to be abandoned. Ted showed no hesitation in making the offer to pick up and drop off his uncle.

The journey took them across the nearby unmanned railway crossing, which had gates which drivers would open and then close after they had passed through. The Webbs were familiar with the times and schedules of the trains to and from the west, but none were due at that hour of the night, so it was likely that Ted opened the gate, dropped his uncle home and then planned to close it on the way back. It was a dark night, and on any night such as this, the lights from a passenger train would be visible anyway along the lie of the land if there was one approaching. But an unscheduled goods train was making its way along the tracks that evening.

The locomotive was travelling from Westport to Castlerea to collect the following morning's newspapers. It chugged along the quiet countryside, slicing through country roads. Dimly lit because it was carrying provisions and supplies and not passengers, it came out of the darkness and collided strongly with Ted's car as he crossed the line at the crossing. Mere seconds before or after, and we would never have heard of the incident, and the trajectory that impacted the Webb family and Mayo football would have been avoided. Such was the impact of the collision and the shock at what had happened, the Peugeot ended half a kilometre down the tracks when the engine was finally able to halt.

TO THIS DAY, in his honour, the Ted Webb Cup is held in the west, but it is surprising the number of people who are unaware that the cup is not named after some retired GAA veteran official, but a dashing star who was once the future of Mayo football. A man who lived in colour and dreamed in colour, who had been cruelly snatched on a black night.

There had indeed been great hope that summer. Galway had made it to the previous two All-Ireland finals and in the second of these, had shown serious signs of the decline from their great teams of the mid 60s. But at least they still mattered, even if it was only to the point of getting to the business end of the championship. In an era when Connacht teams only hoped to make a final appearance was in a year when they played an Ulster team in the semi-final, Galway had at least managed to break that duck and get to the last day of the championship on two successive years. Mayo on the other hand had shown immense promise at underage. The mid 70s was a brash new world of Showaddywaddy, the Bay City Rollers, and ABBA. The world was experiencing an oil crisis, The Troubles were at their zenith in Northern Ireland, but out west, in the aftermath of Tedd Webb's passing, football success seemed secondary.

In 1977, the misery continued when Roscommon travelled to Castlebar and beat Mayo by three points, 0-16 to 0-13. The Mayo team showed a massive 10 changes from the team which had succumbed meekly to Leitrim the previous year. One of those changes was the selection of minor and under-21 centre half-back, Con Moynihan who was played at centre half-forward. Nonetheless, he made a major contribution, hitting six fine points.

In 1978, a scintillating run through the league before Christmas saw them qualify for the semi-final against Down in Croke Park – a game they won by a narrow two points, 0-10 to 0-8. In the final, they would grace the all-conquering Dubs and nobody gave them a prayer. Almost 40,000 went into headquarters to watch the decider and it was a cracker, however the result was never in any doubt. The Dubs led by five points at the break, and finished the game with the same advantage, 2-18 to 2-13. In the Connacht Championship, Mayo opened up with a handy win against Leitrim in Ballina (2-18 to 1-8). This saw them qualify for a semi-final showdown with a powerful Roscommon side who beat them 1-12 to 1-9 at The Hyde. The Rossies beat Galway in the final before going on to be demolished by a powerful Kerry side in the semi-final, going down 3-11 to 0-8 at Croke Park.

With such behemoths as Dublin and Kerry ruling the roost, expectations elsewhere around the country were low, but the highlight of 1978 was also the highlight of the end of the decade, when the minors went on to win the All-Ireland title for the first time since 1970 with a scintillating display against Dublin in the curtain-raiser on All-Ireland final day.

★ ★ ★ ★ ★

JIMMY MAUGHAN GREW up with us in Ballinrobe, a sportstar with a bit of swagger about him. Whether he was playing soccer or gaelic or hurling or basketball, he had a style about him and a dimple that you would only ever see as it shimmied past you on whatever court or pitch you met him. He hailed from New Street, behind which were some rows of houses where members of the Travelling community had been settled. Jimmy had grown up in this area and was one of just a handful of settled Travellers to partake in team sport in the town.

He was about four years older than me, but to a generation of kids in Ballinrobe, he was pure Harlem Globetrotter. Back then, there wasn't much to do in the evenings in Ballinrobe apart from make your own sport. Later on, the town would have its own Sports Centre with indoor pitches, courts and a gym. Back then, the only place for sport after dark was 'up the basketball' – the term we used for the disused railway warehouse at the abandoned railway station.

We used to play indoor soccer there as well, and every so often a stray shot would hit one of the few bulbs that lit the place. It was into this unusual setting that Jimmy Maughan conceived the skills that led him to becoming an unlikely hero for Mayo football in the 1970s. Austin Garvan, who sadly passed away in 2022, had taken over the Mayo minor team for the 1978 campaign and immediately set about making an impression.

They knew there was something special about the side with the manner in which they despatched Leitrim in the opening game, scoring a whopping TEN goals in a 10-11 to 2-5 victory in Ballina. Roscommon were not as accommodating in the semi-final at Hyde Park, but Mayo emerged victorious on a 2-10 to 1-8 scoreline. Galway in Salthill stood in Mayo's way, but the visitors brushed aside the maroon challenge with a comprehensive 2-6 to 0-4 victory.

Although confident in their own ability, meeting Kerry in the semi-final was probably going to be a bridge too far for the westerners, but on a rainy day in North Dublin, Mayo built up a five-point lead at the break. However, the warmth of the dressing-room must have lulled them into a false sense of security, because within five minutes of the restart, Kerry had that lead down to a solitary point. Mayo fans watching in Croke Park and on the live broadcast as gaeilge on RTE feared the worst.

But they had not reckoned for the composure and resilience of this Mayo side – exemplified by goalkeeper Sean Warde, who pulled off some miraculous saves to keep The Kingdom at bay. However, it was the arrival of the Mayo subs who reignited the challenge and when the man-mountains, TJ Kilgallon and Tom Byrne arrived, Mayo were back in business. They hit 1-2 between them to give

Mayo a 1-10 to 0-10 victory and send them into the All-Ireland minor final for the first time in four years.

The achievement became momentous, given the poor fortunes of the senior team at the time. To have the chance to play the curtain-raiser to the clash between Kerry and Dublin was a massive fillip to the boys from the west, but they knew too that The Dubs support would be packing the Hill for what they hoped would be a momentous Dublin double over the teams from west and southwest.

However, in Mayo, it was the curtain-raiser that caught all our interest. Dublin were seeking their eighth title while Mayo went off in pursuit of their fifth. Mayo had one enforced change for the final as Paraic Corcoran was ruled out with a leg injury and he was replaced by Kilgallon. It lashed rain on the morning of the match and the pitch was soft underfoot. Back home, we all watched and hoped for a mention of Jimmy Maughan... which came early on when his shot hit a post. The next mention happened in a flash.

The ball was played in front of the Dublin goalmouth, Maughan got it in his grasp, and was immediately swallowed up by a number of Dublin defenders. There seemed nowhere for him to play it, but then in a flash, the ball nestled in the Dublin net – Maughan's sleight of hand catching them off guard. So fast was his deft touch that the cameras were barely able to capture it. Years of mastery with the big orange ball in the dusty confines of the goods' store had fine-tuned him for this moment. A goal of audacity and skill that summed up the Ballinrobe man whose silken skills enabled him to pivot and pirouette in the square until the ball was in the net and nobody was any wiser.

'Maughan had his back to the net and he just palmed the ball in with a swift accurate flick of his hand... one of the most delicate goals ever seen in Croke Park,' read one of the reports. Others such as Peadar O'Brien in the *Irish Press* said that from where he was sitting in the Croke Park press box, it *'looked like Maughan had blatantly thrown the ball to the net'*. However, to suggest that would be to not know Jimmy Maughan and the box of tricks instilled in him by basketball coach and teacher, Noel Ansbro in Ballinrobe. Noel who passed away a few years ago, had as much of a hand as anybody else in that goal.

That was a final full of drama and tension, but we were thrilled that the one Brazilian moment had come from one of our own, a lad from the town, a star we knew to meet on the street. The goal sparked Mayo into life and ensured that despite wasting many chances, the teams were level at 1-4 apiece at the break. For a generation born in the mid to late 60s, it was a novel feeling to be in contention at half-time of a late September decider. However, misfortune soon followed and when Jimmy Lyons was stretchered off with a dislocated shoulder, Mayo's day threatened to fall apart.

Lyons was replaced by the bulk of Tom Byrne from Kiltimagh. There were hopes that his introduction would mirror that of his performance in the semi-final, but The Dubs soon roared ahead with two goals to send them six clear. However, what was to follow was a glorious comeback that sustained Mayo football through this depressing decade. A storming run from Achill's Kieran O'Malley ended with a low shot to the net. With a strong mist falling, Dublin looked rattled and a Griffin point reduced the deficit. A free from Adrian Garvey became a hot potato in the Dublin defence; it was grabbed by Tom Byrne, who shot firmly to the corner and Mayo were ahead. When the Dublin goalkeeper dashing from goal lost control 25 yards out, it broke to Byrne who fired home with aplomb to give Mayo the win they so richly deserved.

Despite being devastated, the Dublin fans on the Hill gave the Mayo team a rousing applause as they completed the lap of honour, as did the Kerry fans who were delighted to see their old foes lose at any level. Unknown to The Dubs though, their day was to get much worse – Kerry had the most comprehensive victory ever in an All-Ireland final, beating Dublin 5-11 to 0-9 in a humiliating defeat for the team from the capital.

But we were happy out… for the last time in that decade.

★ ★ ★ ★ ★

IF STEVEN SPIELBERG ever centres a *Jurassic Park* movie on Mayo football and attempts to see from where the DNA of Mayomania emanated, he would not have to go much further than the 1980s. The impression that Mayo folk have been infatuated with winning Sam Maguire since 1951 omits the inconvenient fact that for about 25 years, interest in the county team on a widespread basis was very cyclical, and appeared in peaks and troughs.

Before the wall-to-wall, heartache and thrill of more recent times, things were bleak enough in the county.

The talent was there, but consistency and unity were lacking.

Between 1951 and 1989, Mayo won just six Connacht titles. Think about that, six titles in 38 years – Galway had 21, and Roscommon had nine during those days. So, it is safe to say that the work done by Liam O'Neill in the mid 80s or O'Mahony in the late 80s was when the thought of Mayo as a national force was revived.

When I look back on the 80s, my abiding memory is of rain and Peig Sayers and endless days learning in the CBS in Ballinrobe. And of Eugene McHale dancing around like he'd won the World Cup – and the Mayo influence on the GAA moment of the decade, that Seamus Darby goal for Offaly, replayed a thousand times.

Kilmaine's PJ McGrath was the man in black on the occasion of the 1982 All-Ireland final, when Kerry, aimed at five in-a-row, were shocked that Darby was not penalised for a push on Tommy Doyle as the lofted ball headed towards their goalmouth in the dying moments of the game. Perhaps, since the 1950s, there had not been such an important Mayo role in a key moment in Croke Park.

PJ McGrath played football with his local club, Kilmaine and was a member of the Mayo senior panel in the mid 60s, having also played full-back for the Mayo junior team in the same year. After he hung up his kicking boots, he became the man in the middle, refereeing games from the 1960s to the 90s.

However, down Kerry way, PJ is solely remembered as a Mayo man who they feel cost them their glorious place in history when PJ did not penalise Seamus Darby for an alleged push on Tommy Doyle in the build-up to the last gasp winner which denied The Kingdom in 1982.

Speaking in 2011, the affable McGrath told Radio Kerry's Weeshie Fogarty that he is still adamant that he made all the right decisions that afternoon. 'It keeps coming up for me. Someone said recently when Kilkenny were going for their five in-a-row that I should referee the final of the hurling to make sure they wouldn't win it,' he joked.

'I don't believe there was any push. If there was, I'd have given a free. I'd have not worried at all about giving a free, in or out. I did it as fair as I possibly could because anything you do in an All-Ireland final would be judged by everyone for many years afterwards.

'Darby was vastly experienced and he made himself comfortable when the ball was coming to him, so he'd be in a position to shoot afterwards, and that is what an experienced player would do. I agree that he made contact with Tommy Doyle... he bumped off him and I couldn't see any free in it.

'I certainly didn't expect a goal to come off it. If you were a Kerry man, it was a freak goal. If you were an Offaly man, it was the goal of the year.

'Kerry had chances afterwards which they did not take. Bomber Liston came flying across the pitch in that last minute and I know if he got it, it would have been straight over the bar, but he did not get the pass.'

PJ said that the furore after the final did not impact on him at all.

'I refereed the semi-final in '83 between Cork and Dublin and that went to a replay in Cork. I went to Australia with Heffo's Compromise Rules team in 1986, and the following year in '87, I finished up,' he said.

★ ★ ★ ★ ★

IT IS DIFFICULT to believe that Mayo entered the decade searching for their first Connacht title since 1969, once again highlighting the bleak competitive wasteland of the 70s. In 1980, their Connacht journey saw them heading to an inevitable beating at the hands of a Roscommon side who were by far the best in the province at the time. The match, on the weekend after the death of John Morley, was played in a daze. Mayo opened their account beating Sligo 2-11 to 1-7 in Markiewicz Park; and brought the Connacht Championship to Crossmolina for the game against Leitrim which they won by nine points. Having scored 3-28 in their opening two games, they were to be held to just eight points by Roscommon in the final at Hyde Park when the home side rattled 3-13 past them.

The Rossies went on to the 1980 final to play Kerry, but just when they seemed to have the champions on the ropes, they descended into a shell and surrendered a great chance to win an unlikely All-Ireland.

Nonetheless, it showed that a team from out west could come through and challenge the best in the business. Maybe in 1981, the winner of Connacht could put a nail in that Kerry coffin? The provinces were due to meet in the semi-final that August. But first, Connacht had to be conquered. As we entered that summer of hope, there was plenty to distract.

The then Lady Diana was walking up the aisle with her prince; the Pope got shot in St Peter's Square; Ireland was Eurovision crazy staging the contest for the first time in a decade, and Charlie Haughey was about to blow his first election as Fianna Fail leader. It was into this Bucks Fizz *Making Your Mind Up* craziness that Mayo set out on their Connacht campaign. Once again, the team toyed with our hopes, having an impressive run in the league, the high point of which was toppling the much-feted Dublin in the quarter-finals. However, true to form, we ran into the Rossies in the last four, and were treated to a five-point defeat.

The defeat was not unexpected, nor was reaction to it in any way overly pessimistic. However, our other neighbours, Galway won the other spot in that NFL decider (by beating Kerry in the semi-final) and they restricted the free-scoring Roscommon men to just three scores in the final, winning 1-11 to 1-2. So, the omens pointed to there being two strong teams in Connacht that summer in '81– and Mayo was not one of them.

Galway showed their ability when they thrashed Leitrim by 16 points to set up a semi-final between Mayo and London. Up to that point, Connacht Championship games for the Londoners had been played in Ireland, so there was a novelty when they hosted Mayo on their ground at Ruislip. The occasion was a unique one, with people from all counties turning up for the encounter. Burger vans and pints in plastic cups were the order of the day. Obviously, given the originality of the occasion, Mayo played with a complacency that haunts all teams travelling overseas before then and since. It is as if the distraction of the travel takes the eye off the ball. Mayo went on to kick almost 20 wides and prevailed at the break by just a point. However, in the second-half, they got their goal boots on and emerged 3-11 to 1-4 winners.

Chastened by their performance, they came home to a media that expected that the final would be a showdown between the powerhouses of Roscommon and Galway. However, the form book was ripped up a week later when Sligo took Roscommon apart in the semi-final, scoring a remarkable 2-9 to 1-8 win against the team who had nearly been kings just 10 months beforehand. It was a remarkable performance, sending Sligo through to their first final for six years and reviving hopes last seen in that hot summer of 1975. Free-scoring Galway were licking their lips in anticipation of another Connacht title.

But first, the Tribesmen had to come to Castlebar to take us out of the equation. Just like in '75, the sun shone brightly, and the vendors cleaned up as fans turned up in droves. From that blue sky emerged an unlikely hero – Willie Nally leapt time and time again to claim balls he should never have won. Jimmy Burke crashed home a goal in the first-half as Mayo tore into the visitors, building an unexpected five-point gap at the break. Galway were rattled but they had the firepower to recover in the form of Gay McManus and Stephen Joyce. Inevitably, they came back and when Joyce netted midway through the half, it seemed that Mayo's gallant efforts would be for nought.

We comforted ourselves with the belief that at least we had given it a good shot. But the Galway net had some sort of magnetic attraction for Aghamore men that day and a goal from Jimmy Lyons put us right back in the mix. A point clear in the closing moments, a Ger Feeney free into the Bacon Factory End seemed to take an age as it soared through the air, before splitting the posts and inspiring a roar that could be heard all the way to Moore Hall. Galway were stunned and had no time to reply.

Mayo had made it back into the Connacht final, with a chance to gain revenge for that frustrating final of 1975.

If the excitement of the Connacht Championship that summer had caught the imagination of the country, then expectations were brought back down to earth with a dreadful final played in Castlebar. Sligo tried gamely and indeed had many chances to score throughout, but were profligate with their finishing, and Mayo, with their experience, picked them off, ending up eight clear, 0-12 to 0-4.

To win a first provincial title in 12 years generated a celebration; then, there was the excitement of knowing we were heading in to an All-Ireland semi-final, against one of the greatest teams of all time.

Kerry had won the previous three All-Irelands, and buoyed by a seemingly endless conveyor belt of talent, allied to some wily old heads who had survived from the class of the late 70s, it seemed likely that they would encounter little difficulty in winning a fourth successive title. Nonetheless, the green and red flags went up around the county and special trains were laid out for the clash which generated little interest in The Kingdom, who were waiting for grander things. Consequently, only 25,000 filed into Croke Park on that day.

Mayo wore a white kit that day, and Kerry donned the blue of Munster and the champions tore into us. Creating goal chance after goal chance, they looked every inch the powerful side they were. The brightest moment Mayo had enjoyed in a semi-final for over a dozen years came when Eugene McHale was fed the ball in front of goal, did a little shimmy that sent a Kerry defender and half Hill 16 the wrong way, before flicking the ball into the net. A well-worked goal, but what made it remarkable was not the score, but the celebration.

McHale leapt with joy, punching the air, not once, not twice... but three times, as he circled around to meet the congratulations of his teammates. In that one moment, to the roar of the Mayo fans who had made the journey, it was a guttural expression of years of hurt. If we could have packed up and gone home at that stage, there would have been dinners eaten in Harry's of Kinnegad with a great sense of satisfaction.

Kerry could have had six or seven goals in the game, but in the end the scoreline was Kerry 2-19 to 1-6, and The Kingdom went on to win their fourth title in-a-row beating Offaly in the decider. It seemed as if they could not be stopped.

The following year, Mayo as Connacht champions got out of the semi-final in Carrick-on-Shannon with just a goal to spare against Leitrim, but they were no match for Galway in the final in Tuam, when they went down to a heavy defeat. The Tribesmen were out for revenge after their surprise reverse in Castlebar the previous summer, and they tortured Mayo in a 3-17 to 0-10 victory.

★ ★ ★ ★ ★

1983 BROUGHT FURTHER disappointment for Mayo, going down by three points in the Connacht final to a Galway side who went on to contest a feisty final against Dublin which saw The Dubs lose three players to red cards and still prevail. The repercussions of that 'Twelve Apostle's defeat were to haunt Galway for years and they were not back in an All-Ireland final again for another 15 years. However, in Mayo in the early 80s, there was a sense that something was building; even though there was surprise when the minors came from nowhere to win the title in 1985 with a squad that had shown little promise en route to the decider.

Our minors weren't given a prayer in that year's championship. In their opener away to Sligo, it needed a last-gasp Pat Walsh free to snatch a draw. Nor was there any hope when we allowed Sligo to hit four goals in the replay in Castlebar a week later and were seven behind at the break. What odds you would have received at that stage if you were told that a few months later, London-born and Lacken-raised Michael Fitzmaurice would be receiving the cheers and plaudits after leading Mayo to an unlikely title. Sligo went goal-crazy, but Mayo's 3-10 was enough to see them through.

In the final, how two teams of high calibre could manage to hit just eight scores between them seemed unbelievable, but Mayo emerged, their 0-6 bettering Galway's 1-1. Michael John Mullen from Kilmaine turned on the fireworks and scored two goals in the 2-12 to 2-8 semi-final win over Meath; on the day when the game was a curtain-raiser to Mayo's infamous clash with The Dubs in the senior semi-final during which John Finn had his jaw broken. Mullen was a talented soccer player who had gone for trials with Aston Villa around the same time... and those soccer skills were evident in the final against Cork when he was sent through in space with only the goalkeeper to beat.

A lesser player might have hesitated and picked up the ball and tried to round the advancing goalkeeper, but Mullen was coolness personified and he waited for his moment, and side-footed the ball assuredly past the Cork custodian and into the net. It was a goal that smacked of confidence, and was one of three that Mayo scored that day in a 3-3 to 0-9 victory that looked more comfortable than it was. Just six scores in the final were enough to bring them victory.

It was a remarkable success with a team that delivered, but looked most unlikely all the way through. A line uttered by team manager, Mick Burke about having to forge a winning team from the selection you had has become immortal.

'You have to dance with the girls in the hall, you just have to dance with the girls in the hall...'

★ ★ ★ ★ ★

IT WAS A cold wet day; the wind blew across the cinder track at Claremorris, marked out in lanes. When you qualified from your local Community Games run on grass using flags and markers for guidance, you were never prepared for the jump to these facilities. I was running for Ballinrobe and made it through the heats to the final. Drawn in lane four, I looked down the track to where I would hare to. To focus on that, use the calves to spring myself forward and go like the clappers.

The first races had been OK, but this was the one. I looked to my right, where the lads were equally nervous. To my left, the runners were like a set of steps, leading to an upstairs landing. Running in the outer lane was a lad who looked like he was two of us stacked on one another. The countdown began, the whistle blew and we were off; arms flailing, the feeling of leg upon ground. But while we were three-quarters of the way up the track, we could see the white ribbon being breached, and an official grabbing the hand of the winner – the lad from lane one, the giant, whose stride was twice ours and whose power propelled him towards that finishing line.

I got to keep the race card with my number on it. It gave the result of the final. Myself a few back, but the winner, written simply as… '1st P Brogan, Knockmore'. I didn't know it then, but I would spend the rest of the decade knowing who he was, and cheering him on as our great green and red quest continued.

★ ★ ★ ★ ★

JUST LIKE IN 1981, Mayo getting back into an All-Ireland semi-final created what was probably the start of the Mayo fever which we have to this day. Nowadays, an All-Ireland semi-final is just a point on a journey for us entitled group of Mayo fans. Back then, getting to the last four meant that there was only ever going to be one topic of conversation for the height of summer. If you could call it summer… 1985 was one of those miserable stop-start summers. Not an ideal time to be selling cheap t-shirts.

It was also the summer when another Mayo pipe-dream was coming to its zenith, and steamrollers and tarmac contractors rolled layer after layer of hardness onto a runway on the top of a mountain near Charlestown. That too was made steadfast to last 30 years and bring home a whole new generation of supporters from far flung places across the globe. That tarmac was also the foundation for a newfound confidence in 'Brand Mayo', one that has stood the test of time to the present day. Perhaps it was in that newfound belief that we could build an airport and be able to honour our heritage, that the roots of Mayo-mania originated.

That summer of '85, as our minors made their way through the championship to enjoy an unexpected lap of honour on the last Sunday in September, there was a freshness about Mayo football that would spark a revolution that would keep the county mattering and engaged for the next 40 years.

For myself and my friends, several of whom were on that minor panel, life was about to get exciting. We were departing school and heading to college in Galway and elsewhere. Soon that portion of our lives when we would exclusively be in our home county would be gone, and our identities would morph into whatever communities we nestled in along the way. I headed to Galway and, more than a decade ago, realised that I had spent more time out of Mayo than in it, yet nothing would ever diminish the love for my own place and the tribal role it played in shaping me throughout life.

In those years before the Charlton era and the arrival of the Celtic Tiger, hope was limited. Few of those I met on the waiting line for work outside the Cricklewood Cafe in the mid to late 80s felt that they could ever prosper back home. Nor could they ever foresee the standard of living in Ireland matching that of its European counterparts.

Liam O'Neill had taken over as county manager in 1982 on the back of the low-ebbs of the Kerry drubbing at Croker in 1981, and an even more dispiriting thrashing by Galway in Tuam in 1982. It was into this environment that former Galway star O'Neill arrived, having played a key role in Knockmore's ascendancy. What was needed was someone to tap into the rich well of young talent that was sprung from the 1978 minor win and other successes, the likes of Kilgallon, Ford, Durkin, Flanagan… Maughan.

Kevin McStay recalled how he had never even trained with the seniors before he was thrown into the melting pot of a Connacht final against Galway in 1983 alongside another debutant, Padraig Brogan. The experience was not lost on them though because the same year, Mayo claimed an under-21 title, beating Derry in the final with a team of players, many of whom became household names in the years after.

Success did not come easy though for O'Neill, because Mayo were beaten again in 1984, so in a sense, '85 represented the Last Chance Saloon for the Galwayman. This meant he had to dabble in the transfer market, so to speak. Former Offaly star Sean Lowry moved to Crossmolina earlier that year to take up work at the Bellacorrick Power Station. In his mid-thirties, Lowry had retired from inter-county football when he transferred west and an Indian summer in the green and red couldn't have been further from his mind. He had his Celtic Cross and his memories, and returning to try to win another was not in the equation.

'Liam O'Neill came knocking at my door. I had given up football and was just playing with Crossmolina,' he explained. 'It was a great way of getting into the community anyway and they were so welcoming and looked after us. Liam O'Neill came to me around May.

'Eventually he came around the second time, so I said, "Listen, I'll give you a hand for a few months and whenever you are out of the championship, then I'll skedaddle". When I did go to Mayo training, I couldn't believe how good they were. I said there was huge potential here. I couldn't get over how they weren't thinking of winning.

'I told them, "If we had this team in Offaly, we'd definitely win the All-Ireland" which I'm sure of still. It's definitely a year that got away.'

BILLY FITZPATRICK, WHO was still performing miracles at club level was cajoled back into action, while Martin Carney found a new life for himself in the backs.

The league saw draws with Monaghan and a defeat by the Rossies. In the Centenary Cup, the team had novel pairings with vastly different results. They hit 5-12 against Kilkenny, with 2-5 of this coming from Kevin McStay. But in the next round against Limerick, they lost 3-6 to 0-5, an inauspicious manner in which to prepare for the forthcoming championship.

Fortunately, they were drawn away to Leitrim in the semi-final and won easily 2-11 to 0-05, with Henry Gavin hitting 1-3 and Eugene McHale coming on as sub and scoring 1-1. In the final at Hyde Park, Mayo hit 2-11 again and, once more, the opponents didn't get into double figures, with Roscommon responding with only eight points.

'Lowry gave a fantastic speech that day in the dressing-room, where he insisted we were as good as any team he had ever played for,' recalled Kevin McStay. 'In my innocence, I believed him and we nearly took the door off the hinges as we tore out onto the pitch.'

The manner of the victory had everyone talking and there was genuine excitement that something good was happening in Mayo football; the unexpected progress of the minors an encouraging and distracting sideshow.

This was a summer where myself and my schoolmates were to head off to college in Galway, so in order to make a few quid, we bought a box load of white t-shirts and got a local artist to do a colourful 'Mayo are Magic' emblazoned on the front. It was a line to which the cynics responded, 'They're fuckin' magic alright, watch them disappear from the championship'. But we were undaunted and persevered and sold hundreds of them, oblivious to the fact that one wash later, the artwork would probably disappear.

The 1985 semi-final was against a Dublin side still managed by Kevin Heffernan, a team that had won the All-Ireland just two years earlier, their fourth in the previous decade. It was a team that included the likes of Brian Mullins, Barney Rock, Ciaran Duff, John O'Leary, Gerry Hargan and a young Charlie Redmond. Mayo were rank outsiders but it hardly mattered to the thousands of green and red clad supporters who made the long pilgrimage to Croke Park. They got in early too and watched as the minors despatched Meath to make it through to the last Sunday in September. There is something uplifting about seeing minor and senior teams line out on the same pitch, a sort of overwhelming satisfaction that progress is being attained, for the now and the hereafter.

Like every Mayo trip to the capital, there were moments of hope, especially early on when Noel Durkin got on the end of a wayward free from McStay and fired past O'Leary into the net. The ground erupted, but it proved a false dawn as The Dubs came roaring back, goaling and leading by six points at the break. Mayo fans were resigned to another chastening defeat; and hoped it would not be a scoreline that would replicate that of four years previously when Kerry had destroyed them after a promising start. That six-point lead for Dublin became seven, but, just like the Mayo teams of recent years, there was nothing like a bit of mad chaos to kickstart them back into it.

The centre of the field seemed to be flagging, but a ball of energy was released when O'Neill sent on Padraig Brogan and Big Tom Byrne, the man who was instrumental in the minor comeback against the Dubs in '78. With seven minutes gone in the second-half, Mayo began to dominate and The Dubs would not score again that afternoon. McStay, Padden, Brogan, Kilgallon and Byrne all fired over points to reduce the lead to two. When Brian Mullins sent through Anto McCaul on goal, we were sure our goose was cooked but somehow the ball bobbled past Lavin, and wide of the post and the gaping net. But there was to be more drama. Billy Fitz turned back the years when he entered the fray and his point generated a roar that could be heard back west. With 28 seconds on the clock, Kilgallon struck a sweet equaliser and in the dying moments, McStay had a chance, but the ball squirmed from his grip and the final whistle blew a second later.

For a county scarce on even moral defeats, a moral draw seemed like a victory and there was a bounce in the step of every Mayo fan as they left Dublin that evening to head west and to start the search for the tickets for the replay. But there was more drama for the intervening weeks. The question on everyone's lips was…

'Who shot JF?'

Five years after TR Dallas serenaded the country and hit the top of the charts with his cash-in on the Dallas phenomenon, *Who Shot JR Ewing*, Mayo had its own whodunnit. While that oil and riches mystery was eventually solved and pinned on Bing Crosby's daughter, our Mayo side had its own drama, and one, to this day, that has probably had a longer run than Agatha Christie's *The Mousetrap*.

IN THE DRAWN game on August 18, John Finn's jaw was broken in an off-the-ball incident. Every Mayo fan knows where they were the day this happened, live on TV in front of hundreds of thousands, yet only a handful know who was the perpetrator. Overnight, Finn became a household name. Radio phone-ins described the act as 'shocking' and 'thuggery' which left him unable to eat solid foods for the best part of a month and out of the game until well into the following year.

The player himself was plagued with requests to spill the beans, to 'out' who had done it to him. It was not as if any extra spice was needed for the replay, but a desire for retribution was in the air. The following day's *Evening Press* even went as far as to name a player who might have been involved. Everyone had their theories; even to this day there are people who swear black and blue that it was this one or that, even players who were not even on the pitch at the time of the incident. You can well imagine that if such an incident was to happen today, it would be caught on several of the high-def cameras and on thousands of phones, but all we had to go on was the slightly after-the-fact image of Finn being down.

To the player himself, the saga was surprising. And he didn't even know the extent of his injury until after the game when the stadium was emptying out and half the fans were tucking into chicken and chips in Harry's of Kinnegad.

Speaking some time ago to Vincent Hogan, Finn recalled the events of the day.

'I had a shower after the game and got dressed,' he recalls. 'But I knew as I was cooling down that there was something wrong. As my body was relaxing after playing a pretty hyper game, I could feel myself getting sorer and sorer. I remember saying it to the lads, that I thought there might be something seriously wrong with me.

'Then the X-ray just confirmed my worst fears. And I was kept in for a few nights. The big problem for me was that I couldn't play in the replay. That was the only issue for me. I remember crying in the hospital when I realised. But then you had the media hype afterwards, which I thought blew things out of all proportion.'

The heat of the media dance made him distinctly uncomfortable. Because he was the victim of the incident, he felt the glare was on him to an unfair extent. His privacy was invaded, as pundits and fans and former players had their say on what they thought happened and what should have been done about it. But behind it all was a man who had played for his county since he was 13 and who was facing the possibility of missing out on the biggest game that the county had played in decades. He felt too that there were some people who thought that he had provoked the matter in some way and that the injury had been caused by some form of retaliation. Nothing could be further from the truth, he said.

'It wasn't nice actually,' he stresses. 'Because you'll always have knockers and I knew there would be a lot of people saying "Well, maybe he did something to deserve it". That wasn't the case though.

'Put it this way. I know exactly the lead-up to it… and I know exactly why it happened. I know exactly who made it happen and, of course, I know exactly who did it. But I'm not going to name names. Let me just say that there was pressure coming from beyond, from a particular person.

'I know quite a few of that Dublin team well. And all the guys of that period, including the fella who hit me, are decent, nice guys. I've played golf with a lot of them since. And I feel confident saying that what happened to me wasn't intended by the fella involved. Plain and simple. It worked out a lot worse than he'd ever have imagined.

'Well, I do remember when JR Ewing got shot and, for the whole summer, no one knew who did it. I suppose this was the same thing, except it's gone on for many years. Unfortunately, it's the one thing that the game is always remembered for. In hindsight, it's probably the one thing that I'm remembered for as well. But I actually played for Mayo for 10 years after that.'

But missing out on the replay broke his heart.

'I remember sitting in the dug-out for the replay and that was tough. I could feel everyone looking. The only way to avoid that would have been not to show up for the game at all. And to do that would ultimately have only led to more talk. I'd have been adding to the mystery.'

MAYOMANIA WAS born and our t-shirts sold like hotcakes with no consequences for Revenue or the dole payments. Being on the front-line of selling merchandise, and flush with pound notes, I managed to get two tickets for the replay. The Nally. In an effort to impress the girlfriend of six months, I got them upgraded to decent seats in the Hogan and was cock-a-hoop when she agreed to travel. We'd get the train up, bite to eat… and the match. Last of the big spenders… know how to show someone a good time. Yeah, right.

Ahead of the replay, Sean Lowry approached O'Neill with a different game plan, telling him that they should play faster ball to the inside line and trust Willie Joe Padden and TJ Kilgallon to look after Brian Mullins and Jim Ronayne, instead of crowding the midfield sector.

The only trouble was, by the time the replay came around, Lowry was abruptly dropped.

The argument abounded that because he had not scored in the first game, he was a luxury the team could ill-afford, but this could not be further from the truth. His experience and ball-winning and sheer physical size was something that would occupy defenders in a way that few could. However, the die was cast and they took to the field without him.

Mayo played well in the first-half but a one-point half-time lead was a poor return for their dominance. Although Padraig Brogan hit a wonder goal for Mayo in the second-half, two Kieran Duff strikes at the other end finished their ambitions.

'I think Liam O'Neill lost the run of himself,' says Lowry, who didn't get off the bench. 'I think there were outside influences. I don't want to come across as bitter, I was just disappointed because it was a team that was fit to win an All-Ireland. We were well fit to do it. Dublin and Kerry were tired teams by that stage.'

Prior to the game, sitting in a restaurant in the centre of town, the girlfriend, another Mayo woman, told me that I was getting the red card. It was all 'it's not you, it's me', space and the usual palaver. But sure, I had to agree with her. There seemed little point in contesting the decision. But what always bothered me was why she chose to tell me before the match.

Was it to add a little more drama to an already dramatic day; maybe a fear that she wouldn't go ahead with it in the elation of an historic win. Perhaps, she knew that it was a very Mayo thing to add misery to misery, so that even if we had won, I'd be sad. (I hasten to add that we are now great friends and laugh about it all)

AS THE SLOW train eventually arrived back in Claremorris that night, both I and Mayo had been dumped unfairly out of our respective championships. I hadn't even the luxury of a replay. As I walked herself to the lift she was getting home, I passed by the athletics track where Brogan had beaten me five years earlier, and my heart swelled with pride that the man who had scored the best goal of that day, had at one stage, shared a sporting moment with me… even if he was five metres ahead of me at the finish.

The roads were quiet that night, but the moon was bright, so I decided to walk as I made my way thumbing along the lonely roads of South Mayo. My own relationship aside, for Mayo football, it felt like a day that represented the end of something.

In my miserable state, I opined that perhaps we had come the nearest we would ever come to reaching an All-Ireland final again. That there is a reason we could not have nice things. As I waited for the lights of any car to break the darkness along the roads of Hollymount and Robeen, these were the thoughts that filled my mind.

Little was I to know that contrary to my beliefs, this day was probably the beginning of the greatest sporting obsession in the long history of the county.

★ ★ ★ ★ ★

IT WAS A Monday night. Hot, sticky. Back in the days before we knew there'd be a price to pay for the great weather. There was a novelty to that summer of 1989.

For the first time on the FM wavelength, you could soar out past the low 90s and find stations… Irish stations. Some were faint, but some were crystal clear, broadcasting in local voices from the heart of our community. We had grown up with summer radio. Radio Luxembourg on 208, and clearer sound right from when Radio 2 was 'cominatcha' in 1979; when every summer job was spent painting or cutting grass or banking turf to the cyclical playlists of the chart music on the national station.

But there was a new buzz on the airwaves and because of this, we listened in the morning, right through the day and into the early evenings, marvelling at this sound coming from the heart of our own community.

It was July, and the evening presenter on MWR was happy out with his new station in life, to pardon the pun. He had just been handed the sheet off the fax machine. The Mayo team for the replayed Connacht final against Roscommon had just been announced, and he read it out with great glee, although it was obvious that sport was not his strongpoint.

'…Irwin, Browne, Forde, Flanagan, Noone, Kilgallon, Finn, Maher, McHale, Dempsey, WillieJoe, Durcan, Fitzmaurice, Burke… and McStay.'

He had been reading out requests all evening 'for Bridie in Aughagower… for Mattie down in Kilmaine', but here was something different. Something beyond Mattie and Bridie, something everyone wanted to know. He enjoyed it so much that he read it out three times, milking the county's newfound ability to bring team news to the masses in ways that were unprecedented. Up until then, you had to wait for the Tuesday or Wednesday morning rush of local papers for your diet of county team gossip. Indeed, many is the county player who found out he had been dropped from the team when the local paper dropped into the town newsagent. Local radio changed that dynamic… forever.

'Listen, I'll read it again for any of ye who may have missed it when I read it out earlier.' And so, he did.

Our man was flying now. So, he decided to go a bit further.

'Isn't it mighty to be able to get the Mayo team like that. Only mighty… now, I am wondering, if there any of ye out there who might have the Roscommon team? If ye do, sure ring it in to oh-nine-oh-seven- three-oh-wan-six-nine. That's oh-nine-oh-seven- three-oh-wan-six-nine… if ye have the Roscommon team.'

The phones hopped.

Listeners had their Roscommon teams all right. Several of them, in fact. Our presenter was inundated with line-ups, many of them featuring Roscommon players who had been dead for donkeys' years. Players who had won All-Irelands with Roscommon in the 40s were surprisingly getting a recall for the '89 match. There was a Ulick Magee at full-back, a Phil McCracken at centre half-forward, and Mike, one of the Hunt brothers named as corner-forward.

By the time he had read out the third different Roscommon team, the penny dropped. Needless to say, our presenter never asked the public for direct information again, but the episode provided light hearted relief in the height of that football-mad summer, when the country was changing, and when it seemed, though we could be mistaken as we were so often in the past, that Mayo were back.

★ ★ ★ ★ ★

HAVING SO NEARLY overthrown the Dubs in 1985, it was determined that '86 would be our year. There was the added incentive that it would be that one-in-three years when Connacht winners would play Ulster, and on most occasions when this has happened, the Connacht team had prevailed and found themselves in a handy All-Ireland final. If we would only win Connacht, we would have another shot at Dublin or Kerry in a final, and anything could happen. But first, Connacht had to be won.

We had shown that we had some bright recruits coming through and we sailed all the way to the league semi-final, only to be pipped by Monaghan. The championship brought us to Ruislip for the yet another sunny day, where the pitch was swamped with the smell of cheeseburgers and hot dogs and warm pints in plastic glasses.

There was not to be any away-day panic this time and we won, 3-14 to 0-4, with a performance that suggested normal service was resumed. The reward was a home semi-final with the Rossies, and given the gaps between the sides a year earlier, Mayo expected to win this easily. There was a warning, though. The Rossies had walloped Monaghan in a pre-season friendly and had impressed in the league. On a scorching day in Castlebar, a sloppy start had an understrength Mayo side five behind after a quarter of an hour, and although some sharpshooting by Brogan in the second-half drew us level, two late, late points by the McManus brothers, Tony and Eamonn sent us packing from the championship.

The loss of key players such as Flanagan, Kilgallon and Maughan unsettled the side and so the great progress of 1985 was sent packing. It didn't help that the memories of that hot day in 1975 were raised by the fact that Mickey Kearins was the man in the middle, although on this occasion, his performance was not as startling as it had been 11 years previously.

Once again, a dominant Mayo had failed to turn possession into scores, a malaise that would haunt us on many occasions in the future. To make it worse, the old enemy Galway went on to beat Roscommon in the final and took Connacht's place in the semi-final against Tyrone. However, surprisingly, they made a mess of it and went down by three points.

★ ★ ★ ★ ★

BY THE TIME the 1987 Connacht Championship came around, I was working on the building sites in London, stripping out buildings such as that owned by ballerina Margot Fonteyn and converting them into high-end apartments for their new Middle Eastern owners. On hot days in Hackney, we slogged for the Green Macs pulling cables through tunnels just a metre high, beneath the streets of London, the dampness dripping onto our bare backs as we scurried like rats dragging the cabling from one underground pit to another. There is nothing like the frantic busyness of a London workday to prepare you for the absolute deadness of a Sunday afternoon.

Back home, Mayo had, after an indifferent league campaign, won their place in the Connacht final by walloping Sligo 3-17 to 0-6, a result that did little to endear us to our foreman who was from Collooney. Not helped by the good weather in London that day, the radio signal on LW was barely audible for the provincial decider, so on a lonely Sunday in a dank bedsit on Olive Road in Cricklewood, we tried to take advantage of the good weather to hear Mayo blow another final, losing out 0-8 to 0-7 to Galway in a terrible game in Castlebar. In the era of mass communications, perhaps it is hard to get a sense of the low that descends on those who are far from home when their native county fails to win.

Back then, when the signal died at the full-time whistle, there was nobody to share the result with, to dissect it with, a thought that came back to me on the day of the 2020 final when the world had suddenly become a very different place. But more of that anon.

The experience of the low after that has informed me much in the years since. For most back then, it was something to hold onto, a short reunion with your core identity in the midst of so many cultures. Just one thread on the great patchwork quilt. On days like that, it was hard to imagine that following Mayo would ever amount to anything above endurance, a torture forced upon us by accident of birth.

★ ★ ★ ★ ★

IN 1988, THE mood was not helped by relegation in the league after defeats by Dublin, Kerry twice, Meath, and Armagh, but the team found their mojo out west, storming through the province, with handy wins against Leitrim, Sligo and Roscommon. However, a powerful Meath side awaited in the semi-finals, and they handed us a five-point defeat. If the feeling abounded that the 80s was going to peter out in another decade of disappointment, then a surprise was just around the corner and another key moment in the creation of the fanaticism that has hung around Mayo football to this day.

For many modern followers of the green and red, this is where the memories began. It was the year that started with hope and ended with hope, even if there was a penultimate disappointment in between. The gap from 1951 to 1989 is mammoth, so it was understandable that when the chance came to become fanatical about the team, tens of thousands grabbed the opportunity with both hands. And like so many seasons, the hope came out of nowhere.

The league campaign had not been awe-inspiring. John Maughan was injured and never to play for his county again. John Finn and TJ Kilgallon were also struggling with injuries. There was not any new name coming off the conveyor belt. The Mayo of 1989 was a certain case of, 'From the people who brought you the disappointment of '88'.

Once again, it was a year of the 'soft route' to an All-Ireland final as, once again, it would be the Ulster champions we would face in the semi-final. If only Connacht could be conquered again, then maybe there would be the prospect of a day out in Dublin in September for the first time since people lived their lives in black and white.

In all of the years since that win in 1951, Mayo had never even met an Ulster team. It was as if fate had ordained that our search for ultimate glory would not be a soft option. Any year that we had escaped from Connacht, we were facing the behemoths of Dublin or Kerry.

To make matters worse, we did not have the option of a provincial game against Sligo or Leitrim or London. If we were to win Connacht, we would have to beat both Galway and Roscommon. Thankfully, Galway were in a bigger mess than us, having had a nightmarish league campaign which saw them plummet into Division 3. But if there was ever a red rag to hold to the Galway bull, it was the sight of a Mayo jersey.

That animosity was on display from early on the drawn match in Tuam, where an upper-cut to Kevin McStay's jaw saw him depart before the break. A man who was no stranger to sneaky punches to the jaw, John Finn was introduced in the second-half and it coincided with a Mayo revival. Finn's attitude had an inspirational impact on the Mayo side, and they rallied well, and were on course for victory until they let in the swarthy Gay McManus for an equalising goal in the dying seconds.

However, it was obvious that this Mayo team had more about them than a Galway side still psychologically smarting from the 'Twelve Apostles' defeat in Croke Park six years earlier and they were not flattered by the eight-point gap at the end of the replay, with goals from McHale and Finnerty carrying the day.

Although Roscommon had not won Connacht since 1980, Mayo were still wary of the hungry threat that they carried and in a poor but honest game in Castlebar, the home side shot 14 wides and were grateful to 'keeper Gabriel Irwin when he made several late saves to deny Roscommon a smash and grab. The save from Paul Earley in particular was spectacular and Mayo were glad to get the replay a week later at Hyde Park.

If people were disappointed with the drawn game, the replay was a classic for the ages. I still cannot watch it and believe that Mayo got out alive. The two sides locked horns for 100 minutes of drama; gold dust to the new radio station MWR which had come on air just a short time earlier and which had not covered the drawn game, but decided in the hectic days beforehand to broadcast the game live from the Hyde, with cub *Western People* reporter, Liam Horan drafted in to man the mic. A lifelong friend of mine, there was no better man to take on the challenge, not knowing that what lay ahead of him was a 100-minute challenge and analysis before and after to bring the drama of the contest across the region on 96.1.

The game went this way and that on a sweltering day and, when Tony McManus scored a penalty in injury time to give his side a one-point lead, Mayo fans feared the worst, but they had not reckoned for Micheal Collins, who goaled to send Mayo back in front. But the celebrations were short-lived as Mickey Kearins, (yes that Mickey Kearins) called back play having whistled for a foul, leaving Michael Fitzmaurice with the pressured task of having to kick an equalising point.

Into extra time, and Roscommon seemed stronger, but the best chances came Mayo's way and many were missed. However, substitute Brian Kilkelly ran onto a Willie Joe knockdown and pushed it into the path of Anthony Finnerty and the Moygownagh man poked the ball into the net. Fitzmaurice pointed again soon after and when the long legs of Liam McHale ran loose through the heart of the home defence, he gave Jimmy Burke the simple task of goaling – but Mayo don't do simple and Jimmy seemed to stumble and fall onto the ball, pumping the shot into the net.

At this stage, Liam Horan's larynx was in shreds with the drama but the new medium had arrived at the birth of a new hysteria. Hearts raced across the province and now the region and the country had seen that Mayo were back in the last four and with a decent chance of making the decider.

'I tried to dwell on the positive aspects of the game, the great scores, the super-human efforts, the high fielding, the man-to-man tussles between the likes of Glennon and Noone, Maher/McHale and Killoran/Newtown, and Jimmy Browne and Tony McManus, the man who had complete control of my voice every time he came within 25 yards of the ball,' recalled Horan.

'Although a novice, I had no difficulty in maintaining the flow because the players made it easy. On the Saturday evening, I had gone through some old programmes to build up a data base to fall back on during any lull in the game, but I didn't refer to that store of information once. Which is just as well, because a fair few pages of it blew out the window of the commentary box during the second-half.'

He says now that a valuable lesson he learned was that his passion for Mayo was overwhelming during the commentary, forgetting that a fair few of the MWR listeners were from Roscommon, so there were deafening silences for a Roscommon goal and ecstatic elation during a Mayo one moments later.

What Horan achieved in that historic broadcast was to create a valuable conduit between the game and the listeners.

'You were my eyes today,' a grateful fan told him in the days afterwards.

Horan has been involved in communications roles for various Mayo squads since then, but his role in '89 was key in creating the manic devotion to the idea of the chaotic pursuit of glory that has lasted to this day, despite the substantial disappointments. In one sense, he and other devoted Mayo scribes such as Sean Rice, Ivan Neill, John Melvin, Terry O'Reilly, Mike Finnerty, Tom Kelly, Aidan Henry, Colm Gannon and Ed McGreal, to name but a few, have fed the hungry beast that is the thirst for information surrounding Mayo football. Horan's commentary and MWR's broadcast was followed that night by an open-ended analysis programme, broadcast from the studios in Ballyhaunis. Local fans could not believe what they were getting – a service before its time, and months ahead of the establishment of other legalised radio stations around the country.

★ ★ ★ ★ ★

BUT THE SEMI-FINAL awaited.

Ulster champions, Tyrone were favourites to get through on the basis that they were more experienced and, in the opinion of many, rather unfortunate not to have won the All-Ireland a short time before. They were, however, surprised by Mayo, who won that game because they believed they could win. No one will forget the determination on Willie Joe Padden's face as he returned from the sideline, having undergone emergency repairs to his injured head and wearing headgear like an Indian topi, to resume his convincing performance. That was Mayo... confident, impressive and close to ultimate success.

The 38-year wait for a place in football's showpiece had ended in a hard-hitting uncompromising semi-final in front of 48,000. This had been Mayo's seventh pilgrimage to headquarters since 1951, so to finally make the breakthrough saw the county go... MAD.

WITH FLIGHTS OPERATING from the then Knock Airport (now Ireland West Airport) it was mooted that the team would fly from Mayo to Dublin for the final. Carried on sound waves of enthusiasm from the new energised radio spectrum, the mania speed throughout the region. The new radio station considered broadcasting the final but because of logistical difficulties, it was deemed to be a non-runner, although live 'on the whistle' reports from a nearby building were arranged.

The fever pitch that was reached in Mayo in those hectic weeks in the summer/ early autumn of 1989 went a long way to ensuring Mayo got close to winning an All-Ireland, but also provided valuable lessons in ways in which a county should not prepare for an All-Ireland final, lessons no doubt learned by the Mayo manager, John O'Mahony, who was to manage Galway to Sam Maguire less than a decade later.

O'Mahony recalls how he and his teaching colleagues in St Nathy's in Ballaghdereen broke up for the holidays in June and it was then he set about plotting Mayo's Connacht Championship campaign.

'It was as if it wasn't a priority until then, and my next encounter with reality and the real world was walking back though those gates of St Nathy's a couple of days after the All-Ireland final.' In between those two dates, O'Mahony, like the rest of Mayo, was to partake in a summer of drama and excitement like no other in his native county.

'In between wasn't a total blur," he recalled. 'But the memories are confined to Mayo and football, to injuries, to draws and replays and with training. There was the great momentum when Jimmy Burke sealed our Connacht final victory over Roscommon with that unusual goal in extra time; or when Michael Fitzmaurice put us three points clear against Tyrone in the semi-final and guaranteed our place in the final.

'There were the difficult moments when I had to tell a player he was dropped for Sunday or, worse still, that he is not in the official sub list, and will have to take his place among the spectators even though he had put in as much effort as the players on the team; the uplifting moments when Micheal Collins, even though he was not in the starting 15 for the Connacht final replay, got up at the team weekly meeting the day before the match and said how much it was going to mean to him to win a Connacht medal the following day.

'That for me showed the depth of character in the panel and was illustrated on the pitch the following day when Micheal came on for the injured Frank Noone and scored what would have been the winning goal only to have it disallowed. There was also the never-to-be-forgotten impassioned speech of Frank Noone when he left his stretcher and dragged himself across the pitch to exhort his teammates to greater effort.

'Once he had spoken, no one else had a need to say anything,' said O'Mahony.

★ ★ ★ ★ ★

HOWEVER, THE REAL story of Mayo's championship drive in 1989 emanated from the disappointment on the bus, on the return journey from Croke Park, after the narrow semi-final defeat to eventual All-Ireland winners Meath the previous August. All the players felt they did not play as well as they could, and would have loved the chance to play that game again that Sunday evening.

But there was no second chance. The flaming passion though lit the flames of the assault on Sam in 1989. In early January, at a team meeting in Bonniconlon, the squad and management felt that they had a right good chance of winning an All-Ireland that year.

However, to have mentioned their ambition in public might have seen them laughed out of the village, so external expectations were low.

'The New Year resolution that we made that day was tested many times up to the final the following September,' recalled O'Mahony. 'It was a rocky road and it was important that we kept the faith.'

TJ Kilgallon's year seemed to be in ruins when in Mayo's first league game after Christmas, he was victim of one of the most brutal tackles that O'Mahony had ever seen. The perpetrator was not even booked, but TJ was in the operating theatre two days later and the prognosis was a spell of at least six months out of action. However, the skill and determination of medical team Gina Carney, Frank Davey and TJ himself, defied those predictions and he was sprung from the bench against Galway in the Connacht semi-final replay. There was a togetherness about the squad that built up right from that moment, until they collapsed on the turf at the end of the final the following September, a camaraderie constructed from the 103 training sessions that they held during that campaign.

For the first few weeks, it was beach work, hill work, all about building up the stamina that would stand them in good stead that summer. After 45 minutes running on steep hills in Tony McHugh's field, they often finished off with 10 60-yard sprints up a cliff-like hill. Many of them collapsed by the top, but they were picked up by colleagues and encouraged to keep going.

But there was plenty of work going on behind the scenes too.

Times were different to these days. This was, despite the memories of golden sunshine and melting choc ices, still the end of the 80s, when the economy was poor and jobs were not plentiful. There were a good few of the panel unemployed at the time.

'This was a major concern for all of us,' said O'Mahony. 'It is very hard for a player to perform to his full potential if he has no job to go to the next day. A number of people helped us in this regard and in other ways during the year. People who had nothing to gain except they knew they were helping Mayo to success. All of those people in particular were very much in mind when the final whistle blew in Hyde Park signalling our first back-to-back Connacht titles since 1951, and again in Croke Park, when we defeated Tyrone in the semi-final.'

Cork were bidding to win their first final since 1973, so they were hungry for success. In the final, Mayo fell behind by three Larry Tompkins points, and one from John Cleary, after just eight minutes, but a fine effort from Willie Joe stopped the rot. Cork gave a masterclass in point scoring, and went in two points clear at the break, a dogged Mayo staying in touch and belying the tag of being no-hopers.

However, Mayo fans were in dreamland with their first attack of the second-half, when the ball was worked through to Anthony Finnerty; a quick shuffle of the hips and he was through on goal, where he fired to the roof of the net. The place erupted. From having trailed for the entire game, Mayo were a point clear without even having gotten going. Dave Barry soon equalised and it remained tit for tat; a McHale point narrowing the gap to a point for the 3/1 outsiders.

A Maher goal chance went begging before a Fitzmaurice free gave Mayo the lead once again. Then came the moment that haunts Mayo fans ever since. A Durcan pass put Finnerty into space once again, and his driven shot across the face of the goal went a foot wide of the far post. A goal at that point could have sealed the deal for Mayo.

But it was not to be.

Cork rattled over three more points, some which resulted from tired play, and it was those three scores that created the gap held to the end. It might be too easy to suggest that the reasons for Cork's victory were that their forwards played better football; that they scored 16 points from play; that four of their original attack took their points extremely well and that they won the battle in the last quarter.

Yet it seems a valid argument, if one considers that Mayo's original forward line scored just three points from play. Michael Fitzmaurice scored seven, six from frees, and a '50'. Sub Anthony Finnerty scored our goal, and midfielder Liam McHale scored our other point.

There is no doubt that as Mayo reflect on the afternoon's performance they will remember when Fitzmaurice and Greg Maher hit the post in the first-half, when Tony Davis blocked a great shot by Greg Maher in the 25th minute, and when Liam McHale shot tamely wide just two minutes later.

In a game without a single booking or nasty tackle, the sad reality was that Cork scored 16 of their 17 points from play, and we got just five. A weakness that went on to hamper us again and again in the years to come. The general consensus after the '89 final was that we were a force coming, that more finals would be on the cards, given the strength of the squad that was emerging.

One would never have foretold that it would be another seven years before we would set foot in a decider again.

★ ★ ★ ★ ★

SIXTEEN SECONDS… JUST sixteen seconds.

Croke Park was humming with excitement. A strange light fell across the ground. It was a brighter stadium in those days before the looming stands joined forces at either end. There was a richness to the colours of both sides lit by the dropping sun behind the Hogan. Both sets of fans were elated in equal measure – a Mayo side seeking their first victory in 45 years had given themselves a strong platform on which to snatch Sam.

Just a short while earlier, they had been six clear of a street-wise and toughened Meath side. A county that had come lately to renewed success and which had a hardened reputation as a side unfazed by any other. But such a hardness does not desert a team easily and as the minutes ticked down, so did the deficit. Mind the gap… as it was wound down by a Meath team like a fisherman reeling in a salmon. Mayo had been superb, but when you are superb and not seeing it out, there is always a hope for the other side…and so it proceeded.

Six became five… five became four, four became three and… before we knew it, it was down to a single point.

To a Mayo following starved of success, once the advantage hit three, we knew we were vulnerable to a sucker punch. When it became two, fear of a major concession would have devastated us; when it became one, a long punt could undo us.

Time was almost up… the tide was only going one way, there was time for one more Meath attack; if not an attack, more so a hit and hope effort from Colm Coyle… from midfield, he lifted a hopeful ball into the centre of the Mayo goalmouth. For those of us who were there, the greatest fear was that goalkeeper John Madden would misjudge the bounce and it would rise up into the net, and win Meath the All-Ireland in the cruellest fashion. But instead, it hit the hard turf and with defenders and attackers and goalkeeper floundering, it evaded every touch from the crowded square, and bounced over the bar.

The likes of it had never been seen in an All-Ireland final, but this was Mayo and their misfortune. For all their effort, we sensed this was going to end in disappointment. Meath had their tails up. We were devastated, there had been stops and starts throughout the game, and referee Pat McEnaney would surely play three minutes, sufficient time for the momentum to carry Meath into a lead… but then 16 seconds after the 70, the long whistle blew and both sides looked stunned. A draw does not leave any side satisfied; the momentum carriers feel denied; the long-time leaders feel deflated.

But 16 seconds… probably the shortest added time in any final in modern times. And barring 1982, the strangest end to a final in many years. In hindsight, we see this with some rose-tinted glasses. If the bounce had been anticipated and attacked rather than being feared, if we had been cuter when six points clear – there was a line ball kicked outfield rather than in-field at that stage. Looking back at the video, I struggle to see how we failed to win it; and in another viewing, I am damn glad that McEnaney didn't allow the three or four minutes of additional time that were probably warranted and which would have eliminated the need for a replay and the psychological damage that was to bring with it.

IT ALL STARTED out so differently – Mayo, who John Maughan had dragged from the depths of Division 3, led Meath 0-7 to 0-4 after a dominant first-half and they reinforced their dominance early in the second when a Ray Dempsey goal put them six points in front and en route to ending the famine. We led by four as the game entered the final 10 minutes.

John Casey remembers being hooked ashore at that stage and selector Tommy O'Malley telling him, 'We have the All-Ireland...' but points from John McDermott, Trevor Giles and Brendan Reilly brought The Royals back to within a point, before Colm Coyle scored that most speculative of points to save Meath's skin and ensure they got another bite at the cherry. So, what happened Mayo?

What caused us to run out of steam just as had happened in the decider seven years earlier? In that last quarter, just about everything that broke behind midfield was easily picked up by Meath and, whether it was a series of bad tactics by Mayo or just that they were running on empty, this was the main reason why Meath were able to stage their recovery. They were kept in the game up to that point by a defence in which Martin O'Connell had an absolute stormer. True, Mayo played right into Meath's hands by repeatedly kicking high balls into men who couldn't win them, but even when Mayo forwards did win possession, especially in the second-half, they found it extremely difficult to create space for themselves and the fact that they could manage only one point (as well as a goal) in that second-half says it all.

Indeed, Colm Coyle at right half-back had probably his worst game in a Meath jersey... and yet he was the one who made a draw possible with his speculative kick from 70 yards which was allowed to bounce over the bar in the last minute. Afterwards he admitted that it was a punted pass rather than a scoring attempt.

'I thought I saw two Meath forwards near their goal and one of them seemed to be inside the defence,' he explained. 'So, I thought if I could kick it into the danger zone something might happen.' Coyle wore spectacles in everyday life and he jokingly commented, 'I did not have my glasses on, so I honestly did not know what the hell was happening from the final point to the final whistle'.

But his kick earned a cool million quid in the bag for the GAA.

WHILE THE FIRST day will be remembered for Mayo letting it slip and Coyle's freak equaliser, the replay will be remembered for a much more serious event. Meath were installed as strong favourites, but some commentators declared that Mayo should not be written off. Maughan said after the drawn game that they would regroup and see what they could take from that first encounter. Other commentators opined that they could not see Liam McHale having the dominance in the replay that he enjoyed in the first game.

How prophetic they were – after six minutes, Maurice Sheridan dropped a free-kick short into the Meath square and, out of nowhere, pandemonium reigned as players from both sides started swinging and trading punches. It should have been a forgotten incident, but it exploded into a brawl. It seemed to emanate from a non-malicious tackle by Finnerty on Darren Fay that was construed as being much worse than it was. Finnerty admitted later that he did lift his elbow in the hope of popping the ball out from Fay's grasp, but that instead, it looked like he caught him in the face.

When Dempsey barrelled in from behind, all hell broke loose. Finnerty got a box in the ear, McHale leapt in but was doing more pushing than punching. Meath attacked en masse and punches rained in from behind the Mayo players. The referee could (and probably should) have given several players from each side their marching orders and we could have been left with a high-profile version of the Kilmacud 7s.

Instead, he opted to send-off one player from each team, which happened to be Meath's hero from the drawn game, Colm Coyle, and Mayo's talismanic midfielder, Liam McHale. To be fair, McEnaney had met both teams before the final and warned them that if a brawl broke out, he would send off two players. So Maughan warned Mayo players not to get caught striking players, just to push instead. However, the memo did not seem to have been received in Meath because they hunted in packs in the knowledge that if it's a case of one-in, all-in, as in the end they will only lose one player. A gasp went around the ground when McEnaney raised his hands to the stands to indicate Coyle and McHale were sent off. A general consensus was that the punishment, if it was to be tokenistic, was damaging Mayo even more, given McHale's dominance of his patch in the drawn match.

As the action returned, it was Mayo, yet again, who settled into the game quicker and dominated the first-half with PJ Loftus rattling the net three minutes before the short whistle to put them 1-5 to 0-2 in front. However, moments later

Meath were awarded a penalty which was duly dispatched by Trevor Giles to leave just four between the sides at the break. A couple of Tommy Dowd scores helped peg Meath back to within a point before James Horan extended their lead. From here on out the game was filled with drama.

Graham Geraghty latched onto a long ball before being fouled; however, the young supremo had the speed of thought to take the free quickly and put through Dowd, who fired home Meath's second goal to put them into the lead for the first time heading down the home stretch. James Horan then levelled for Mayo, as the game looked to be heading towards another draw and extra-time. That was until Brendan Reilly stepped up to kick his first point of the game in the final minute to hand Meath their fifth All-Ireland title.

The summer of '96 was the sort of year that would dispirit fans. The manner of the defeat; the beginning of a series of unfortunate events that fed into the narrative of the newfound ridiculous curse; or that Mayo could not finish out a game having had two opportunities to do so. Certainly, with the sense of injustice that existed after the final, it was felt that the team would either crumble with the legacy of it; or come roaring back.

It was the latter that prevailed.

★ ★ ★ ★ ★

HOWEVER, WHAT WAS to emanate that autumn was to resonate ever since in the mind of every Mayo supporter. Thereafter, the Murphy's Law of inevitable defeat was uppermost in the thoughts of even the most optimistic fan. Expectations had been low in the years building up to it. After their loss to Cork in the final in 1989, John O'Mahony had written that it was going to take some effort for Mayo to build on the performances that had thrilled the nation. And how prophetic he was.

In 1990, they were surprised by their old rivals Galway in the Connacht semi-final in Tuam, a result which underlined their desperate record at that venue. After defeat to Roscommon in the 1991 Connacht final, O'Mahony was swiftly given the boot, a decision which Mayo supporters were to spend the next 15 years cursing, especially seven years later when his exciting Galway team won honours. Mayo won a couple of poor Connacht Championships in 1992 and '93.

After that, the just retired Jack O'Shea came in as manager. Mayo won the worst Connacht Championship of all time in 1993, beating Roscommon on a highly instructive scoreline of 1-5 to 0-7 in Hyde Park. The extent of their battering against Cork in the semi-final presumably made them wish they hadn't. They shipped a historically embarrassing 20-point defeat which saw fans streaming out well before the end as the scores screamed in. It was after that period of underachievement that Mayo rocked up in 1996, and buoyed up by the seeming unfairness of that autumn's final, it all fuelled the Mayo response in 1997.

Following a league campaign that included a win and a loss against Clare, Mayo escaped relegation with an eventual three-point win over the Bannermen. However, the prospect of a preliminary round championship opener against Galway in Tuam ought to have filled us with more dread, given that the Tribesmen were building something special, based on the golden generation of Hogan Cup heroes coming through from St Jarlath's. But a four-point win there had us dreaming of Connacht titles again, with Leitrim and Sligo in our path to retain the title.

We had seven points to spare over Leitrim but the Sligo match was a much tighter affair, from which we emerged with just the minimum gap of victory. Now just a gallant Offaly side stood between us and return to that a September's decider. The game produced poor football on a dour day. Cold drizzle, no goals and not even the blaze of a good row to warm us. Mayo defeated Offaly 0-13 to 0-7. We duly advanced to a second successive All-Ireland final, an achievement which was as much a testimony to this team's doughty persistence as it was of promise of a rising tide in the west. The final against Kerry could have been a classic, but was far from it.

Before the final, the survivors of the Cavan and Kerry teams who contested the Polo Grounds final 50 years ago were presented to the crowd. It was accordingly ironic that the match which followed was as forgettable as its illustrious predecessor had been historic. Dermot Flanagan pulled up after only four minutes and had to be replaced, raising questions about whether he had been fully tested before the match, given the reported difficulty with his hamstring. The next injury afflicted Maurice Sheridan, who limped around forlornly after another hamstring had gone 'ping', with the Mayo line apparently unwilling to replace him before half-time. On one occasion he caused panic by arising behind the defence to fist a point when a goal was on, had he two working legs. The smoothness of the switches had a rehearsed quality and Fergal Costello dropped back to the corner with David Heaney moving from centrefield to replace him; Colm McManamon and substitute Horan slotting into the ensuing vacancies.

Once again, Mayo's troubles were exacerbated by the playing of persistently inappropriate ball into the forwards: three times in the first 11 minutes high kicks rained down on Ciaran McDonald to predictably little effect. Then, having conjured a little-foreseen, second-half fight-back which exposed Kerry's nerves and took Mayo to within a point of the rattled opposition, we seemed to decide that 10 minutes of this raised tempo was enough. We accordingly followed a dam-burst 1-2 in the space of two minutes by leaving the scoreboard untroubled for the final 20 minutes.

Looking back on that match, it seems as if time stood still, because Mayo certainly did. Far from the free-scoring side of 1996, we took 23 minutes before we bothered the scoreboard operators, as our Maurice (Sheridan) tried to keep up with the prolific Maurice (Fitzgerald). At the break, Mayo trailed by five points and could have been put out of their inevitable misery early in the second-half if Peter Burke between the posts had not stopped what seemed two certain goals for the Kerrymen. Despite these let-offs, however, Mayo still looked lethargic but picked themselves up to carve several chances and points, eventually winning a penalty in front of the Canal End.

While everyone expected Sheridan to step up, it was Ciaran McDonald who cracked it into the top corner and when James Horan scored a cracker from the right, the margin was down to two points. But Fitzgerald had the last laugh when his free from the right sailed over Burke's bar and Kerry were three clear.

It was no consolation to Mayo fans that they had witnessed one of the greatest All-Ireland final performances in modern history… Maurice Fitzgerald was simply unmarkable.

★ ★ ★ ★ ★

THE DECADE DID not get any better for Mayo.

Galway came to Castlebar the following year, under John O'Mahony, with a team packed with underage stars and promising attackers, and left with the spoils. One of those was Niall Finnegan, the grandson of the man who first lifted the

Sam Maguire for Mayo. With a team driven by the likes of Ja Fallon, Michael Donnellan and Padraic Joyce, it was ironic that O'Mahony would be the first Connacht manager to bring Sam west in 32 years, after many attempts as a player and manager with his native Mayo.

The following year, Mayo, with just six scores (3-3), gained some revenge by sending the Tribesmen packing in a thrilling final at Tuam Stadium, but despite a bright start to the All-Ireland semi-final against Cork, they ended the decade like they had the previous four, without an All-Ireland to show for it.

Mayo were bidding to contest their third All-Ireland final in four years, a state of ostentatious wealth only once previously experienced by the county (1948, '50 and '51.) Back then they won two.

This time they had won none.

In addition, they had ended the Millennium with just the three All-Irelands won back in the mists of time. Was there any hope that they could even become competitive again?

Maybe the next millennium would bring renewed hope.

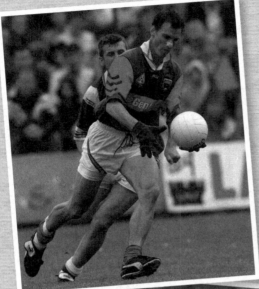

John Casey on the ball against Meath in the 1996 All-Ireland final replay, and three years later in action versus Cork in the All-Ireland semi-final.

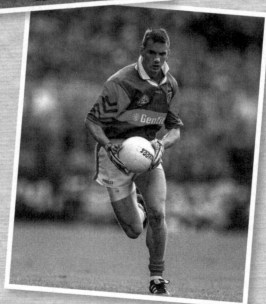

PART ★ SIX

THE CLIFFORD OF '96

THE FOOTSTEPS COULD be heard coming down the corridor. Inside, the lads listened to the teacher droning on. It was an October morning in the then Letterkenny RTC and the room was draughty and warm. Just cold enough to keep you awake, just warm enough to make you sleepy. Footsteps came nearer.

The door opened and in came the Business School Head. He nodded a nod to the teacher who looked up from where she was reading, getting unwritten permission from her to interrupt her class. He spoke.

'Is there a John Casey here?'

They all looked up, as did Casey. A message like this is rarely good. In the days before WhatsApp and SMS and mobile phones and social media, strangers were normally the bearer of bad news. He nervously put up his hand.

'I'm John Casey...'

'Well, John Casey, if it's yourself that's in it, there's a phone call for ya. A Jack O'Shea is looking for ya...'

The other four Mayo lads in the class knew what this meant and let a yahoo out of them. And with that began John Casey's Mayo senior career.

GETTING A PHONE call from one of the greats in front of dozens of your classmates might be the coolest way to get called up by your county, but the memory was even sweeter for John Casey because he had been rejected at 16 and told he was too small. Coming home from that trial, his late father John Joe asked him what happened.

'He said to me what happened and I said, I didn't make it. And he sighed and said, "Sure you're probably not good enough". And I made a vow that day to him. I said to him, I guarantee I will have played for the Mayo senior team before I'm 20 and he said to me, "I'll give you a thousand pounds if you do".

'Now, I never got the thousands pounds off him but I fulfilled the ambition of playing for the county before I was 20. So, it was the kind of a thing that gave me a little drive to succeed.

'Overcoming rejection and resilience is something I point out to my kids; now that you know if you don't succeed at first, you just keep going. Rejection is sometimes the best thing that ever happened to somebody to motivate them, but I know I look back now on players like myself who had been mainstays of the minor team two years after being rejected for the under-16; and then went straight out of minor into the senior ranks.'

At the time Casey entered the senior team, it wasn't the glamour gig it is now. The county's fortunes were at a low ebb. 'We had been trounced by Cork in the semi-final of '93, a game I was at and left early. Little did I know that I'd be togging out with some of those fellas the following year. I find that a bit surreal.

'In my first ever year training with Mayo, it was the year of the World Cup in America in 1994, so that gripped the nation. Combined with that, training with the Mayo team was not as prestigious as I had been hoping it would have been. At the same time, it was head down and shoulder to the wheel for me.

'I suppose, I found out the real thing of how cut-throat inter-county football was. I would have been, I think, pretty much considered a certainty to start for Mayo against Sligo in the championship, and the week before, I got introduced to the A versus B game. I never knew what cut-throat A versus B football was like until that day. I absolutely got the s***e beaten out of me. I was in against Anthony McGarry and he was beating me to a pulp for the ball and I just sat there and took it. And I'm sure they were looking around and wondering if this guy has the stomach for the fight. PJ Loftus and Ray Dempsey and these guys said to me, "Throw a slap back to him, will ya?"

'It opened my eyes a little bit to know that that's what it meant to these fellas, seasoned campaigners like them. They knew they wanted their jersey; they wanted their championship jersey; they wanted their place on the 26 and they were willing to hurt, and nothing was going to get in their way; so that was my debut season.'

In a match we'd all rather forget, Casey came on a second-half sub against Leitrim in the Connacht Final that they won under O'Mahony. He was also one of the few who made his Mayo debut in the Championship rather than the league, having missed out on that early-year blooding. After the Leitrim defeat, Jacko left and matters didn't improve for him under Anthony Egan.

One of the lowest moments was playing in a league game away to Tyrone. When he opened the match programme, the Mayo team was printed as 15 AN Others. 'Our names weren't even in the programme. Now, it's not a major matter, but it just had us thinking that things could only get better than this. We also took a pasting from Galway in Tuam in the Connacht final that year...'

But things were about to change, with the arrival of a certain Mr John Maughan.

'I used to travel with Kevin Cahill, he'd pick me up on the way in from Ballaghaderreen. The message came in from the new manager, Mr Maughan that he wanted us to meet in Castlebar for a 'bring your boots for a light jog' and a team meeting to follow at eight o'clock. Kev and I agreed we'd go for the meeting because he wasn't too fond of the training himself. We landed there at five to eight at the Sportlann. And we saw our Mayo teammates trodding from the back pitch at MacHale Park and all I could see was death in their eyes.

'Liam McHale, Pat Fallon... they came out faces drawn. I was wondering what was going on here? But who comes out after them but Maughan and he was after running the dog out of them on the very first meeting with them. He set the gauntlet down very early to us that if we wanted to be involved, we would have to buy into it.

'The most famous mantra that I will always take with me was from Maughan... "We will be whipping boys for no-one".

'He left us in that meeting in the Sportlann. He said, "Lads, what do ye want out of Mayo football?" And lo and behold, then he, along with his selectors Peter Ford and Tommy O'Malley, walked out of the room and closed the door. But they were outside listening. Then Noel Connelly took the floor with an inspirational speech; what with the likes of John Finn and Dermot Flanagan and Liam McHale there, I was thinking hasn't Noel Connelly a neck on him to be speaking like that and he only just drafted into the squad. But, lo and behold, wasn't Noel named the captain not long after.'

THE TEAM HEADED to London to play their first championship match, a game they won by the skin of their teeth and the width of a post. Casey was injured before he went over, standing in a divot while trying to take out Maurice Sheridan in a club game against Balla.

'I tore the ankle ligaments and missed a heap of games, but I was still able to run, but not kick. We were staying in the Hilton in North London and Maughan said to me and a few other players, "I'll meet ya in the lobby at 9am". I said how do ya mean, sure we're playing championship tomorrow.'

Anyway, there was no getting out of it. We met Maughan at 9am, walked out of the hotel to a big green area in a park. It was a hive of activity and there was a fully-fledged cricket match going on at the park. Umpires in their whites and all, but didn't Maughan go straight over and say, "Hi guys, would ye mind moving your game over a bit so I can have some space here. I've a couple of Mayo players here I need to train".

'I stood back and said this guy has some neck on him.

'He moved the game over to get a few yards of green grass to run the s***e out of Kevin O'Neill and Ronan Goulding and myself.'

Mayo hung on by the skin of their teeth in Ruislip and flew back to Dublin after the match. Maughan told the players that they could have a few drinks as long as they were okay for training. 'Drink whatever you're able to train with in the morning," he said. We looked at each other. Surely he's not going to have us training the morning after a championship match?

'The boys went out and let their hair down; I had a bit of a sore throat so didn't do the dog on it. Fat Larry danced a jig on the bar in The Hairy Lemon at 5am. We were all meeting for Westmanstown at 8.30am. Anyone from that vintage would know that the Maughan sessions were known as "hole openers". But this is the morning after playing championship, and we above in Dublin... so he started us off on the run.

'And I'll never forget it. He said right I want you to run a lap and I need you to be back... inside three minutes. So next thing we start off on this run and we'd gone about 200 metres... and behind us David Brady was trailing by 60 or 70 metres already.

'Whistle blows. Back to the start again… "Brady, how are you going to be back inside that time. You're letting your team down." Maughan roared.

'Race starts again… whistle blows… and this happened about four times.

'At this stage, a few of the front runners, probably me included would have probably nearly had the kilometre ran by that and we were still having to restart it because of the laggers behind, so he had us fighting amongst ourselves. Everybody was getting annoyed, shouting at the fellas that were lagging behind. "Come on to f**k… we're having to do this because of ye and we're having to do it again".

'It was a real team build and bonding kind of thing. But Fat Larry finished the run anyway and he was down on all fours and all I could think about was the boys telling me about Larry dancing in The Hairy Lemon at 5am.

'He was down on his hands and knees… begging for mercy. Maughan was down on him like the army captain, saying, "Ya haven't got the heart Larry… ya haven't got the f***ing heart." And Larry looked up and him and said, "I have the f***ing heart John… I just don't have the f***ing lungs."

'Even Maughan broke a smile for that one.'

THE CHRISTMAS DAY of 1995 was a very different one, as John Maughan had them out training instead of them being at home eating turkey.

'The Christmas Day sessions stand out in the memory because it was unique for anyone in Mayo to do anything like that. He had us out training because he told us we needed it, but I never once complained and I think that summer the whole team reaped the fruits of his work. I don't think anyone appreciates how hard the squad worked. Neither does anyone really know the work that the gaffer did with us and the time he devoted to our game.'

Beating Roscommon and then Galway gave the team serious momentum. The victory against Kerry in the All-Ireland semi-final really pushed the Mayo name into the limelight. And especially the name of John Casey, who was fast becoming that summer's superstar. In a report of that Kerry game, Casey was described as the *'sharp pin on the seat of Kerry's trousers'*, scoring four points and drawing fouls that resulted in another four for Maurice Sheridan. He was the focal point in a summer of expectation.

'The final against Meath is a game I've never watched back on video. I ended up getting a virus between the semi-finals and finals. Of course, it was all kept behind closed doors. I wasn't able to train. I didn't have it to lose but I lost almost a stone in weight…

'The build-up experience alone was just as bizarre. I have memories of the Mayo team in 1989. They got on their coach to go to Knock Airport right outside our shop. And I would have been standing there as a 15-year-old with the mouth wide open. I was a Mayo fanatic and my father used to bring me everywhere and anywhere to every single game and whatnot. And then, all of a sudden, you realise… *Christ… I'm actually on the team coach*'

Living and working in a shop in the middle of a town in the middle of the hysteria meant Casey had no escape from it all.

'I suppose, being in the middle of Charlestown in a shop with the doors wide open… it opened an avenue for absolutely everybody and anybody to walk in and access me. Yeah. And that's what happened. We lived above our shop. But even when I was unwell, I would have had my mother come on up, "John, there's a lovely little lad from blah, blah, blah to see you downstairs". And I said to my mother I'm not well. I said I can't go down and see him, as I'm sick. And she goes, "But he's after coming all the way from blah, blah, blah".

'I remember the cameras were following me around the place. And would I do ads for this, and would I do ads for that? At the time, I would have thought it was water off a duck's back stuff. But ultimately, it had to have had an effect on me because I was only 21, and I was trying to *try* to get my head around it. If I could change it now, I definitely would have managed it a bit better.'

He managed to try to avoid the headlines, but having his dinner in the Broadway Restaurant a few days before the final, a copy of *The Star* was in front of him and the temptation to open it was too much. Inside were final previews from established stars and they were all predicting a Mayo win and John Casey to be the Player of the Year.

His head was spinning.

THE BUILD-UP and the atmosphere were factors unknown to the Mayo side. Meath were accustomed to the noise of Croke Park through Leinster finals and their other big games there. When Mayo ran out for the final in front of a full house, Casey recalls the decibel level.

'My head nearly shook off my shoulders with the noise. It was like somebody had banged a big drum in your ear. I remember trying to call Ray Dempsey but he couldn't even hear me. I had to grab him to get his attention.'

At the end of that pulsating draw, emotions were mixed.

'After the game, I was not in a great place? Yeah. I felt I hadn't done myself justice. All I remember is realising that whenever I got the ball, I didn't just have Darren Fay to contend with. I'd have two or three other Meath lads. That was, I suppose, Sean Boylan with a plan to stop me doing what I had done to Kerry in the previous game? It was very successful.

'There was serious deflation after. I got taken off when we were four points up. I just remember on the sideline people grabbing me like a victory hug. And can I remember the last few minutes and the Meath comeback? Absolutely not. I just remember thinking *We've left this one behind us lads.*

'I think I gave away a few bad passes and then I passed when I should have a shot. I can't remember, but I get vivid flashbacks sometime from that game and the drawn game, when I should have shot. It was all just a daze.

'The next year, we ended up beating Galway in Tuam for the first time in a long time, and there were Mayo supporters coming onto the pitch and taking clumps of grass for having buried the Tuam hoodoo. I was thinking this is pure madness. In that year, Offaly won the Leinster Championship and they had a strong team.

'We played them in the semi-final and tactically that day, I saw the strength of our team. James Nallen was detailed to sit in front of our full-back line because Offaly were going to bomb in everything, and Nallen cleaned up, like a Henry Hoover in front of our defence.'

THE FINAL PITTED Casey against many of the lads he played with in Tralee IT, where he lived with Galway's Padraig Joyce. 'We used to collect Joyce in Tuam on the way down to Tralee every Sunday evening. Some craic we had with him. He never stopped talking once he got into the car.'

Joyce was abroad in that summer of 1997 but he messaged Casey to "Beat those Kerry fuckers because I'll be coming back next year and Galway will be taking the country by storm". How prophetic were Joyce's words! The next summer, he scored the goal that won the final against Kildare and saw Galway win two of the next four All-Irelands.

'Little did I think I'd end up playing in an All-Ireland final against eight of my Tralee teammates, including the brilliant Seamus Moynihan. In the first minute I got the ball, I grabbed Moynihan's arm and took him to the ground and bought a very cheap free. I remember patting Moynihan on the back and saying, "Seamus, I got ya bad there". He was a lovely fella. I threw the ball to Ciaran Mac, thinking he'd put us on the scoreboard, but he kicked it wide. I was thinking *Oh no...* and from that moment, I knew that we weren't on song. We played horribly bad. I felt like I was running in a cauldron, that the wind was taking the ball away from me.

'I was mad leaving the field, not just because we'd lost an All-Ireland but because we'd left our performance levels behind us; we missed free kicks and played so poorly. I had played in two under-21 finals in 1994 and '95 and a senior in '96 and 97. If you count replays, I had played six All-Ireland finals in two years and the record stands as drawn two and lost four. I was wondering if there was some sort of football God up there who didn't like us.'

JOHN IS ANOTHER player who dismisses this idea of there being accumulated baggage from losing finals. 'I would always have felt that had we taken that All Ireland in 1996, it would have opened the door for numerous to follow. Look at Dublin, what happened to them? Cluxton's free in 2011 opened the door for them. They were in a bit of a doldrum and all they needed was that one; they just wanted to get over the line and then it just releases all the pressure.

'When I played in those finals, I wouldn't have been bothered by Mayo not winning in '89. Would I have been massively aware of the history? I think they are probably more aware now because social media gets slapped in your face.'

In 1998, Galway were about to be launched and they came to Castlebar and won, though a tiring Mayo team almost caught them. 'We felt the strain of having been to the well and back in 1996 and '97. I had many great battles with Gary Fahey down the years. When we played them in Castlebar that day, it was the first time I felt that my legs were gone. Even though we almost caught them, they were a phenomenal team. It was May 24, 1998... and that was our season cooked until the following October.'

When John came to the realisation that his Mayo days were coming to an end, it was a difficult time and there were some dark moments.

'It was horrible because you must remember that I was only 24. I realised I had problems with a thing called a pronate heel in early 1999. John Maughan was doing everything and anything to get me sorted. Even sent me up to Dubarry in Athlone to get a special boot made, because any football boot was rubbing against the heel and causing me grave irritation. That made me put pressure on the sole of my foot, which made a Morton's neuroma grow on the sole of my foot. I was basically in agony from two places and I couldn't train as a direct result. I knew I was in trouble, but Maughan came to me and said, "We are going to win the All-Ireland this year and I need you to be part of it".

'Consequently, I used to get a double injection into the foot to even play league games, because I wasn't able to walk. My plan was to do the year, then get fixed by the surgeon in the off-season and then *I'll be as right as rain for retaining the All-Ireland in 2000.* We won Connacht, again beating Galway in Tuam, but we lost to Cork in the semi-finals.

'During the surgery, without my knowledge, my Achilles tendon was removed to get to the bone. My game was based on sprinting and getting the ball, and I remember my Achilles tendon feeling like an absolutely overstretched bungee cord… I had no flexibility in it whatsoever.

'And so, the realisation that I might never play football again for Mayo was very hard to take. I was 26 in 2001, when Mayo actually won the league beating Galway, and I remember being at the match, having rushed there from hospital where my brother-in-law had been seriously ill, and watching the game and thinking there were players out there who wouldn't lace my boots who were after winning National League medals. I mean that in a nice kind of way. That was the realisation for me.'

Nowadays, the GPA provide the supports for players coming to the sudden end of their careers. For John Casey, there was nothing like that at the time.

'I had absolutely nothing to fall back on. I had to stop playing and I wasn't able to do a thing. The county board washed their hands of any responsibility of my health status. I tried to stay fit in the off-season by playing the odd game of soccer for Charlestown Athletic to get around a little bit and, of course, I got to score a couple of goals every now and then for the soccer club.

'And I remember getting a letter from the county board to tell me that they'd noticed that I'm doing well on the soccer pitch. They had watched me putting two needles into my leg for a whole year and now they were telling me that it's not their responsibility. So, it was a bit bittersweet like that, and I'm thinking Do I go to war here with the organisation?

'Or do I just, you know Drift away into the abyss?

'I was a bit bitter about it because of the lack of understanding and the lack of admitting accountability.

'I got a little bit of reprieve with the club as I ended up winning all of my proper club medals as a goalkeeper for Charlestown but I used to feel like, no disrespect to goalkeepers, but a d***head. I used to think I should be off up the other end of the field, lashing the ball into the back of the net and setting up scores… and tackling and tracking back… and instead I'm standing here between the sticks.

'I just had to embrace it… I had no choice.'

JOHN CASEY SAYS he's made his peace with the disappointment of that now and is thankful for the lifelong friends the game has given him all over the country. In particular, he loved meeting the Galway 1998 team on their 25th anniversary in Croke Park in 2023.

'All right, I would have been very, very bitter for a while. Yeah, I was bitter because… number one, I didn't win an All-Ireland, and… number two, because my career was cut short. And number three, because I felt that the powers-that-be didn't probably control my situation, as well as it should have been controlled. It definitely wouldn't happen in the modern era what I did to myself.

'I would have given one of my limbs to win that gold Celtic Cross. And that's what I was willing to do then.

'Now, when I am above in Croke Park, I am in awe that I actually was on that grass in that intensity competing for the biggest prizes, and that is something that I will never get sick of. You see the belts and the Mayo team going toe-to-toe… and I gasp for breath.'

CHARLESTOWN IS NO stranger to being under the microscope. Right from the moment distinguished local journalist John Healy used it as basis for his seminal work, *No One Shouted Stop*, it was seen as the poster boy for the decimation of small towns. Healy's words were prophetic and Government after Government struggled to ensure that every summer brought a brain drain from the towns and villages depriving them of the opportunity to retain their people. Trains and boats brought the best people from these places; but often those left behind were not lacking anything other than the freedom to go. Many were held by family ties, by land and by fear.

Casey's shop stands in the heart of it.

When I talk to John, not even nine months have passed since his father, John Joe passed away. A native of the town, John Joe had opened shop and tapped into the local pulse every moment of his working life. Hardware is the software of the rural people. In this small town and in my own, the need for paint and nails and brass screws and washers and calf nuts are the oil that lubricates the community. Here in the heart of the town, the Casey family fulfilled that need and earned a living from it. Drapers also played a vital role in the life of the community. Gentlemen and women, they clothed the generations, conscious of the economic constraints, always willing to aid those who struggled.

Up the street, Eddie Fitzmaurice was one such draper, a fellow retailer of the Casey's. In 1998 when John Casey was midway through his career, the 83-year-old was found dead; bound and gagged on the floor of his bedroom, undoubtedly assaulted, but dead from hypothermia. It was an act that shocked the community, and is a crime that has remained unsolved. It galvanised the town and made it aware of the vulnerability of their most vulnerable.

Right where John talks to me, through the trees lies the cemetery where lies John Joe, and further over, the grave where rests Colm Horkan, a friend, clubmate, mentor, all round good guy who was shot dead while on duty as a member of An Garda Siochana.

'Colm was a very good friend of mine, a clubmate and I soldiered with him on the pitch. Where I'm standing now, if the leaves were gone off the trees, as they will be soon, I would be able to see his grave. Our club is honouring his memory as best we can, and on the way soon, we will have the Colm Horkan Memorial Pitch, to be known locally as Colm's pitch.

'His funeral was a very humbling experience. Six of the Mayo lads carried Colm's coffin. A State funeral, the guards were in charge. But they gave us special permission. The Horkan family insisted that the GAA have a big part in carrying Colm, so we all helped. Not fully from his own house because it is a bit of a hike from the church, but from the outskirts of the town. We took turns in groups of six. As did six Mayo players... David Clarke, Aidan O'Shea, Tom Parsons, James Horan, Colm Boyle and Cillian O'Connor.

'People were doing anything they could to help the family. I know their dad, Marty is mad into the GAA, as Colm was. He was one of our own. One of our diehards. This was a fella who was loved by our community. We had to give him the send-off he deserved.'

THIS IS THE first year that John has spent without John Joe. The mantle has passed and now he stands at the heart of his community, talking football and inspiring young players. His children are equally fanatical about the green and red, but obviously were not born when he was in his prime.

'They have a great interest in the game, and they see a top player and they will ask me, "Were you as good as this lad or that lad?"

'And I tell them, "Listen guys, for a few months, I was the country's David Clifford," and I start laughing and they say, "No way, ya liar ya".

'And I say, "Well maybe for a few weeks... maybe for a few weeks".'

Alan Dillon celebrates after hitting the net against Kerry early in the 2004 All-Ireland final and (below) beats Marc Ó Sé to the ball in the final two years later.

PART ★ SEVEN

ASKING QUESTIONS

I LOOKED AT my phone. There were 10 minutes gone in the 2004 All-Ireland final. Through the horse-trading of tickets, I had managed to get myself a seat about two behind the Mayo bench. I could see too that they were equally stunned.

The game was barely on, yet the game was surely over. Kerry, whose bus I had seen entering the ground to little fanfare an hour or two beforehand, had taken a sledgehammer to a bunfight and had dissected Mayo's hopes of avoiding losing their fourth successive All-Ireland final. Mayo arrived looking to end a then 53-year wait for a title, but they only momentarily teased their supporters when, after five minutes, Alan Dillon stunned the stadium with a clever shimmy and a shot to the net.

However, it was a brief titillation, because we only scored four more points in the half, by which time Kerry had hit 1-12. Here I was with a front row seat to disaster, and I flung my programme to the ground at yet another inevitable Kerry score. 'For f*** sake,' I mouthed to myself, then discovered that the RTÉ crowd camera had me in their sights at that time. Within 10 minutes, my phone hopped.

I looked down at it… 39 text messages. My noted obscenities had been seen around the world. Lads I hadn't seen in years got in contact to remind me of my misery. But no court in the world would have convicted me of gratuitous profanity because of what we had endured in that short time.

Largely regarded as one of the most disappointing All-Ireland football finals for many years, Kerry racked up a total of 1-20, the highest team score in an All-Ireland football final since the time of 'Bomber' Liston and the 5-11 that decimated Dublin in 1978, and the stadium was one-third empty by the time referee Pat McEnaney blew full-time.

We bravely attempted to stay the pace with Kerry, but were regretfully found wanting in too many important areas for such a major game, particularly in teamwork, finesse and, most importantly, the need for a greater number of scoring forwards, something Mayo teams have lacked for a long time. There were times in the second-half when Mayo looked totally disjointed, leaving their bewildered supporters to wonder what had happened to the form which took Maughan's men past Galway, Roscommon, Tyrone and Fermanagh.

WE HAD BEATEN Tyrone, helped no doubt by the cunning of John Maughan, the team's charismatic, shorts-wearing leader during the late 90s and again in 2004. David Brady recalled how Maughan succeeded in winding up his men before the 2004 quarter-final by saying that the Tyrone players had cheered when they drew Mayo.

'I remember we had training on the Monday after Tyrone beat Laois fairly comprehensively. But in those days, the draw was made half an hour after the game finished and John Maughan brought us into the dressing-room and he said, "How dare they, how dare they?" And he said it five or six times and we were saying, "What is he on about?"

'He says, "When the draw was made, yesterday, the roar went up in the Tyrone dressing-room when they got Mayo".' Maughan alleged his source was a Croke Park steward standing in front of the dressing-room door.

'By Jaysus, we were like raging bulls for the whole week,' said Brady.

Mayo were considerable underdogs heading into that quarter-final against the defending All-Ireland champions, but they ran riot in a 0-16 to 1-9 win, bringing an end to a tumultuous year for a Tyrone side who had so tragically lost the brilliant Cormac McAnallen on March 2. The respect between the sides was helped by the fact that Maughan and several of the Mayo players had attended McAnallen's funeral. When Tyrone returned to National League action for the first time after his passing, it was in Castlebar. The night before that game, the Mayo squad joined their opponents at a remembrance Mass in Ballintubber

Abbey as the GAA world stood shoulder-to-shoulder with those still stunned by the passing of the Tyrone man.

Mayo, meanwhile, had come into the championship against a backdrop of unease in Maughan's second year back at the helm, the previous campaign having ended in huge disappointment as they were dumped out by Fermanagh in the qualifiers. And when Mayo travelled to New York for their Connacht opener at the start of May 2004, they did so without the talismanic figure of Ciaran McDonald. The Crossmolina playmaker had brought an abrupt end to his county career in April 2003 after being booed throughout a league defeat to Fermanagh in Charlestown, and had allegedly vowed never to kick a ball for Mayo again. Knowing what his talented clubmate had to offer, Maughan launched a low-key charm offensive. It took time, it took patience, but eventually it paid off.

'I was a year-and-a-half trying to get him back, travelling around every building site trying to find him,' Maughan told *Balls.ie*. 'Eventually we managed to coax him back, but it wasn't easy. The length of time it took probably tells you there were plenty of times I thought it wasn't going to happen. And then, one Wednesday night, he turned up at a challenge match against Kildare in Leixlip, and that was that.'

McDonald would wind up with an All Star for his exploits that summer, his creativity key in unpicking Tyrone when that quarter-final clash came around.

'Tyrone's biggest strength is their collective structure and at that stage they were fantastic tacklers,' says Alan Dillon, a then fresh-faced 22-year-old who ended up with six points to his name after an inspired performance. 'We had a lot of work done even before Connacht.

'When we were in New York we were training away in the Catskill mountains, and conditioning-wise we were hitting peak form at that point. But then, we knew Tyrone probably as well as any other team because we played them at under-21 level earlier in our careers. We weren't surprised we beat them because we had beaten them at underage but, that day in particular, we knew we needed to get out of the blocks pretty early because their bench was pretty loaded.

'In previous games, Peter Canavan was their go-to man when things were getting a bit tight, so we needed to be in a position that when he came on, that his influence wasn't going to be as strong as in previous times.' Canavan came on ahead of schedule, replacing centre-back Shane Sweeney in the 23rd minute, but not even the great man – or a second-half wonder goal from Stephen O'Neill – could swing the momentum their way.

THE HUMILIATION OF defeat in the final in 2004 was tempered by the belief that never again would a Mayo team fail so badly in a decider, that lessons had to be learned about what had happened and why; was it fitness, tactical underachievement, a general underperformance, over-hype or were we just unfortunate to meet a Kerry team that was superb and who would have probably hammered the lard out of any team that was put up against them on the day?

It was a beautiful evening, and the sun dropping down lit up hues of blue and gold and orange, momentarily distracting us from the memory of what had happened. I wondered just how much more the Mayo heart could bear, but vowed to be back again for whatever it brought.

★ ★ ★ ★ ★

SOME SCORELINES JUST cannot lie.

I remember playing an under-14 hurling county final against Tooreen back in the mists of time. In at full-forward, and probably the same size I am now, I scored two of the six goals we struck that evening. Tooreen replied with four of their own. The game ended Ballinrobe 6-0, Tooreen 4-0. It wouldn't have been out of place at Wimbledon, that scoreline, and does little to deviate from the quality of the fare on show.

That minor scoreline of 0-6 to 1-1 in the Connacht minor semi-final in Mayo's victorious year of 1985 is also an outlier. The scoreline of 4-15 to 3-5 isn't much different. In fact, it's the kind of scoreline you'd see in the Cumann na mBunscoil games played at half-time at Croke Park.

But for that scoreline to be in an All-Ireland senior football final beggars belief.

It was Ronald Reagan who spoke of having that deja vu all over again, but it was surely the same for Mayo fans and players by the time 10 minutes elapsed in the 2006 All-Ireland final. Just two years after the horrors of the 2004 final, the hostelries of the road home were caught on the hop by the number of Mayo supporters who took off early, and who were well past Lucan when the final whistle blew on an unusual but, once again, ultimately depressing All-Ireland day from a Mayo point of view.

Thirteen was the unlucky number that day – after 13 minutes we were 2-4 to 0-0 down. In the end, we lost by 13 points. To complete the surreal nature of the day, in the remainder of that first-half, we scored THREE goals against Kerry in an All-Ireland final, but were still six adrift at the interval – and we made no impact in the second-half.

Given what had happened to us in the final of two years previous against the same opposition, we were mindful of the awesome scoring power that Kerry possessed, but not even in our worst nightmares could we have imagined that so soon in a final would our hopes have been dashed again.

Our finals have been populated by moments like this – the Michael Murphy goal in 2012; the Bernard Brogan goals, the 15-second Dean Rock goal in the winter final of 2020.

Murphy's Law must have been constituted in our county.

Just as in 2004, David Brady was sent in to steady the ship and cool the head when everyone around him was losing theirs. I love the line he says, that he wasn't sent in to win the game, but 'to look for survivors and recover the bodies'. However, his performance was one that should not ever be minimised in the context of the defeat.

With Mayo on their knees and 10 points adrift after as many minutes, from the moment Brady was sent in from the bench until two minutes into injury time when Kerry got a late goal, Mayo held Kerry for the intervening 60 minutes, scoring 3-5 against 1-11 for The Kingdom. Brady's role in that amazing and almost hidden statistic is one of the few bright jewels to be extracted from a disappointing afternoon in Croke Park.

He curbed the influence of Kieran Donaghy to such an extent that he limited the towering Kerryman to two points. Would Mayo have won if he had been in from the start? It's hard to say. But the role of Brady throughout was symbolic of the season and the craic that was had in the semi-final against Dublin. Indeed, he was central to what was probably the highlight of the year – the march to the Hill and the subsequent thrilling victory over Dublin in the semi-final.

IN THE SAME way you'd urge on a fight in secondary school when you saw two fella flaking each other, so too did the hairs rise on the back of our necks when we saw the Mayo players leave the photo-bench and head towards The Hill on that warm August day.

There was something different about Mayo that afternoon, from the moment they ran onto the field and began warming up in front of The Hill. Its throngs of blue-clad fans were disgusted and made their feelings known. Eyebrows were immediately raised, as Mayo conducted their pre-game drills in front of the Dublin supporters. Although it looked like a psychological ploy, Conor Mortimer said afterwards, 'I didn't know anything about it... I think beforehand somebody came in and said Dublin were warming up at that end... I think David Brady said, "No, f*** it, we'll go down that side..." so then, we went down'.

Ciaran McDonald backed up Mortimer's claim that the decision was a spontaneous one.

'We came out of the dressing-room and we just went left after coming out of the tunnel. We got down there and people said there'd be Holy Hell. A few of the senior lads were saying what are we going to do? I said we had to stay now, we couldn't be going up the field like a shower of pups.'

Nevertheless, what ensued has gone down in Mayo footballing folklore. Dublin got wind of Mayo's antics and started walking down to the Hill 16 end arm-in-arm. Mayo though held firm, as Dublin had no option but to conduct their pre-game drills alongside Mayo. If anything, the Dublin arm-link looked ridiculous and just highlighted their indignation. With both teams warming up and setting down cones in front of The Hill, the rest of the stadium looked on, roaring their encouragement at whatever side they followed.

It was pure theatre.

Balls were flying everywhere as both sides threw shapes. Not one of them willing to give any ground, and The Dubs showed how rattled they were when Dublin manager, Paul Caffrey, unnecessarily slammed into the back of Mayo trainer, John Morrison. With such chaos, it was only a matter of time before someone got hurt, and this happened when one of the stray footballs struck Mayo dietician, Mary McNicolas, knocking her to the ground. With both teams refusing to budge, she received treatment while the teams continued to warm up around her.

Whether it was the psychological shenanigans beforehand or not that inspired it, but we were flying and got off to the better start as it looked like Dublin had been rocked by Mayo's warm-up move. Seventeen minutes had elapsed before they got on the scoreboard, when Conal Keaney got them off the mark and Mayo led by 0-4 to 0-1. A goal from Keaney five minutes later drew The Dubs level, 0-5 to 1-2 and the great scores and skill continued from there.

Outstanding scores from Alan Dillon, Conor Mortimer and Ger Brady kept Mayo in the game, while Alan Brogan was on fire. Ciarán Whelan was very lucky to stay on the field after a strong tackle on Ronan McGarrity which added to the drama of the day. Just before half-time, with almost 35 minutes on the clock, Mayo manager, Mickey Moran introduced Kevin O'Neill. Mayo trailed by a point in stoppage time of the first-half, when the ball was fed into O'Neill who showed every ounce of class to draw Mayo level. They weren't finished there as Mortimer kicked another great score to give Mayo the lead at half-time, 0-9 to 1-5.

The anticipation of the second-half was at maximum levels. The third quarter was nearly all Dublin. The Boys in Blue got off to a blistering start. A goal from Jason Sherlock after good work by Kevin Bonner and Alan Brogan gave Dublin a three-point lead. That lead was to be extended to seven by the 46th minute, when Dublin led 2-11 to 0-10.

Incredibly, Dublin would only score one point in the last 25 minutes. Mayo rallied from that point on. Andy Moran was introduced and goaled in the 50th minute... 2-11 to 1-12, game on. A cracking score from Alan Dillon followed in the 54th minute to make it a draw match. The scores dried up, but the quality didn't. The intensity of the game remained as both teams battled to get to a final with Kerry.

Mayo managed to edge in front with a Conor Mortimer free in the 56th minute. They led for the first time since Sherlock's goal and the momentum shift was finally completed. Dublin needed something special, and it was their main man who delivered it. Alan Brogan put The Dubs level in the 66th minute, their first score in 20 minutes... game on again. Would The Dubs get the momentum back?

Were they going to win it in the most dramatic way possible? But a Mayo side who had been disruptors all day had not read the same script. We gained possession right back at the left corner-back position with two minutes of normal time remaining. We worked the ball up the pitch until O'Neill managed to ship the ball off to McDonald, when one of the finest left boots in football put Mayo back in front with a really classy finish for the ages. Mayo were a point ahead with 70 minutes almost up. There was hardly time for more drama?

Or was there? As the clock struck 70 minutes, Dublin substitute Mark Vaughan stood over a '45' close to the right-hand touchline. It was a very difficult kick for a right-footed player, but Vaughan was known for his big boot. He caught it well, it looked on target, the ball looked to be dropping over the bar before, agonisingly, hitting the crossbar. One more free would arrive, a further distance out to the left of the posts. Vaughan stepped up again but failed to take the opportunity.

The final whistle blew about a minute later and Mayo were in the All-Ireland final. It was heartbreak for The Dubs and sheer elation for Mayo. It was a win that made us believe that anything was possible; that if we could beat Dublin like this in their own backyard – for the first time ever in the championship – that this might be the year.

The hype machine went into overdrive.

Mickey Moran had managed to produce a team that indicated there was nothing to fear from facing Kerry in the decider; that the ghosts of 2004 were vanquished in Shakespearean style.

But how The Bard adored his fantasy and tragedy!

★ ★ ★ ★ ★

IT'S THE SUMMER of 2023. At this time for many years, he was making waves, preparing for big clashes, making a nuisance of himself against big names. Asking questions of their capabilities.

Twenty years earlier, just before the All-Ireland finals of 2004 and 2006, he had made a name for himself pulling on the Mayo senior shirt in a championship match, not knowing that he would go on to become one of the best-known players in the game, as part of a Mayo team that gave great entertainment and created the bond with its supporters that has stood the test of time.

This summer of '23, he is suited and booted, with a folder of sheets and bound reports in front of him. He is listening intently, taking notes. The creme de la creme of RTE management and one of its biggest stars are rolled into Leinster House for a series of hearings initially into a wage overpayment to Ryan Tubridy. But the quiet questioning of the committee has unveiled a trapdoor that flings the executives into a maelstrom of lavish spending, of slush funds. It unveils a culture within the national broadcaster that painted a picture of a world far removed from the 'cost of living' crisis that is endemic in households across the nation.

While many of the politicians repeat questions that had been asked before, or jump at their chance to be in the national limelight from the televised proceedings, Alan Dillon is, as he was on the pitch, the epitome of efficiency and high standards. His questions, delivered without histrionics, cut straight to the chase. He elicits information from the reluctant interviewees with the minimum of verbiage, but with the maximum of cunning. Like his football play, he makes it all look so easy. His link play looked effortless until you tried it; his articulation and polite incisiveness on the committee winning the praise of the national media who covered the hearings in minute detail.

This is Alan Dillon's life now.

Not the first or last politician to come from a sporting background, but none are as recent as him. It seems like only yesterday he was terrorising defences; a linkman who always gave an option for a return pass, who scored on the biggest stages. Who became a genuine hero for the Mayo army as it made its mark in the opening decades of this millennium. In his 16-year career with the Mayo senior team, he scored an impressive 3-225. The three goals, we all remember, the points scattered over a consistent career during which he became a role model for other young players fascinated by his displays.

But those scores aside, they don't take account of the mayhem he caused for opponents – the assists he engineered and the frees he won when his progress was stopped by foul play.

From his 2003 championship debut against Sligo, where he lined out at left half-forward, scoring a point, he went on to make 66 championship appearances – those 134 appearances of which six were in All-Ireland finals at headquarters.

In that time, he won eight Connacht senior medals, including the five in-a -row from 2011-15 and was a two-time All Star (2006 and '12).

However, the losses in six finals should not be Dillon's legacy. Everybody who has worked with him at club and county levels testifies to his dedication. Everyone I spoke to for this book detailed the sadness at his retirement, because when Dillon was on the team, he brought a level of preparation that ensured standards were high in those around him. In one sense, the arrival of James Horan and his requirement for higher standards was a match made in heaven. Dillon knew what was required and what he was prepared to do to match those requirements. After the shock of that Longford defeat, he was one of those who stood up and said that the team wasn't working for each other; that a greater collective responsibility was required if success was to be achieved.

In that Longford match, a truly sliding doors moment for Mayo football, he was one of just a handful to justify their selection that day and was not behind the bush when it came to outlining how he felt. 'In terms of fighting performance, we don't seem to be fighting for each other as a team, as a unit. We lost the individual battles last Saturday evening, not enough lads were digging out the guy beside them,' he admitted.

'Everyone is too focused on themselves, not the team. In championship, you have to be thinking of how the team can benefit.'

WHEN IT CAME to the finals, opponents knew the importance of Dillon and smothered him, knowing that if they nullified his threat, they were half-way to beating Mayo and ridding them of a serious offensive option. The Kerry team that won in 2004 and '06 knew that this course of action was necessary; as did Jim McGuinness in 2012.

Few played such a key role in getting Mayo to those finals as did Dillon, who was Mayo's Mr Consistency throughout so many journeys into summer. Remember the great game against Dublin in 2006 when Mayo marched into The Hill; that day also generated great football from the victors for whom all their scores were good ones. Alan Dillon's shots that day were all difficult to execute, yet he got them over in a tense, high-odds game. In 2014, he was on fire against Kerry in the semi-final and Cork in the quarter-final with a spattering of scores from play.

Of course, we all recall that splendid early goal in the 2004 final that was akin to Ray Houghton's in Stuttgart being too much too soon. To score a goal that soon in such a game had us dreaming temporarily, the optimist in us charmed by the smart manner in which he converted with a confidence past Diarmuid Murphy that was his hallmark in games before and after. For a youngster (he had just come of age) to give us a memory for all time was remarkable and kept alive a game that ran away from Mayo thereafter.

Indeed, in a showreel of proud Mayo moments, it is up there with Keegan's 2017 goal against The Dubs. But to think that a dozen years later, he was still contributing is a testament to the condition in which he kept himself. He is still as lean as a pin in his neat suits, looking for all the world that he could tog out again next year and 'do a job for ya'.

When he was introduced in that game in 2017 with a quarter hour remaining, The Dubs knew that a quality player had come onto the pitch, evidence of which was provided when he kicked the equalising point moments later. But he didn't last long, and went off injured. If he had managed to stay on, what might have been? At the stage in a game when many players are losing their heads, coolness is called for – Dillon had that in spades. He would have exploited the exhaustion, the tension, the late-game indecision and fear, but it was not to be.

DILLON WAS A key reason why Mayo made it to the number of finals we did. He was a star performer who lit up many a summer's day on the odyssey. We can never forget the manner in which he seemed to pass the ball between the sticks, rather than any lash and hope. His shimmy sidestep too would send marching armies lurching left or right, skills honed on the pitch at Ballintubber going to good effect on the big pitch above in Dublin.

There is no doubt also that the great success enjoyed by Ballintubber was down to the inspiration he provided to those around him. It was very noticeable that his club captain, Jason Gibbons mentioned this in his acceptance speech when they won the senior title in 2014, an acknowledgment of just how integral he was to the cause. To get the praise of your club is praise indeed. When Dillon retired in late 2017, he did so with the humility for which he is renowned.

'Playing the game, representing this team, giving my all and never letting go has meant everything to me. If asked to write a script for my career back in 2003, there is no way I would've been able to imagine this journey but now I feel it's the right time to step away.

'The wins and losses will be remembered, but what I'll remember most are all my teammates who I can never give enough credit to from over the years...

'Thank you to the people of Mayo for all your support over these years in the good and challenging times. It's been a humbling experience and made me realise how lucky and privileged I am.'

ALTHOUGH ACADEMICALLY GIFTED, with an MSc in Pharmaceutical Science from the Royal College of Surgeons Ireland, a Postgraduate Diploma in Education from NUI Galway, and a BSc in Applied Mathematics and Biology from Maynooth University, he opted for a life in the public eye when he chose to go into politics.

'Playing at the highest level of inter-county football required huge levels of personal dedication, a willingness to make sacrifices every single day and an unrelenting focus on improving preparation and performances,' – so began his pitch for a place on the Fine Gael ticket in Mayo.

His roots in the party run deep – his uncle Ollie was chairman of the FG branch in nearby Ballyheane and his aunt, Kathleen Coady, widow of former FG Cllr Liam, worked for Enda Kenny as his secretary for years. In fact, Liam was also Enda Kenny's driver and trusted confidante. Kenny had served as a TD for Mayo all the years since 1975, the year of that famous Connacht final loss to Sligo.

On the day that he was picked by the voters for his latest off-field Mayo team, the country was racked by a storm – Storm Ciara unleashed its ferocity on the west coast. In Galway, plans to open the long-awaited but much criticised European Capital of Culture designation were in tatters when it was felt that the location known as The Swamp might actually turn into a swamp when the wind and rains hit. At the same time, in Navan, Mayo were playing a Meath side looking for their first win of the National League.

At the break, Mayo led by 0-7 to 0-1, aided no end by Storm Ciara but it did them no favours in the second-half as Meath rallied for a single-point victory. It was a day they could have done with Alan Dillon, but that time, he was in the process of trying to hold onto the Mayo seat held for 64 years by the Kenny family, Henry and Enda. No pressure, in your first election and without knowing if football allegiances would trump political ones.

His demeanour, friends and wide circle of contacts made sure his message got out, and he pulled in transfers from the most unlikely of sources; from Sinn Fein and from Green Party candidate, Saoirse McHugh.

His transfer-friendly nature meant that even the most hardened political opponent would not begrudge him some sort of a placing on the ballot paper. With a first preference vote of 5,198, he pulled in another 5,779 transfers, showing that the effort he put into the canvas reaped rewards.

'This is one of the greatest achievements of my life, above my sporting achievements. I would say there was an appetite for someone who's credible, has integrity, has shown a willingness to fight for the party before. That's what people want in an ideal candidate. As a young person, we all face challenges in terms of housing, childcare and sustainable jobs. I think the electorate related to me in that way,' he said afterwards.

ALAN DILLON MAY not have won a Celtic Cross in his time with Mayo, but there are plenty of signs he is endeavouring to ensure that dozens of them come Mayo's way in the future. Not long after he retired from inter-county, he became involved with the county coaching think-tank devised by coaching officer, Liam Moffatt. It has been a long-held fear in the county that once this golden generation dries up and fades away, so may the county's hopes of being sustainably competitive.

Dillon has loads of ideas on how this can be combatted, and the idea of keeping good players around appeals to him. 'Lads and girls coming out of school; where are they looking to go to college? If they are looking to do a college or science degree in Dublin, let them know that the same degree is available in Galway.'

Dillon knows what it is like to be studying away from home and having to grab lifts to training from the likes of James Nallen. Dillon is envious of how Kerry and Cork, and now even Limerick, manage to keep their top inter-county stars in college in the region. The development of the ATU brand across the colleges of the west is a blessing to this objective as they offer hundreds of new courses across a range of fields.

'Players who are travelling home find it harder to get the balance right; the rest, the recovery, college work and performance because there are so many stresses and demands on them. If this impacts on preparation for try-outs in league games, it has a roll-on effect on the championship as they may not be tried and tested by the time early summer comes around,' he told the *Examiner's* Kieran Shannon. He feels that to bring Sam West, there is a need to keep the players west.

He enjoyed his time with Mayo – it gave him the profile for what will undoubtedly be a lengthy political career representing the west, especially now that an extra seat has been added to the county.

'Every session, I enjoyed going out and trying to get the best out of myself. If you think about it, you only have a short window of a career. The most you can hope to get is eight or nine years. I got 16, though the last three I was not near the peak of my powers. But it's not the journey, it's every session, every match… it's seeing how the team evolves.

'That's the one thing I take the greatest pride in, when we got the group of lads together around 2011 and seeing how the younger lads integrated and bought into the set-up. The trust, the unity, the honesty. From talking to other people who have played with Mayo teams, they don't understand the bond that squad had and still has.'

Dillon thrived in the challenge of trying to find his way around the variety of massed defences that the Mayo coaches would come up with; he was energised by the training sessions, the constant challenging of each other to be better and stronger and smarter; to see opportunities and close off others; to hone his skills to the best he could, so that on days like those days when he was on fire in Croke Park, when you tried things, they worked.

The end, when it came, brought sadness to many fans for whom Dillon was always a possible solution to whatever the Mayo problem was. In 2015, he did not start any match; he had a starring role in the win over Tyrone, while in the final, he arrived late and left early – injured entering and injured departing, but not before he had hit that crucial point against The Dubs in the drawn game. What we would have given to have had him in the replay when the difference between the teams was minuscule – his presence might have been enough.

'I probably chanced my arm a bit in 2017. I knew the gas and legs were gone in 2016, but I had an inkling that we were very close. I could still read one or two steps ahead, but the body couldn't get there. I still felt that if an opportunity presented itself, I could definitely do a job, but I knew mid-season that it was definitely the last year.'

The force of nature that was James Nallen about to surge up the field.

PART ★ EIGHT

THE JOY OF SIX

IT IS THE summer of lockdown and the boreen cul-de-sac where I live near Claregalway is crawling with walkers and runners; people for whom finding a satisfying space in which they can carry out their limited exercise brings them to unlikely places. Back then, I cut the grass every four or five days; ironically it is manicured to within an inch of its life at a time when nobody should or can call.

The world is at a standstill and those of us upon it are shuffling around in a five-kilometre circle in which, for now, we must live our lives.

But every day, there is the sound of sharp running. Good running.

Not a shuffle, but a practised pace. A regular foot-beat strum out on the dusty road; a familiar sight that brings back memories of a man breaking a tackle and cleaning out attackers. It was James Nallen, strong and as fit as he has ever been. Beanpole, but layered in muscle. Still having that rangy look that saw him drag a Mayo jersey on over his head over 130 times; different fabric jerseys for different managers and regimes, with different outcomes.

Nallen was a player with grace and power, normally not bedfellow attributes. The master of breaking that tackle and finding the spaces that such a larceny creates, he drives forward with the momentum that carries him. Like a lion pouncing on a gazelle in the wilderness, he comes out of nowhere to take the ball, his strong running standing to him time and time again, for club and for county.

Running hard is no stranger to the Nallen psyche – as a young lad, like many of us, he spent summer Sundays traversing the county taking part in the many community sports days that were de rigeur in that era. In the times of shop-less Sunday, when the world 'closed shut' right after last Mass, the community sports day was manna to young boys and girls who just wanted to run and jump. You did not even have to specialise to have a good day out at them and travel home with the jangle of a few medals or the glamour of a wooden plaque for your efforts.

Nallen was no different. His long rangy reach made him ideal for a scatter of disciplines. From the long jump to the sprints, he mastered them all, carrying a strength and athleticism that he brought with him to this day.

'Like anything, in your formative years, you go wherever you're brought. My dad was very interested in sports. He would be more into weight throwing, the 56lbs throws and events like that. He would bring us all to a sports day... places like Hollymount, Glenhest, Bofeenaun and Westport. There were four of us, Micheal, Tom, John and myself, and there would always be a bit of competition to see who did the best on the day. You just took part in whatever was there for your age group. When I was young, that was our Sundays, rather than going to football matches. That gave me a good athletic base.'

Such a base gave him the ideal foundation for playing football, which started in national school.

'John Cosgrove, a teacher in Crossmolina NS, would organise a league among the higher age groups – third, fourth, fifth and sixth classes on a Friday afternoon – and that was big for us because winning the league in school was the thing at the time. Then my first memory of playing for the club would be the under-10s tournament in Castlebar.' Playing for Mayo was in the distance for the young Nallen.

'Playing for the county wasn't an ambition then; not because I didn't want to play, but because I didn't see myself in that bracket. Everything is a step-by-step approach. Your first ambition is to make your own club team. There were a whole pile of other players in that age bracket who were a lot better than I was. I was a late bloomer and I was probably a bit shorter. I probably had a growth spurt at 16 to 17 to 18, but definitely at that age, I didn't see myself featuring.'

FOOTBALL WAS IMPORTANT in the Nallen house. But even at home, hard work was a hallmark before play. The fields would have been cut of silage and shorn like a buzz haircut before they were suitable for kicking football with his brothers, all of whom combined to give his native parish their greatest glory.

He had two uncles who played for Mayo – Fr Jim, who played on the junior team of 1957, and his Uncle John who played for Galway, Mayo, Meath and Cavan.

'I wasn't aware of their achievements when I was really young, but I was when I got a bit older. I suppose this is because I didn't see them playing or wasn't around for games they played. It was of a time when you don't have the clips on YouTube to look back on.'

It is surprising to remember that James never played minor for Mayo, and that he had not yet played under-21 by the time Jack O'Shea took notice of him, in the Crossmolina 1993 run to the last four of the championship.

On the back of the form in the club championship, he caught the attention of Jacko, who was based in Leixlip; and as James was in Maynooth at the time, the former Kerry great used to give him a lift down on Friday evenings. He was in the squad for the winter but was not in the squad that went down to Leitrim in that summer's Connacht final. Soon, Jacko was gone and had been replaced by Anthony Egan, Eugene McHale, Hugh Ludden and JP Lambe. He made his debut against Roscommon, but most of it was a blur for him.

'I got concussed that day. Sometime in the second-half, I got a knock. It was only towards the end of that half that I realised that I was on a football pitch, so have no idea how I played in the interim,' he laughed. In the next game against Galway in Tuam, there was still a sense of a disjointed set-up.

'From a team sense, we didn't really know each other. I remember in that game, one player shouting 'No 10' before passing the ball. That's how well we knew each other. It was the end of one era and the start of another. You had the older team finishing up and the structures were just not right to bring it to the next level.'

IT DEFINITELY SUITED Nallen that John Maughan was then appointed Mayo manager in 1996, given his appreciation for the rigours of physical exercise, but there wasn't an immediate sense that the team was about to embark on an adventure that brought them agonisingly close to an All-Ireland title.

'John was a young guy and he brought freshness and was very positive, and we trained extremely hard. I liked the shorter runs and John liked the long distance, the endurance effort. There was no doubt who was in charge and there was no doubt that we were fit. It was a young enough group with some experienced lads thrown in as well. It was dogged.

'I was based in Maynooth, so I might have missed the midweek stuff as, at the time, Dermot Flanagan organised training up in Dublin for the city-based players. Shamie Rogers, who was a friend of his, organised the training. He was following whatever template was sent up by John Maughan.'

Mayo at that stage were playing in Division Three of the league that year and were only scraping by teams. They were getting the right results, but there were often one-point or two-point wins.

'You couldn't say at an early stage that you knew where you were going to go. There were no spectacular performances, it was just dogged,' he remembers.

Mayo played Derry in a couple of challenge games that year and they did not do morale any good. 'Physically, it was men against boys for a lot of us, because a lot of us weren't long out of the under-21 grade and they had won the All-Ireland in 1993. But then we got the win over London in the championship and we built from there. Every game you were winning was building your confidence. There was no expectation.

'Then, all of a sudden, we beat Galway in a Connacht final which was fantastic for the group to win something. We were on the right path, I guess. Then, the win against Kerry in the semi-final was huge for us… I'm not sure when we had beaten Kerry in the championship before that day.'

Hi recollection of that win over Kerry sees him modestly omit any mention of his great goal which has to rank up there with any of those iconic moments that we have witnessed while following the Mayo cause.

To watch it back on video is a delight… Nallen got the ball on his own half-back line, passed it off to James Horan, himself no slouch… and Nallen set off running. All those Sundays of sprints in uneven fields across the county in pursuit of medals were made for this; his long legs ate up the ground as Horan moved it on to McHale, who loped up the pitch before passing to the now flying at full speed Nallen, who lashed it into the Kerry goal.

The fact that it was against Kerry in an All-Ireland semi-final made it even better. This team which had struggled against London and was rattling around in Division Three was now scoring worldies against Kerry.

'Tactically and management-wise, that day, we got it on the money. The goal wasn't part of the plan,' he laughs. 'It was personally satisfying and exhausting. I nearly ran into the goal. I went as far as I could, and the other thing I remember from that was telling Colm Mac to get back because I hadn't the legs to. When you consider they scored a freakish goal immediately afterwards, it gave us some momentum.'

FOR MANY MAYO fans, the arrival of this classy ball-playing talent at the heart of the Mayo defence was a bonus on that day against Kerry. Our expectations had been low given our most recent performances in the last four. It had been seven years since the last semi-final victory, and 38 years before the previous one. But while a win is a win, it was the manner in which Nallen imposed himself in that game that made people sit up and take notice.

'The final against Meath is one that got away. A missed opportunity. Probably we didn't expect to be where we were, six points up with 20 minutes to go. We tried to win from that point by containing and that doesn't work with that kind of time on the clock. It wasn't the plan.

'The schemozzle tarnished the replay, but there was still a lot of good football played that day too, and we had got ourselves into a good position there as well. But we got hit by a goal that day, that if you were being picky should have been called back. But the row at the start had a big impact on us more so than Meath.'

The next year, Nallen played a key role in the march to another final, in particular in the semi-final against Offaly where he cleaned up in front of the defence. 'For that final, we had the experience of 1996, so the expectations were different straightaway. The effort was immense, but we were flat on the day. We overshot everything rather than taper it to be on the money in the final.

'It's only when I'm doing something like this interview for this book that talk or memories of those finals comes up. My dad has passed on and my mother is in a home, so life has moved on… it was of its time. I moved on quickly enough. You need another game to get the last game out of your system, so it is always good to have that not to be the last game of the season. It moves you on and you are on to the next competition. We were fortunate to have some great success with the club.'

In terms of the Mayo cause, there are few like James Nallen, who put his body on the line so many times. At the end of his illustrious career, he had won one national medal in the Pat Holmes-managed side of 2001, but he had also played in five All-Ireland finals.

At club level he had much more success with Crossmolina, winning Mayo Senior Championships in 1995, '99, '00, '02, '05 and '06, as well as Connacht Senior Club Championships in 1999, '00, '02, and an All-Ireland Senior Club Championship in 2001.

JAMES NALLEN HAS often used the word 'completeness' to relate to his perception of what defined success. His drive to win an All-Ireland with Mayo was a project that he hoped would result in such a completeness. If the completeness he spoke about was not reached with his county, it was fulfilled with his club, who not only proved themselves the best in Ireland, but did so by beating one of the greatest club sides of all time.

That Crossmolina side was the typical parish mix of brothers and friends; of experienced heads and young lads full of the energy of youth. Around that time, the synergy of their development propelled them into a side to be feared. And they did it at a time when vast tracts of the country were curtailed by the Foot and Mouth outbreak. The All-Ireland club finals back then were the mainstay of St Patrick's day afternoon viewing. However, with events of that Spring decimated or else held with disinfectant-soaked foot-mats, the game was put back a month to April.

Central to that success was the silken skill of Ciaran McDonald whose dexterity and uniqueness of talent and character drove Mayo for the best part of that decade. McDonald was Man of the Match in that club final for Crossmolina, and Nallen counts it as a pleasure to have played so many years at club and county level with one of the most skilful players of the modern era.

'His skill level was that far ahead of others. Some days he'd be toying with defenders. He just had the skill and the natural talent. When it came to work on the field and in training, he'd lead by example on that front as well. It wasn't like he was looking for handy ball, he'd go and win it.

'The best thing about playing for him was that he always wanted the ball. For a defender or a midfielder, when you have possession, you're looking to move it on to someone and then support again if you can. That was one thing you were certain with Ciaran, he'd always look for and demand the ball. He was always making that run into space which was great.'

Regarding the hype that emanated around Mayo teams at the time, James was fortunate to be away from the goldfish bowl that was Mayo.

'For a lot of my Mayo career, I was based in Kildare, so I wasn't getting that distraction, and more often than not, it was a *distraction*. I'm sure people mean well, but it is taking energy from you; even saying the same stuff over and over and over again. Good managers now have the role of looking after the complete person, and not just the footballer. It's part of their role, making sure that it's not *all* the players have in life.

'There is no question that being a sportsperson at that level is very selfish because if you want to be good at it, you need to commit time to it. And that means you're not doing other things that other people want you to do. It is more suited to a single lifestyle rather than married or coupled.

'If anything, it is demanding more these days and that's something I'm not so sure about. I'm not sure would I want to give more. When is enough *enough*?'

For the copycat finals of 2004 and 2006, James Nallen feels that for the latter, there was an element of naiveté about Mayo and their strategy. 'We had different management in '04 and '06, but for the second of those finals, we were naive. I think there were learnings from 2004 that we didn't learn. You can throw responsibility around between team and management, but in my view, management drive whatever happens. The performance against Dublin in the semi-final might have masked issues and there might have been a case where being carried away with that caused us to lose sight of where we were really at.'

Johnno came in in 2007 and there were indications that the Messiah was back. The first year saw a decent league campaign, but defeats by Galway in Salthill and in Castlebar the following year preceded a 2009 campaign where he did not feature.

'I knew that was it. I was feeling tired of it at that stage. To some degree, 2009… there were sprinklings of hope and new talent. It wasn't difficult to hang up the county boots. It's hard if you were forced to through injury or if it's at an early stage where you feel you have more to give.

'But I was done at that stage. I wasn't finishing strong.'

He doesn't have any regrets about his Mayo days now, because he doesn't think about them much at all, though he acknowledges that his life would have been different without Mayo football.

'I definitely liked the team sense and the athletic aspect of it all. I've no regrets in that regard. I'd love to be sitting here with a bag of medals, but the reality of it is, there are 30 lads who get a medal every year and The Dubs have monopolised that for the last decade.

'So, most of the players I know in the *country* are without medals.'

★ ★ ★ ★ ★

EINSTEIN WASN'T MUCH of a footballer; he probably was building a house or drafting a Theory of Relativity or something, or he had a 'brother at home' who was… but his definition of insanity was rocking around the brains of Mayo fans in the first dozen years of the new millennium. His declaration that insanity is doing the same thing over and over and expecting different results, is not in the Mayo handbook. In three deciders, Mayo boosted by hope and hype and expectation saw their chances blown away by a combination of stand-off defending, complacency and an absence of game smarts.

There seems to be a club formed – a sort of Hall of Fame celebrated in many places, apart from Mayo; a club of which membership is restricted to a disparate group of young to middle-aged men, all of whom share a unique characteristic. Members include Johnny Crowley, Dára O Cinnéide, Kieran Donaghy, Colm Cooper, Dean Rock, and man who joined its ranks in 2012, Michael Murphy. All of them have on their CV, an achievement that will see them have to pay for their own pints if they ever venture Mayo way. Each one of them has played a part in breaking Mayo hearts by scoring uncharacteristically, but ultimately match-defining, early goals against the green and red in All-Ireland finals.

From the previous two chapters, you will have ascertained the frustration at the similarities between the defeats in 2004 and 2006, but when Mayo next came calling to the decider in late September of six years hence, it showed that few, if any, lessons had been learned about the importance of keeping cool heads, taking it steady and easing yourself into a game without giving anything too handy away.

A lot had been written about the new cynical Mayo that had come through in 2012; a team that was not going to be bullied; that had a bit of attitude and shit-housery about it. In fact, we celebrated our ability to forego the Mr Nice Guys tag, sure that with its dismissal, our chances of winning would increase.

But adding cynicism to your arsenal is only worthwhile if you consign naïveté to the bin, but this Mayo side did not, and they missed the opportunity to capitalise on what was their most winnable final they had ever played to that point.

True, there were fears for Mayo in the build-up to the final in 2012, but if they had eliminated the horror start from their repertoire, the outcome would have been a lot closer than the gap that was held throughout this game by a strong Donegal team. A lot has been made of the fact that Mayo won the last hour of the game, but such victories are pyrrhic and meaningless if the first 10 minutes are a disaster, as was the case here.

Just two minutes had passed before the net bulged as it struggled to contain Michael Murphy's rocket. Seven points down after 11 minutes, it should have been the sort of chaos that Mayo relish, but their play was riddled with mistakes and poor decision making. Frees were wasted as we started to panic and the quarter hour had passed before we bothered the scoreboard operator. Some sublime play followed as we reduced the deficit to three at the break, when Ger Cafferkey was assigned to mark Murphy. To be fair, he did well, holding him.

We continued to hit some bad wides, and our scores seemed to be in response to Donegal points, and the clock ticked down with seemingly little change in proceedings. Donegal's fitness had been much vaunted all summer, but it was Mayo who looked stronger in that last quarter – it was what Mayo were doing with the ball that was costing them. Fitness is a key component in any victory, but technique is king, and we were sadly lacking in that department.

The mood in the ground that afternoon, at the break was that it was still there for the taking. To be just three points, one score behind, after the psychological pummelling we had taken in the first 11 minutes was admirable, but we needed to take advantage of whatever came our way in that second-half. Yet, when they fell to Enda Varley, Michael Conroy and Barry Moran, we missed all three as our composure withered and Donegal's belief was reinvigorated.

Although, we were to have plenty of further opportunities for mournful reflection in the years after, it was on days like this heading back west, that I pondered our inability to place one good performance on top of another. The great performances just show the level of talent that exists in the county; the bad performances just frustrate the loyal fans who are lulled into the belief that this is the time. Perhaps when the time eventually comes, the 'this is the year' brigade will be minuscule and a win will be secured from an unlikely falling over the line scenario.

Perhaps the real damage to Mayo's hope that year were not solely the Murphy and McFadden goals which applied the coup de grace, but the game against Down earlier that summer when in a comprehensive victory, Andy Moran did his knee.

If he had been available to play in the final, his ability to win possession in tight areas would have been invaluable against the system that Donegal deployed. Mayo had gotten through the Dublin semi-final without him, although there had been fears that his absence would have been costly. But it was in the final that I think we illustrated that we could not win the day without him. On days like that for any full-forward line, it is difficult to get the freedom you need. There were times that day when Cillian O'Connor was swallowed up, set upon like a swarm by the likes of Thompson and McHugh and the McGees, making it almost impossible to make good ball stick. Moran on the other hand was able to wrestle possession, to grab and to hold and to set up quick plays.

You might think that this is just a minor straw to grasp at, but in the days afterwards, an analysis by Ed McGreal of the *Mayo News* showed that of the 2-11 that Donegal scored that day, 2-7 came from ball that did not stick inside with the Mayo forwards. In effect, the Mayo forwards were like a rebounder for their own attacks, as ball that went in, came out as quickly… and was turned into direct plays that generated Donegal scores.

LEST WE LEAVE 2012 thinking that nothing good came of it, it is instructive to remember just where Mayo football had come from in the years at the end of the previous decade. Mayo were truly in the doldrums after the 2010 season. After losing to Sligo in the Connacht Championship, they were gone from the championship by June after losing to Longford after extra time in Pearse Park. John O'Mahony, who had led Galway to glory and was hoping to do the same with his native county, stepped down immediately afterwards.

But Mayo's recruitment of players was in a decent phase, although results might suggest otherwise. Andy Moran, Aidan O'Shea, Keith Higgins, Donal Vaughan, Kevin McLoughlin, Chris Barrett, David Clarke, Séamus O'Shea and Alan Freeman all started against Longford and went on to play big parts in the

Mayo story. The county board turned to James Horan, who had played such a starring role in the 1996 and 1997 final runs, but whose managerial experience was limited to looking after Ballintubber.

The impact was instantaneous and before 12 months were out, Mayo were Connacht champions and had beaten the All-Ireland champions, Cork. Within two years, they were in Croke Park, playing Dublin, minted as All-Ireland champions in 2011 and the toast of the city, in an anticipated semi-final. With just 20 minutes remaining, Horan's Mayo were 10 points clear of Dublin, leading 0-17 to 0-7. The All-Ireland champions were taking a pasting in front of their own fans.

A shot by Jason Doherty skimmed the Dublin goalpost and a goal there would have put the game to bed. But this is Mayo, and it flew just wide, sparking Dublin into a revival. The style of this Dublin team was looser and less orchestrated than that which went on to win eight All-Irelands in the next 12 years. It was instinctive and reactionary, and it brought them back into the game. The next seven scores went to The Dubs, and The Hill was alive with the sound of recovery. Dublin had staged a Lazarus-like comeback that seemed certain to carry them into the final.

Two points clear, David Clarke saved them with an instinctive reaction to a Brogan piledriver, and relieved, Mayo saw out the victory with two late points from O'Connor and Seamus O'Shea, 0-19 to 0-16. Dublin were devastated, and Mayo were ecstatic.

On that evening, with the sun lowering itself behind the Hogan Stand, you would never have predicted that that Dublin side would only lose one more game in the championship in the next 10 years; while in that time, Mayo would still be scrambling around for that first victory since 1951.

Tom Parsons on the ball against Dublin in 2019, in the All-Ireland semi-final, after fighting back from horrific injury, and inspiring a whole county.

PART ★ NINE

TICK TOCK

74.05 READ THE giant clock on the scoreboards at either end of the sweltering stadium, the sweat on every brow dripping on that unseasonably hot afternoon in 2013.

Dublin players were out on their legs, two were effectively walking wounded, barely able to drag themselves around the pitch as the Mayo comeback continued. Three points down, deep into injury time, Cillian O'Connor brought it back to a two-point deficit with a free, but a goal was needed if they were to get a result.

The four minutes of added time had passed, and now right at the death, Mayo had a free not far from goal after Enda Varley was fouled. Mayo trailed by two points.

One half of the stadium bayed 'go for the goal.'

Bulge the net at that stage and the bonfires could be lit on the roads west. But there was something less urgent about the way Cillian O'Connor was approaching it. Granted, with so many bodies ahead of him, there was only a 10 percent chance that it would sneak in, but a powerful shot could deflect. In hindsight, so many things could happen.

How many Mayo fans had dreams of that free ricocheting into Cluxton's net and ending that long wait. 'Go for goal, you have to go for goal,' bayed many fans, because with the four minutes up, there seemed little chance that referee Joe McQuillan would prolong affairs once the ball was kicked out. It was as well to lose by two points as one. But it would be a mistake to think that this game was lost in that last passage of play. If Cillian had hammered a shot at the packed-up Dublin goalmouth, and the ball was cleared easily, he was likely to have been vilified for taking that option.

It is highly unlikely he would have scored a goal, but O'Connor later told *the42* that he would have handled the situation differently if he had the time back.

'I just said to Joe McQuillan how long was left and his answer was 30 seconds. Then Barry (Moran) shouted how long was left and he said 30 (seconds)… and Donal Vaughan came running in and he said 30 (seconds).

'It was obviously rolling all the time with people in the way… me moving, steadying, taking my time and doing my routine obviously. He was including all of that… I wasn't.

'If I could go back now, knowing that the game would be blown from the restart, obviously I would have thrown caution to the wind and tried to go for the goal. But I thought there might be a passage of play. My understanding was that there would be another little bit of time. If we had maybe won the kickout and scored an equaliser, it would have looked like a good decision.'

But O'Connor is refusing to blame anyone for the incident.

'Joe McQuillan, he didn't do anything wrong either. There's no point dwelling on it and I wouldn't be pointing the finger at anyone and I wouldn't be in any way sour or bitter. At the same time, you have to remember that there were 13 or 14 people on the line. The game wasn't lost in the last passage.'

He took his point… 2-12 to 1-14, and Cluxton took his time with the kickout and the whistle blew within seconds. Another cruel way to end an All-Ireland final for Mayo. Another devastating defeat to add to the list.

THE DAY HAD started well for the Mayo fans when the minors, a team containing the likes of Tommy Conroy, Conor Loftus, Stephen Coen, and Diarmuid O'Connor engineered a three-point win over Tyrone. A minor-senior double seems on the cards many times for teams, but is rarely executed, and despite our joy at their success, we wondered if fate would be kind enough to grant two Mayo victories on the one day. To have achieved that would paint the county as a powerhouse with a thriving academy.

The positive buzz got through to the seniors as they prepared for their bow. It also bolstered them into the right frame of mind in order to avoid the early-start disasters of their three most recent encounters in the decider. We hoped too that any potential loss would not take the gloss of the achievements of the minors in securing that Tommy Markham Cup. Once showered and changed, they sat and watched and hoped that one day, they would be out there trying to break Mayo's long wait.

The senior match was a stop-start physical collision of footballing giants – Mayo gutted after their failure against Donegal the previous year were baying for success, and were begging to revel in their second home, Croke Park. For them, the pressure was intense. After a comprehensive win against Donegal in the quarter-final, they had the air of champions-in-waiting, which is the last role they wanted to play. With Dublin not as impressive en route to the final, it could have been said that Mayo were definitively the best team in the country that year. But Dublin had won the league, and were the team with recent All-Ireland success under their belt.

However, it was dawning on a lot of Mayo fans that deserving is never enough, that wins have to be earned. These things aren't just handed out to those who think they deserve it.

Songs and books have been written, and curses invented, to try and explain why Mayo haven't won an All-Ireland in all those years.

When the story of the team that broke the hoodoo is written, will the simple explanation be that they were the best team out of the 32 that entered. This was a year when they tried to make that case. They had marched all the way to the final with an aggregate winning score of 67 points.

The stats and figures were scary. Galway overpowered by 17; Roscommon thumped by 12; London beaten by 16; Donegal, the holders, flattened by 16; Tyrone outfoxed by six. Five matches with an aggregate winning total of 67. Mayo believed that this could be the campaign, but Dublin's conveyor belt of talent was rolling... and waiting in the freshly-mowed shorter grass.

HORAN HAD EARNED huge respect for Mayo, but ultimately this loss was added to the list of near September misses. It hurt, especially considering the green and red felt that the Dublin scalp was attainable. 'We had enough ball to win the game, we just made too many basic mistakes,' Horan lamented in Croke

Park. 'We turned over the ball too often, the ball wouldn't stick inside for us and Dublin were launching counter attacks. That was basically it, nothing more. A few mistakes let us down and in the second-half Dublin came with a surge and got ahead and we were chasing then.'

He must have been frustrated though when watching his team fail to open a good lead when they were on top in that first-half. It was a big call from him too to take flu-recovering Freeman off just before the break, when maybe sticking with the full-forward would have paid dividends, while moving Keith Higgins to the full-back line took some of the gas out of the Mayo engine in the half-forward line. Especially when Eoghan O'Gara was hobbling around and Dublin were effectively down to 13 working players.

The hope was there after Andy Moran's goal which brought parity after a torrid period in the second-half but it was a temporary relief. The owners of the next score would be boosted by it, and as it happened it was Dublin who engineered a smooth passing movement to enable Bernard Brogan to flick the ball to the net.

The lead was cut to two points twice in the frantic last quarter as Dublin, with all five subs on, grafted to hold onto their advantage... to that dramatic last gasp moment, when Cillian stood there with the ball in his hand for what seemed like an age.

AT THE END of 2013, with the associated disappointment and frustrations, there wasn't much strong confidence that the team could mount a third successive assault on the championship. Surely, there wasn't another year left in this merry-go-round. Teams are cyclical and Mayo had been there and thereabouts for the guts of a decade. Surely, we opined, that the time would come again when Mayo would not matter, just like they didn't for most of the 60s and all of the 70s.

That our time would pass unrewarded, that maybe for those of us following them for so long, the possibility that it might not happen in our lifetime was a real one.

Little did we know, that mattering would be the default status for a long time yet.

★ ★ ★ ★ ★

IT'S THE WEEK of my 49th birthday and I wake up in a white room, the early morning sun blasting off the facing wall. A cacophony of beeping machines give their own dawn chorus. When the consultant comes in and asks me if I know where I am, I tell him with strong certainty I do.

That I am in IKEA and I'm looking for a pencil and a yellow carrier bag. He looks at those around him and I know that's the answer he feared he would get.

For the next month, this isolation room in the High Dependency Unit at Galway's University Hospital is my home, as I battle to recover from a sudden onslaught of viral encephalitis, an illness in which effectively, your brain goes on fire, and you enter a world of tormented hallucinogenic dreams while you are wide awake, and from which just two percent emerge without any serious damage to their brain or physical functions.

I overhear the condition being mentioned by a trainee doctor so know full well the possibility of what lies ahead. I had previously written articles on the condition involving sufferers trying to be treated as adults and I realise that these are my last days of normality. Staring at the suspended ceilings, I try to figure out how my spirit will soar through them.

There are days of which I have no memory and others which are crystal clear. There are nights when the repeated tormented imaginings shock you awake even though you fail to sleep. There is no pain, no sensation, only the realisation that your mind is messing with you. I don't eat because they don't know if I can. I have a procedure to take a sample of spinal fluid which if I move a millimetre this way or that, could result in total paralysis.

I lie still.

I HAD BEEN in London the previous weekend to watch a laboured penalty shootout win for Arsenal over Wigan in the FA Cup semi-final. I had suffered from a chest infection for a few weeks before that, but was sure I'd shaken it off in time to get to Wembley to see Arsenal edge closer to ending a nine-year-long quest for a trophy, so my immunity had been low. The new Wembley as is its wont, was dull and dark.

Its towering stands not allowing in the great sunlight that used to pepper the great afternoon Wembley occasions of my childhood. The day is miserable, the mood is frustrated and teetering on anger. The game is delayed to allow a deserved tribute to the victims of Hillsborough, which had happened on the same day 25 years earlier. Then the game starts and Arsenal go a goal down and the crowd are restless.

'Wenger out' dominates the chanting, but on 85 minutes, Per Mertesacker throws himself at a cross two yards from goal and it crashes over the line in a style that former Mayo forward, Jimmy Burke would have been proud of. Extra time doesn't separate the sides and the penalty shootout with its ominous repercussions for Wenger is eventually won, with one kick being taken by Kim Kallstrom, a player who Arsenal bought in the previous January transfer window, not knowing he had a broken back.

By the time I get back to my hotel, I'm feeling elated but exhausted and grab a few hours ahead of the red-eye flight back to Shannon – a journey on which the doctors believe I picked up the virus. Two days later, my world changes forever when I begin to lose any sense of who I am. The neurologist uses some conversation on sport to ascertain where my brain function is at.

There were days when I dreamt I woke up in 2024, and not 2014, and I ask if Mayo has won the All-Ireland yet? Other days, there in the silent dawn light of a secure hospital unit, I wonder if I had already passed on. There in HDU, my Mayo-ness means I am inundated with football questions.

Will we, could we, should we? I opine as best I can.

One of the main nurses who is minding me is the wonderful Mary Lucy Morahan with strong Mayo heritage. At night, she monitors my vitals; she encourages my wife, Bernadette with every update of my condition. She is a welcoming face through the darkness when I try to convince myself that the horrific stories that run through my mind are wild dreams, but I endure them while awake as the virus lights the gorse of my brain. Mary Lucy's dad was Dan The Street Singer from Louisburgh; her uncle Fr Leo Morahan in whose church, Bernadette and I were married, was chair of the Mayo County Board in the 1970s. Another sign to encourage me. To explain the context of my medical episode, I often joked with her and others that I had always feared that I would never see Mayo win an All-Ireland in my lifetime.

In good health, the chances were long, but in this new incapacitated state, the odds were not great. To put it bluntly, they had to do it this summer.

No pressure, lads.

I RECOVERED FROM the encephalitis in the heart of the summer of 2014, with my mind thankfully clearer, but with a massive appreciation of the reality of life for those who suffer a brain injury and have to battle the prejudices of perception for the rest of their life. My recovery was so complete that myself and my wife give presentations to medicals at conferences. Having someone who was as far gone as I was, able to articulate the reality of the patient experience in critical care was seemingly not that common, so hopefully the experience is worthwhile.

But back to Mayo.

I spent the summer thinking I was alive and unscathed for a reason. If I was spared; if the grim reaper was wearing green and red socks, he was keeping me alive for some purpose. This had to be the year and the team's performances were not dissuading me from this fact. By the time I left hospital a few stone lighter, Mayo were set to face old rivals Kerry in another Croke Park showdown in the last four.

Bring yourself back to half-time in that drawn game at Croke Park and check your emotions. We were trailing by four points to Kerry, we had scored just once in that second quarter and once again, one of our talismanic players, Lee Keegan was unjustly sent off for unwisely flicking out at Johnny Buckley – a yellow card at worst. All six of the Kerry forwards had scored, so they were on fire and we looked shellshocked. There was only one way this game was going and it was not Mayo's way.

I wondered if the Grim Reaper was just having me on.

It was just the sort of chaos that Mayo revel in – but then the chaotic is not a sustainable tactic to pursue. The need to get yourself into trouble so that you can engineer your way out of it might be fine for James Bond or Indiana Jones, but not good for longevity in this game, although it was a scenario we were to see so often in the following years.

Contrast that quarter with the next.

Mayo hit 1-8, the last of those scores coming when Cillian O'Connor slotted away a penalty awarded for a blatant barge on Donie Vaughan as he prepared to pull the trigger on a shot at goal. Mayo were cooking – it seemed like we were finally going to get one over on The Kingdom.

But then, Kieran Donaghy, the tormentor of 2006, came on.

It seems remarkable to think that in some quarters, Kerry's need to fling on the big man looked like a weakening act of desperation, but once again, the sight of a Mayo shirt got him flying. He set up James O'Donoghue for a goal and, suddenly, we were hanging on with three minutes left and injury time to come. O'Leary levelled it up and we had to pray as a last-gasp massive free from Bryan Sheehan dropped short and into the hands of Seamus O'Shea.

It was the best game in headquarters for some time and everyone eagerly anticipated that the replay would be just as exciting for the more than 50,000 fans who would flock to it. The only problem was that the UPC Knights and Penn University were slated to use the ground the following Saturday for a US college football game and the GAA didn't want to push the reply back to the next Saturday in case the Dublin-Donegal semi-final game needed a replay. Limerick's Gaelic Grounds was mooted, but there was uproar that the game being staged in a neighbouring county would give Kerry an advantage.

Ticket fever would be at a zenith as the Ennis Road venue could hold only 46,000 – about 20,000 fewer than would probably be needed given the quality of the drawn game.

If the drawn match was a classic, there was also plenty of interest on a sunny Limerick evening in a game which was a classic for the ages in terms of drama, discipline, and off the pitch intervention. Some described it as the greatest two-game saga in the history of the GAA, but there have been many contenders for that.

BUT AT THE end of a very first All-Ireland semi-final to be held in the Treaty city, Mayo's hopes were undone and we were left managerless when James Horan, just a few hours after the game, stepped aside from the task that had consumed him for the past four years. When he took the job, Horan had vowed to make Mayo perform consistently

Speaking to me for this book, Edwin McGreal, who covered the Mayo decade for the *Mayo News,* said that the arrival of Horan was a key turning point

'I think the appointment of James Horan in 2010, taking over from John O'Mahony began the modern or current era of Mayo football, and one of the stated aims at the outset was to make Mayo consistently competitive, because you'd obviously had the 50s, 60s, 70s where there were more fallow points than there were high points. The 80s we began climbing up, but then the 80s, 90s and

Noughties, there were highs and lows, yo-yo kind of performances.

'You could be in an All-Ireland final or you could be knocked out in the first round to a team you shouldn't be losing to; so you had Mayo in 2006 in an All-Ireland final and then losing in Derry in 2007. You had Mayo losing an All-Ireland final in 1996 and '97 and then losing in Connacht to Galway in '98. Obviously, Galway went all the way, so there was no shame in that, but nevertheless under Horan, Mayo made six All-Ireland finals and from 2011 to 2021, they made 10 All-Ireland semi-finals, 2018 being the odd year when we lost to Kildare. That is an incredible run, so for being so relevant for so long and so consistently, it brought a fan-base along with them, a fan-base that was always there," he added.

The magnitude of Mayo's resilience is evidenced by the fact that this was still less than 12 months after the heart-breaking end to the 2013 final when opportunity presented itself and was scorned by circumstance. Now, the vast tome of Mayo misery had a stablemate – the two games against Kerry in 2014, when arguably the side were on their way to being the best Mayo team since 1951. Two minutes into extra time in the Limerick game, Mayo led Kerry by two points, but from then on, they failed to score, whereas Kerry kicked five points.

Two of those came from dubious frees to add discontent to disappointment. It was one of those days when nothing much came Mayo's way from the officials. Shane Enright, already yellow-carded, should have walked for his foul on Cillian O'Connor which resulted in a penalty in the 18th minute.

At one stage in this game, Mayo led by seven points, but they reckoned without James O'Donoghue who, over the course of the two games, scored 3-9; yet despite this, his duel with Keith Higgins was one of the highlights of the series. If Higgins wasn't on him, he could have scored twice that amount. Two second-half penalties were despatched with aplomb, before Donaghy got in on the act.

Mayo led by 2-5 to 1-5 at half time; 3-6 to 2-8 after Moran scored their third goal in the 51st minute, but were trailing by two heading into the final five minutes. Scores from Conroy and Vaughan forced extra time, where Mayo showed first to lead by two. However, the two controversial frees laid the path for Kerry to pull clear and record an ill-deserved victory.

The defeat in Limerick was harrowing for all concerned, players and supporters. For victory to be dangled in both games and not taken, was a massive blow. An hour after the match, under the Mackey Stand at the Ennis Road venue, a handful of supporters lingered, waiting for the players and coaches to come out so they could mark their Herculean efforts by applauding them onto the bus.

The players were tearful, heartbroken, crestfallen, a few dozen good young men left to deal with another shock to the system, another loss. They held their faces in their hands, rubbed their temples at the unfairness of it all. How could so much effort, and so much determination result in so much pain?

Ahead of them lay another late autumn and long winter; of fellas patting them on the back and asking them what went wrong and would it ever happen?

Two finals had been lost in the previous years, but after a final or semi-final, there is a cushion of condolence; a protocol as you head away from the national stadium. A buzz in the city centre, a few days off. But this was the Ennis Road on a Saturday evening, and the only road was north and home.

For the first time in three years, they would be watching *Up for the Match* from home; there wouldn't be the same buzz.

It would be a brave new world for most of them.

JAMES HORAN FULFILLED his media duties. The usual platitudes rattled out, because later he would be the story. Now is not the time for that, he said to the gathered press, their phones and recording devices under his nose. But there was no way he was ever going to tell the media his plans before he told the guys he had journeyed with. The Corduff bus made the short journey to the Greenhill Hotel, where the team sat down for a dinner in the function room. Afterwards, when the players had dispersed through the lobby, breaking into small groups and chatting with family and friends, they were asked to gather again. The manager wanted to see them in the conference room. When they had all filed in and gathered around, some sitting, some standing, still smarting from the result, James Horan told them that this had been his final year. The band had broken up. The journey had brought them to two finals and a semi-final and, for now, the first Horan era was over.

2014 had come to an end with another chapter in the annals of the heartbreak of the county. For myself, back to perfect health, I wondered if that would be the end of it.

I knew only too well how much toll the body can take.

How much more could we demand off these players? Putting in immense effort and being defied by fortune and fate and football.

★ ★ ★ ★ ★

WHEN YOU'RE A grown man, there are few opportunities for running in public unless you're covered in Lycra or have a security guard high-tailing it after you. Whereas when you're a kid, you run everywhere. At lunchtime in the Christian Brothers School in Ballinrobe, I always ran across the town and home for the middle of the day dinner; then hightailed it back for more punishment.

But as you get older, the chance to leg it down the main street decreases. So, when you get the chance, you take it. I was running the Streets of Galway, a race that's been going on annually for almost 40 years. Starting in the heart of the city, it takes you through the streets normally reserved for stationary traffic, out past the University, past the hospital in which I had spent the previous summer, around and up by Pearse Stadium… and out onto the Salthill prom before finishing at the Claddagh. It's about as much of a Galway thing as you can do. As I passed the hospital, I took a look up at the wing where I had been and hoped that I could transmit the energy I now had to whoever occupied that isolation room in the High Dependency Unit.

It was my first 'Streets' and I had registered for months; having taken up competitive 5k and 10ks since my illness the previous year, I was looking forward to it. For me though, the only problem was that it was clashing with Mayo playing Donegal in the All-Ireland quarter-final at Croke Park. Torn between the two, but not wanting to let down the charity I had promised to run for, I opted for the race. I tweeted beforehand of the tough choice and jocosely asked if anyone saw me struggling for breath on the route, to pass on updates from the match and so it was with the wind in my face and surrounded by a few thousand other breathless runners that I heard the shout… "Mayo HAMMERED them, Dec… HAMMERED THEM"

I was thrilled, although since 2012, the sight of a Donegal jersey didn't so much as strike fear into my heart, but struck memories of that frustrating day three years earlier.

Fresh from the excitement of the thrilling run to the 2014 semi-finals and

215

then the replay, one would have forgiven Mayo for being less than enthusiastic about the coming season. But to do so is to reckon without the great self-belief and resilience that the team and officials of this era possessed. They had gone to the well so many times, the well knew when they were coming.

The Horan era had ended, and the Holmes and Connolly era was just beginning. New managers bring new momentum. I had shared digs with Pat Holmes in Tuam many years before when he was a bank official and I was a young hack with the *Tuam Herald*. Ironically, Pat had the record of being the most successful Mayo manager in decades, having delivered a National League title for the county in 2001 in a dreadful final against a Galway side that went on to win that summer's All-Ireland through the backdoor.

Connelly of course had also been just a bounce of the ball away from being the first captain since Sean Flanagan to lift Sam Maguire. Their commitment to Mayo was not questioned and they had an elite squad to mount an assault on the summit in the aftermath of the 2012, 2013 and 2014 disappointments.

YOU WOULD THINK that if you hit 12-75 in any year's Championship that you would be sucking diesel; that your mojo would be firmly on one side in the Lost and Found, and that you'd have to be leaking scores at a rake of knots to be on the wrong side of any scoreline that season. 12-75 across five games – and none of them against a side you could call a soft touch, even a Sligo team who had marched to the Connacht Final.

Now on a Saturday evening, they were back and in with a shout against a Donegal side who had beaten Galway just a week earlier with a strong second-half performance. They approached the break a point down, but a wonderful Aidan O'Shea goal gave us a four-point lead and a crucial psychological advantage at the break. When Keegan goaled a few minutes later, Mayo were seven clear and never looked back, seeing out the game with aplomb and setting up a semi-final against a Dublin side who were just about to embark on an undefeated run that would last years and see them hailed the greatest team of all time.

How unfortunate were we to have lived in the same time, another era denied.

What a treat we were served up in that first game against The Dubs. When the Croke Park PA alerted the stewards to take up their 'end of match' positions, The Dubs were in the driving seat and looking odds on to face Kerry in a replay of their final four years earlier. Mayo had played a game in which they won loads of possession but were patently unable to turn it into scores. The trusty place-kicking of Cillian O'Connor was keeping us in it with nine scores.

But then the drama started… in just eight minutes, Mayo scored a remarkable 1-4 – points from Andy Moran (three) Higgins and Freeman, before Boyle was caught late by Philly McMahon and went tumbling in front of goal. Penalty.

With the clock winding down, Cillian despatched it coolly. Cluxton's bungled restart was burgled by Mayo and Moran was able to fire over an equaliser. In the last minute. Remarkably, apart from the throw-in obviously, this was the first and only time that Mayo had been level in the entire game, a game of classic intensity and mammoth hits. Nothing was being held back as the sides from opposite ends of the country laid bare their disdain for each other in a footballing sense – two black cards went to Michael Darragh Macaulay and Denis Bastick, while Diarmuid Connolly saw red in the 74th for a swing at Keegan as they brawled on the turf. Joe McQuillan gave loads of time on this occasion, signalling five minutes and when he awarded The Dubs a free to win it, Cluxton failed. In fact, our sub Mikie Sweeney had a late late chance to win it but his tired shot was blocked down.

In fairness, we did well to get out of this one alive, because in the first-half we were pretty tame and fortunate to be just three points down at the break, even if the Connolly penalty was a generous give from McQuillan. It was a period in which we seemed allergic to contesting kickouts because the Dubs were allowed free rein to win all of Cluxton's kicks. When they remedied this in the second-half, Mayo got three points for themselves. However, there is a school of thought that suggested that by not focusing on the kickouts in the first-half, we were using a sweeper to keep the scores down and make sure we were alive for the final quarter, when we would traditionally come alive.

Indeed, if we hadn't been as wasteful in the second-half, we could easily have gone on to win, rather than clinging on fortunately to a draw. It was a pure treat for the 82,000 in Croke Park, easily the biggest crowd in the world to watch any sporting event live that week.

No sooner were fans heading out the M4 than they were planning to get back onto it and the race for tickets began in earnest. The furore over the innocence or otherwise of Diarmuid Connolly dominated the week and gave The Dubs a rebel for their needy cause. But at half past two on the morning of the match, a time when carousers and wildboys are making their way home, the news came through that following a seven-hour hearing of the Disputes Resolution Authority, Connolly was cleared to play. Not much time for preparation, even being awake at that hour would seem reckless the night before a tea-time match, so he was named at No 18, his name eliciting a massive roar from the crowd when it was read out.

The replay was a much better game than the drawn one, and in a tit-for-tat first-half, some excellent scores on both sides saw them go in at half-time, 0-10 each.

But misfortune is never too strange a bed-mate for Mayo and within minutes of the restart, Seamus O'Shea got his marching orders after reacting to a late challenge, and dragging Jonny Cooper to the ground. He was no sooner gone than Cillian O'Connor goaled for Mayo and they led by four. The Dubs were out on their back, gasping for survival, but Mayo failed to put them away. Sloppy play saw balls falling short, passes not sticking. When Hennelly was rushed by the referee into hastily tying his laces, the ball moved from MacAuley to Fenton to Brogan and into the Mayo net. Ninety seconds later, another goal for The Dubs, when Philly MacMahon's momentum carried him and the ball into the Mayo net.

A season's work cut short in 90 seconds. Another example of how Mayo had failed to see out a game, to add to the catalogue of collapses in previous years. To concede 2-1 in four minutes; to not take advantage when they had their boot on Dublin's throat was unfortunate. There was undoubtedly greater exertion in the Mayo legs than The Dubs from the drawn game, as Mayo's late burst eventually took its toll in the replay to devastating effect for their title chances. Mayo looked exposed at the back, but to be fair, the new sweeper system was barely out of the box and they hadn't read the manual.

In the end, they just could not shut up shop in the manner you need to deny The Dubs, if there is such a system.

However, a year later it would emerge that there were serious issues of discontent within the camp; issues that effectively forced the resignation of Holmes and Connolly. Indeed, within two months of the defeat by Dublin, the players took action like the team of 1947 had, by penning a letter to the county board.

THE LETTER, DATED October 1, 2015 went:

We, the current Mayo Senior Football Team, wish to advise the Mayo County Board that at a recent meeting of the 2015 senior football panel, a vote of no confidence in the team's current joint managers Pat Holmes and Noel Connelly was passed by the players. This letter therefore requests that the Mayo County Board take steps to remove Pat Holmes and Noel Connelly from their roles as team managers with immediate effect.

We, the players have set ourselves extremely high standards in the context of our individual and collective approach, and also in terms of team organisation and management. Whilst we would like to acknowledge Pat and Noel for their services this year, as a squad we do not believe that they have met those standards and for this reason we do not believe that they can or should lead this team into 2016.

Following on from the above request and looking forward to next year, we believe that any process to select and appoint a team manager which is absent player input runs the real risk of repeating the mistakes of the 2015 season. We believe that the experience and knowledge gained by the players from competing at the highest level in this sport over the last five years will be an invaluable asset to the County Board in selecting a successful management team. Therefore, we will require player representatives which have input into the appointment of the senior football team's manager. The number of player representatives on the selection committee should be no more or less than the number of County Board representatives, resulting in a 50/50 split. We also request that any independent person(s) appointed to the selection committee is (are) agreed upon by both the Players and County Board representatives in advance.

The panel of players has discussed these matters in considerable depth and the contents of this letter are not expressed lightly. Each of the players on the panel is passionate about Mayo football and wants nothing more than to be successful next year and beyond. However, if the County Board declines to remove Pat Holmes and Noel Connelly as team managers, and if it refuses to allow adequate player input to the selection of a new manager, then with great reluctance, the players feel that we have no option other than to withdraw our services and cease to train with or represent the Mayo Senior Football Team until such time as we are satisfied that these requests have been met.

The players very much want to resolve this dispute in an amicable manner and out of the glare of the media and the public. To this end, we are willing to provide the County Board with adequate time to consider the matter properly. We believe that a deadline of Monday, the 5th October, 2015, at 5 pm will give ample time to review and respond to this letter. We wish to avoid making the resolution of these issues any more public or any more rancorous than it needs to be and we encourage the County Board to try and deal with this matter in private and not in the public arena.

As a squad, we believe that the changes sought by us are in the best interests of Mayo football. We trust that the County Board has the same end goal as the panel and that it will engage meaningfully with us so as to avoid an escalation of this dispute.

Mayo Senior Football Panel 2015

CONNELLY AND HOLMES staying on was untenable in the light of such a letter, and their reluctant resignation followed suit the next day. Stephen Rochford replaced them on the last day of November.

It was a year later before the management pair responded, in an explosive interview in the *Irish Independent*, days after defender Tom Cunniffe said that they were hard done by.

The Castlebar Mitchels man, who left the panel that year to travel to the US, believed the players were unfair on the duo, whose first season ended in defeat by Dublin in the All-Ireland semi-final replay.

'We treated them badly. They should never have had to resign. They deserved a lot better,' said Cunniffe. The response came 14 months after they were ousted – the long grass had grown.

In the interview with the *Independent*, the two former players were forthright in their recollection of their treatment. 'Players have got to concentrate on playing football and being as ruthless as it takes to win. They've got to allow management to manage and keep outside influences away. If they don't, it's unlikely they will be successful.

'In time, memories of the trips abroad and all the other perks will fade and it won't matter how many Twitter followers you had during your playing days. The only question that counts for players on top teams is: have you All-Ireland medals? As of now, no Mayo player since 1951 can answer 'yes' to that.

'We're talking about a small number within the panel. The rest are fantastic and there are fine young players coming along but the danger is that they will be held to ransom by a few inside and outside the group,' says Holmes.

'If a small group within the squad are allowed to dictate the way they tried to when we were there, it's not good for Mayo football,' said Connelly. 'If that situation is still there, the likelihood is that they will win nothing. That's the bottom line as we see it.'

A few weeks after the 2015 defeat by Dublin, team captain Keith Higgins and Cillian O'Connor had sought a meeting with Holmes and Connelly. They met on Sunday, September 27, when Higgins informed them that a vote of no confidence in their management had been carried 27-7 at a squad meeting.

Being forced to resign from county team management, with the players announcing they will strike if you stay on, is a deeply upsetting experience for anyone, let alone a pair who had completed only one season, which had ended in narrow defeat by the eventual All-Ireland champions – a team which would go undefeated by anyone for the next six seasons.

'I took it badly. For a start, it was the shock of it all. You think, where did that come from? One day, you're preparing for an All-Ireland semi-final replay and then you're being told the players want you out,' says Connelly. 'Then you'd meet people and they don't know what to say to you. They were jumping to their own conclusions because no reason was given by the players. It really cast aspersions on our reputations. It was tough all round. For two or three months, it was a horrible feeling.'

★ ★ ★ ★ ★

MATHS PAPER 1 —

Q 1 (30 marks)

There is a Gaelic football match. Thirty points were scored in the game. 21 of those points were scored by one team, and nine by the other. Yet, the game ended in a draw. Please explain.

There are many abiding memories of that game in the first year of the Rochford era, but the one which runs to the top of the queue was the feeling that abounded at half-time. A Mayo curse? At half-time in a game where we had done the majority of the scoring, we went in at the break five points down. It wasn't just that, but the shroud of raincloud darkness that enveloped the pitch right on the half-time whistle created a sense of foreboding around the ground.

Dublin were aiming to retain the trophy for the first time since 1977, so there were many emotional bonds to the successful teams of yesteryear. It was also the year that referees were instructed to add on 20 seconds for each substitute, and 20 seconds for each instance of a goalkeeper or defender going up-field for a placed ball attempt. Previously there was no specific provision for these two events which led to instances of deliberate time-wasting by teams who were leading. Thirty seconds was also to be added each time the Hawk-Eye system was deployed. With these changes in place, it was obvious that the championship was going to run its course and give us value for money to the very last second.

And so it proved.

IT WAS AN inauspicious start to the championship when Cillian O'Connor was black-carded after just six minutes of the opener away to London, which we won handily enough in the sunshine of Ruislip. It wasn't the sort of performance to sound alarm bells, but perhaps we would have been better off if it had been, because bidding for an historic sixth title in-a-row, we were caught napping at home to Galway in the next round, losing by a goal scored by Thomas Flynn when he intercepted a short-kick-out from Robbie Hennelly. So, if Mayo were going to make any impression in the championship, they were going to have to travel the scenic route of the qualifiers.

A home draw against Fermanagh would not normally be the tie to get the heart fluttering, but it was certainly pounding at half-time when the visitors aided by the breeze, led by a whopping six points. Cue the chaos that we needed to get our momentum up. A fast start after the break and a spell where they scored five without reply settled the nerves and when Aido was taken down in the square by Che Cullen, O'Connor stepped up to fire the penalty home. Late scores from Keegan, O'Shea and Dillon rounded off the victory.

Another home draw, this time against Kildare and a master-show from Diarmuid O'Connor, who hit 1-5 before going off to a standing ovation from the 15,000 crowd. In the battle for the last eight, it was Westmeath who stood in the way at Croke Park, and despite Cillian O'Connor and Jason Doherty hitting two goals in the first-half, Mayo were made to work for their win, with John Heslin notching an impressive 10 points for the Lake men.

The wagon trail continued on − it must be remembered that this odyssey which probably warranted its own touring t-shirt, was made against the backdrop of the weight of expectation placed on their own backs by the team's decision to oust the 2015 management team of Connelly and Holmes. But, maybe this was also a motivating factor in their progress.

Now only Tyrone stood between them and a place in the last four.

No doubt exhausted by their efforts to get this far, both sides neutralised each other in a low-scoring game that Mayo won by a single point. If anything, Mayo fell over the line, as Tyrone missed a hatful of chances that would have seen them win the day. But there were also nerves.

On many occasions in this game, Mayo tried to play keep-ball in acres of space, yet still managed to cough up possession. In games as tight as this, both sides needed their go-to stars, and when Sean Kavanagh was shown a red card on the hour mark, Tyrone's cause was stunted. It was his future fellow RTE analyst Lee Keegan who showed bravery and composure to score the winner and set up a semi-final against Tipperary, a game for which Mayo would be hot favourites. But even with victory in sight, there were nervous moments, such as when Aidan O'Shea drove a ball across his own back-line, necessitating David Clarke to show quick feet to save the day.

53,212 turned up at Croke Park for the novel semi-final against Tipp and saw Mayo stutter into action, to find themselves behind by three points after 25 minutes, despite Tipp being a man down when Robbie Kiely was black-carded.

A great run by Keith Higgins and interplay with Aidan O'Shea set up Doherty for a 27th minute goal to tie the game; and when Mayo hit four scores in-a-row, the game was turned on its head – Stephen Rochford's charges led by six at the interval. Tipp reduced the deficit to two but a Conor O'Shea goal in the 64th minute killed the tie. Both sides finished with 14 men. For Mayo, Vaughan was black-carded in the sixth minute of injury time, but we had already used all our subs. However, the hard work had been done and Mayo, a year after ditching their management team for allegedly not being up to the standard required, had kept up their end of the bargain by reaching another All-Ireland final.

THERE IS NO doubt though that the stop-start nature of Mayo's summer saw the pundits strongly favour Dublin in the final. There was a sort of inevitable fatalism among our own fans. That we would perform okay but conjure up some method of not winning it. The shape of the first-half did nothing to dispel those thoughts. Having conceded two own goals, not just unlucky deflections, but decent foot on ball contact, it seemed that the wind would have been taken out of our sails and that nothing was going to prevent Dublin from going on to win that match. It had all started so well.

Tom Parsons and Cillian O'Connor knocked over points, and Cluxton kept out Aidan O'Shea's fisted effort in a nervous opening for The Dubs. Jonny Cooper had to be alert also in blocking a Durcan effort, but Dublin got through that early storm to pose a threat themselves. The first goal arrived in the ninth minute, David Clarke saving brilliantly from Brian Fenton, only for the ball to hop off the unfortunate Kevin McLoughlin and into the net. O'Connor converted his second free. The second own-goal came in the 22nd minute. Dean Rock, who was having an off-day with his place-kicking, failed to hold Diarmuid Connolly's delivery, but spilled the ball into the path of Colm Boyle, and another deflection past goalkeeper Clarke.

Bizarrely, no Dublin player had managed to score inside the opening half-hour, but they led by 2-0 to 0-3. Clarke was called into action again to pull off another brilliant save, this time from Kevin McManamon, as the holders continued to press for a score of their own.

Rock finally got off the mark with a 13-metre free in the 31st minute, and substitute Paddy Andrews, in for the black-carded James McCarthy, fired over two splendid points. Dublin's tackling techniques were exemplary, forcing a series of dispossessions, while the tenacity of Mayo's challenges forced several turnovers as a compelling tie stepped up in intensity.

Dublin turned around with a 2-4 to 0-5 lead, but a Mayo whirlwind produced five points in the opening 10 minutes of the second-half, O'Connor bringing them level. Dublin rallied, but encountered stiff resistance from Durcan, Harrison and Boyle.

However, much of our high-quality work was undone by sloppy distribution, and Jim Gavin's men profited to go two clear through Rock. Alan Dillon came off the bench for his fifth All-Ireland final appearance and shot the sides level for the third time, but once again, Dublin rode out the storm with some heroic defending from Jonny Cooper, Philly McMahon and John Small. When Connolly exploited a poor kick-out to float over a spectacular score in the 68th minute, The Dubs were three to the good and ready to tighten a sky blue grip on Sam, but Mayo's passion never waned.

We battled for possession like men possessed, and carved out the opportunities that were to keep the dream alive. O'Connor's free was followed by a Donie Vaughan special, and in the seventh minute of time added on by referee, Conor Lane, Aidan O'Shea wrestled and battled for the possession that gave O'Connor the chance to arrow over a glorious equaliser from 40 metres.

When Lane blew that whistle, our hearts were still racing.

Mayo were still standing and every second of added time that the new ruling had created was needed. On a slippery pitch, there could have been a spattering of red and black cards on both sides. Ahead of the replay, for which the holders were again strong favourites, there had to be some creeping doubts that for all their ability, were they going to be able to match Mayo's resilience and never say die spirit?

THE IDEA OF playing for an All-Ireland in the winter month of October is not so surprising now, given that just four years later, most of the championship was a winter one; but it did drag the Mayo following into unprecedented game-time, journey time and ticket-buying time. In the game that would see out the final minutes of that year's championship, all fortunate to witness it saw an encounter full of drama, physicality and commitment. Before the game, came the drama that Rob Hennelly would start in goal instead of David Clarke, a move that raised eyebrows, before and after. In a strange development too, former players from Mayo and Dublin were interviewed on the sideline before the game, each casting doubts on the late team changes. All well and good, but the interviews were broadcast on the stadium PA system which allowed the comments to get into the player's heads as they warmed up.

In front of a crowd of 82,249, Dublin wasted no time in injecting the intensity that had been missing a fortnight earlier, racing into a four-point lead, with Dean Rock hitting three – two of them from play. The gamble in bringing in Hennelly failed to pay off in those early stages, his kickouts putting his side undue under pressure and contributing to the concession of some of those scores. Mayo tackled ferociously throughout, but in many of the times that they won possession through this, they easily coughed it up again. But the Mayo men settled, and we were level by the 13th minute with a four-point salvo of our own. Durcan got us going, and Cillian O'Connor stroked over a couple of frees. Rock had just edged the champions two in front when we struck for a goal that still chills the spines.

Aidan O'Shea's off-load was perfectly timed for Lee Keegan coming off his shoulder to fire his shot to the bottom corner of Stephen Cluxton's net. Jonny Cooper made a couple of vital interventions, but his game was brought to an end by a black card in the 19th minute. Nevertheless, Rock continued to hit the target from frees, claiming eight scores in the first-half alone as The Dubs nudged back in front.

COLM BOYLE GOT forward to win the free from which O'Connor levelled for the third time, but Hennelly's issues with kickouts were to have further consequences, contributing to Lee Keegan's unfortunate and unjustified 35th minute black card, and another Dublin score. Replays showed Keegan committed a pull-back rather than a pull-down offence, and so should have received a yellow rather than a black card. Small details, but it stole Mayo's go-to player in a tight match at the very end of the championship. It didn't help that Keegan was vilified by several former Dublin players in the lead up to the match, making it easier for officials to make their decisions. In this case, a wrong one. A handful of stoppage time skirmishes led to bookings for Dublin pair Connolly and John Small and Mayo's Donal Vaughan, as the half ended with bristling tension, the defending champions ahead by 0-10 to 1-6.

Mayo came out for the second-half minus another key player, the injured Vaughan, but charged ahead with scores from the O'Connor brothers. However, Hennelly's game ended in devastation, after he fumbled a harmless Paul Flynn delivery into the arms of Andrews, and dragged down the attacker as he went for goal. The 'keeper was black-carded, with David Clarke coming in to face the penalty, which Connolly drilled clinically to the corner of the net on 42 minutes. Brendan Harrison and Stephen Coen defended heroically as The Dubs swept forward, keeping Kevin McManamon out, and countering for Kevin McLoughlin to cut the deficit.

In the last third of this game, Mayo seemed dead and buried as The Dubs came at us in waves. They had so many attacking options that they just kept unleashing, and yet... and yet, we stood firm, resilient, brave. Rock hard. Dead on our feet, but having the muscle memory to make the block, to deny a chance.

Mick Fitzsimons and James McCarthy stood tall and strong in getting in vital challenges to help The Dubs through a difficult spell, and the strength of their bench came to the fore, with Bernard Brogan and Cormac Costello (two) coming in to kick scores for a three-point lead. Brian Fenton's strong influence around the middle helped Dublin keep their opponents at arm's length, as Costello's third made it a two-point game in stoppage time. Nevertheless, we came back again with a ninth O'Connor free, and he had a chance to send the decider to extra-time again, but his placed ball attempt deep into stoppage time tailed left and narrowly wide.

The following evening, the players received the welcome of the fans at MacHale Park, gutted that it was not a celebration for the ages, each trying to emphasise that the losing of the game had not come from individual errors. In the week afterwards, much was made of the decision to change goalkeepers, when such an avenue did not seem warranted after the first game, but Rochford explained that as the drawn game had progressed, The Dubs were making more capital from our kickouts. He assumed that by the time the replay came around, they would have drawn it up as a key part of their game plan.

'Our analysis on Dublin was that they had pushed with a formation in the first game, pushed four guys inside. They were trying to cut out our short kickout. As the drawn game developed, they were getting more comfort with that, more reward, and we felt it was probably something they were going to maximise further,' he explained. But there was no getting away from the enormity of the decision and its consequences. Granted, hindsight is 20/20, but this loss felt even more self-inflicted than the game where we scored two own goals. Dublin's bench had once again been the difference with Cormac Costello kicking three and Bernard Brogan hitting four. In contrast, none of Mayo's subs added to the scoreboard – and therein lies the difference between losing and winning.

THERE IS A strangeness to the Croke Park press interview room after a final. On the final whistle, you get the lift from Level Seven to the tunnel that wraps around the bowels of the stadium. On days when we won league titles and indeed Connacht titles here, you took your time, and stood peering down at the sight of a green and red-clad player holding something shiny and silvery.

But for us hacks from the west, the sight of another Dublin captain reading a prepared speech had lost its novelty. Down there, as the coaches rev up and the backroom staff start to load the crates of kit and the detritus of matchday, you can hear the stadium noise reverberating – a sound that is immediately cut out the moment you enter the sealed press interview room.

In here, it was deathly silent that day as if everyone was going to be apologetic for another loss. The sportswriters denied the chance to write the story of the glorious conclusion of a Mayo journey, having to fall back instead on the familiar details of a Dublin one – a facet that would get even more wearying as the years went by.

On days like this, you feel tearful because you cannot be sure than such opportunities will come this way again. We tend to forget that Dublin had made controversial team changes that day too, but when you win, the rights or wrongs are not writ as large.

Victory has a thousand fathers, defeat is but an orphan.

★ ★ ★ ★ ★

12, 31, 9, 10 and 12

They read like the Lotto numbers being read out at the end of the news.

The bonus number was 1.

The top line is the gap by which Dublin won all but one of their championship matches in 2017. The single point which was the bonus number for them was a solitary point victory they produced against the only team to give them a game. If that single point victory in the final might seem underwhelming from a Dublin point of view, it was anything but, as it represented their most valuable 'Get Out of Jail' card in the Monopoly game that was their amazing run in the second decade of the millennium.

To underline the level of the challenge that this superb Dublin team got from Mayo, look once again at the margins listed above and then realise that in an enthralling All-Ireland final, The Dubs found scores hard to come by, despite Mayo generously offering them the customary flying start to a final by conceding a goal after just 90 seconds. If we thought that generosity would result in a concession of never to be beaten record proportions, the 2020 final would have said 'Hold my beer' when we allowed them in for one within the first 15 seconds. We Mayo fans have known every kind of emotion in All-Ireland finals in Croke

Park, except the ultimate emotion of unbridled joy.

We have known heavy defeat, unlucky defeat, narrow defeat, but the feeling after this final is one that perhaps most of us will never get over. For the entire match, Mayo played their best football of the decade, matching their opponents point for point; bouncing back when fate conspired against us – this was a game that did not deserve to be won by either side in those dying seconds. Or lost. A replay and more of the same would have been fair justice for the excellence and effort illustrated by both sides.

When Dean Rock nailed that winning free in the last minute, not too long after Cillian O'Connor's free rapped back off a post, we knew that this wonderful team were not going to let Mayo in again; that for all their beauty, they had a cynical side that was able to see out a game. So, the final moments of this classic game had scenes of Mayo players being hauled to the ground in the greatest single demonstration of tactical fouling the football showpiece had seen to that point.

IT HAD BEEN some season for Mayo. The resilience of the Mayo teams, coupled with all the off-field drama of the previous two years once again saw our team choose the scenic route to the 2017 decider, having been knocked out of the Connacht Championship in Salthill by Galway. At that stage, with the qualifiers looming, we wondered when this remarkable run would come to an end. None of us wanted it to, but it was inevitable that at some stage, one summer, there would a no-way-back match that would give an intermission to all the drama that started back in 2012.

In reaching the All-Ireland final, Mayo had to play a championship season that lasted a remarkable 10 games; two of which they lost, and two of which they drew. The losses coming against Dublin and Galway; the first draw coming against Roscommon – a scoreline avenged in the replay at Croke Park when Mayo destroyed their opponents with a flurry of goals in a 22-point victory, just a week after they had drawn. The second draw came against Kerry in the semi-final when they ended 2-14 apiece in a thriller. Six days later, Mayo resurrected this Lazarus quality with a five-point win over The Kingdom to make it back to the All-Ireland final again.

Once again showing that the two best teams were in the decider.

If those who arrived early on that mid-September day were looking for any reward for their punctuality, they were rewarded by the remarkable sight of a one-sided minor match that was illuminated by the brilliance of a Kerry team inspired by a young forward named David Clifford who hit a remarkable 4-4. Indeed, were it not for his willingness to share the limelight with his teammates, he could easily have hit twice that. It was one of the most impressive individual minor performances in the history of the competition – and it was no surprise that within five years he was walking around this pitch with Sam Maguire in his hands. But enough about Kerry.

Back to the senior match.

GPS TRACKING OF players allows the measurement and monitoring of players' speed and distance performed during a game or a training session. Several manufacturers have sports GPS units that enable users to determine speed and mileage. In the dying seconds of the game, the heat map for the device worn by Lee Keegan would show a straight line, a burst at pace for about 10 metres. And from there to the end of the game moments later, it would not register anything.

That sad device, lying on the Croke Park turf, containing a gyro, magnetometer and accelerometer had earned its keep that day, because the man wearing it for the previous two hours had run himself into the ground. No quarter asked or given, the technology within had recorded a successful run at goal, an afternoon of determination, and perhaps for that final 10-metre burst, an act of undeniable frustration.

Despite letting Con O'Callaghan through for that early goal, Mayo did not panic and put the Cluxton kickouts under pressure, creating many turnovers and building a narrow lead that should have been much more emphatic at the break. The decision of Donie Vaughan to follow through on the about-to-be-dismissed Small, when a cool head would have seen Mayo with a strong numerical advantage, is something that I'm sure he still thinks about. But lest we think that was the ultimate turning point, there was hope restored when Keegan took a momentary break from keeping Ciaran Kilkenny in his pocket, to zip through and lash a goal into the net in front of the Hill.

His cheeky celebration complete, Mayo were 1-12 to 1-11 ahead. Connolly equalised for Dublin before McLoughlin gave Mayo the lead again. Rock soon equalised, which was the catalyst for another Mayo burst which saw Cillian put Mayo two clear with seven minutes left on the clock. The next score was always going to be crucial – so The Dubs opted to get the next three (Mannion, McCaffrey and Rock) to lead again. The big screen counted past 68 minutes when Cillian O'Connor popped over the equaliser. In stoppage time, he had a free to give Mayo the lead again, but disappointingly, it struck a post and rebounded to safety.

Diarmuid Connolly had been instrumental in everything positive for The Dubs and when he crumpled easily under a challenge from Chris Barrett, Rock took his time, plenty of it; and ignoring the flying GPS unit, sent the ball between the posts and into the netted darkness of the Davin Stand.

Cue celebrations and a determination by Dublin that Mayo were not going to fashion another attack. Kilkenny was black-carded and the Mayo half resembled a battlefield as every potential recipient in green and red seemed to have been hauled to the ground.

It is hard to know how Mayo could have played better. Yes, there were individual reactions and errors that would not be repeated if the game could have been replayed the next day. Perhaps we could have been appeased by the excellence of their performance. Even watching it back now, it is hard to believe that we played so well, yet once again lost. Once again denied the glory the team deserved; the misfortune they felt coming up against the greatest side of all time.

So how did this loss rank?

Was it a worse feeling that the events of 1996 when not once, but twice we had opportunity, yet went away empty-handed. This felt more gutting too because with every final set-back on this road, we knew that we were watching some players for the last time; that retirements were inevitable. Some great teams, winning teams embark on a journey of success for one, two, or maybe three years. But normally in that third year comes fatigue, a loss of hunger, a desire to change their lifestyle.

Never mind third year syndrome, we were here in 2017 watching a team who had been building for the guts of six years and who had the most disappointing defeats handed to them. The 2017 final felt different because we were contenders right the way through… from the sickening opening goal concession… to the half time lead… to the double-point lead with seven minutes left. Even the sight of the Keegan goal and his cheeky celebration to the Hill felt different. But as long as the possibility of defeat loomed, the more likely it became.

The Dubs started to empty their bench with players who improved their team; ours were brought on to try to keep the energy levels at the equilibrium – that is why we needed the advantage of the extra man, and when it was given to us, we handed it back through a lack of discipline and control.

The Rochford era had brought Mayo the closest they had been to winning an All-Ireland since 1951. On the pitch afterwards, the players with children hugged them; the little ones staring up at the noise and the smoke and the golden streamers strewn along the ground in this cavernous theatre.

The manager too; his heart broken, his tactics almost perfect, he had produced a Mayo performance that had produced the longest championship season ever – 10 games, the vast majority of which were knockout. He had brought 40,000 fans along with him, convinced them that this team was a worthy cause to support; and how those players had reacted.

WHEN NEXT THEY got to a final, the atmosphere would be muted.

Austere.

Sad.

In a world that had changed utterly.

★ ★ ★ ★ ★

THE BALL SOARED high into the evening sky, the propulsion of the kicker giving it the altitude that would maximise its descent back to earth. But it never got to hit the ground. If the panels of the O'Neill yearned for the belt of soft grass, the squelch of the wet ground, it was to be sorely disappointed.

Up it went again… high into the Welsh sky.

Passers-by in a rugby-mad town like Cardiff, saw the man doing this – they assumed the ball was oval and some strange form of Garryowen was being perfected. But no. The round ball was firmly grasped by the big hands just three or four metres short of its downward journey.

He remembered doing this as a kid.

Back then there was always someone around for a kickaround.

Tom Parsons loved a handball alley, and there was one not far from his home in Bellaghy, on the Sligo side of Charlestown. Within those walls, himself and his friends perfected all their hand-eye co-ordination. But over here in Wales, there were no handball alleys.

When you are far from home, these thoughts enter your mind. The loss of something taken for granted. A fellow kicker.

A yearning for home and unfinished business.

IN HIS LIFETIME, Tom would have three Mayo careers.

One he might have. One he deserved; and one nobody thought he would. It was a far cry from the hopeful teen perfecting his catching on the roads and in fields at home. How many balls did he field in those years? Tens of thousands, for hours on end.

'Charlestown had a lot of success, when they won the county title for the second time, the town was steeped in success. When I was 12 and 13, that elevated it a bit. You were at the mercy too of the group you find yourself with and their success. In Charlestown, we had a group of young footballers who were playing 'A' football and were doing well. We played a lot of handball too; in fact it was as if we lived in the handball alley. The amount of time we spent there.

'If you were to look at professionals honing their skills, as a kid we spent hours in the handball alley… hours playing football. Kicking ball out the front of the house before the motorway got lively, kicking and catching. That good hand-eye coordination and good hands really came to the fore and then I started picking up basketball, and that helped with quick hands, catching the ball and breaking the ball. The combination of playing hours on the different sports got me to a stage in my teens where people said 'Jeez, this fella can really catch a ball'. I don't think I was starting on teams at 10. I was a big awkward young fella. I certainly wasn't soloing the ball up and down the field.

'But it's amazing when a kid has one particular skill that stands out, whether that's speed or you can really kick a ball. Mine was this ability to read and catch a ball. So right up until 17, the only thing I did was, they'd kick it out to me in the middle of the field, I'd spring and have good hands and kept it simple. And then sometimes the more talented players would solo up and down the field. When it came to minor or playing senior, one of the best attributes you could have was being unselfish… catching, handing the ball off and doing your job. At 17, I was going in playing A vs B games with Charlestown and because my skill-set of catching the ball was so good, I could compete with any of them. Because I kept it so simple, won the ball and handed it off, I wasn't exposed at all as a young fella. I remember going in, marking Ginger Tiernan; all I did was kept with him, caught a few balls and handed them off. The lads were saying this fella is well able for senior football.

'Much better players than me at 17 or 18 would not have been able to play at that level because their skills would have been exposed, they would have brought the ball into contact and have less time to kick it over the bar. That one skill got me exposure at 17, with the club at senior level, two years minor, straight out of minor into an under-21 team that had previously just won the All-Ireland with Seamus O'Shea and Barry Moran. Those formative years of having that skill-set gave me the break with the Mayo senior team. John O'Mahony would have seen me with the club and he gave me my debut.'

The fact that game was against Sligo made the occasion extra special for Tom. As a kid, he went to home games for both counties, and was a big fan of Eamon O'Hara who he felt could do things that he himself could not. 'He could carry the ball, a real warrior, and then to get a chance to go up against him in my debut… and I did really well. I was starting to have a bit of confidence around the middle of the field and I kicked two points, so that was very special for my family and myself.

'In the next game, against Tyrone, they put a forward out midfield and I was marking him, and I was licking my lips. In that game I had three shots and three wides, and we lost narrowly which illustrated that I had just the one skill-set and the other areas of my game were under developed.'

Sean Boylan was selecting the International Rules squad to head to Australia that year and Parsons caught his eye. For the young lad, it was head-turning stuff. Like Tommy O'Malley's 1970 trip to the US, Parsons was travelling with some heroes; some giants of the game. The likes of Kieran Donaghy who had destroyed Mayo two years earlier, Tyrone's Sean Cavanagh, Galway's Michael Meehan, and Aidan O'Mahony. The future looked bright, especially when his performance caught some eyes down under. There was speculation that he might consider signing a contract with an Australian Football League club, but he was a

Mayo player and said that he had no interest in playing Aussie Rules.

'It was unbelievable. You're not a million miles away from when you'd just be hoping you'd get a game with your club Charlestown and that was a dream in itself; to going to Mayo underage which was nearly a bit beyond my expectations, and then from senior to playing for your country as the youngest player. It all happened so quickly in 2008, which was great, but it was also tough.'

IF 2008 BROUGHT glory and a climb up the ladder, 2010 and '11 brought everything back down to earth. Mayo were knocked out of the championship by Longford.

'In your first year, there's not a huge expectation on you. It's when you perform that people start talking about you. In the second or third year, when there is a bit of heat and attention being put on you, you notice and it takes a great maturity to influence a game if somebody is going to prevent you. So, I wasn't able to adapt with these guys now putting in a system to prevent me from executing my major skill, which was catching the ball.'

Being released by Mayo and dropped from the Championship squad for the game away to London in 2011 came as a shock and gave him feelings of being an imposter. He was awarded a scholarship to Sligo IT on the basis of being a Division One footballer, and was living with Alan Freeman and Aidan O'Shea, but he felt an outsider.

'When you're in college, you're in the elite scholarship programme, but I didn't consider myself elite because I wasn't in the squad anymore and I was working in the bar at the weekend. That wasn't me. I did some soul-searching and I was able to keep focused on education and focus on the career. I now think of professional sports people and how their whole world must end when it's all over.'

To make matters worse, the successful Charlestown team had been relegated just a few years after they were county senior champions, having made three final appearances in-a-row. It was as if his entire sporting existence was in freefall. A lesser man would have walked away from it, but Parsons is not any such individual. For two months running in 2012, he took a flight home from Cardiff to ensure that his local club got back up at the first attempt. It was an effort and a series of performances that was to prove pivotal. Remember too, that Mayo had played and lost in two All-Ireland finals in 2012 and '13 – how crucial would he have been in those games?

In 2014, his form was impossible to overlook. Almost three years had passed since his last game in Monaghan; and when the call came to turn up for the FBD league clash with Roscommon in Ballinlough, it was as if he was being called back into action at Croker. Living in Cardiff, and kicking a ball alone in the park, had made him realise what club meant to him; and having shone in Charlestown's promotion, there was a desire in him to get back into the county set-up. He realised too that the story of Mayo is littered with cases of lads who got a few games for the county and then never heard anything again. He knew he had to be proactive.

He played every game as if it would be his last. His recall was rare, but he was going to grab it like he grabbed that ball out of the air in the park in Cardiff. It is at career-stages like this that the GPA is perhaps most needed, so it is fitting that a man who had been through it all now drives that objective as CEO.

'I hope to ensure that players find contentment within themselves without the game, because to be so selfish and give your county everything and perform to your best is okay, as you see the best sportspeople in the world are very selfish. That's okay to an extent, if that is going to be your livelihood. It's not okay in an amateur game where you need to provide for your family, and your life security. That is a really important part of our amateur game, that we invest in players off the field. The GPA were for me instrumental in making sure I got the bursaries and the scholarships, and elevated myself off the field, regardless of what is happening on the field.'

SO, TOM AND Carol moved to Cardiff and embraced the relative freedom of the city in a place where he was not constrained by being a Mayo footballer. Over there, he was Tom the engineer, the sportsman, the loving partner, the sound lad from Ireland. In Cardiff, Carol was developing her physiotherapy career.

They were happy out. This new-found freedom highlighted the need for players to avoid the limelight from time to time, especially in a county like Mayo where the county team is a constant source of fascination. For players for whom the game is an anxiety, the fact that they are constantly asked about it and have their opinions sought out in a variety of settings prolongs their anxiety.

'They need to escape it,' explains Tom. 'The best thing for me was to escape it and start building relationships with people who looked at me as an engineer and as a person, not as an athlete. That gave me a sense of peace for 12 months, and a sense of being able to achieve things not associated with the game. It moved me into a space of being free, after three or four years with Mayo. That freedom in Cardiff allowed me to train without being in pain and through running, athletics, boxing, and soccer, I got myself in good shape and cleared up some injuries.'

The move probably stopped Tom from falling out of love with the game and took him away from the goldfish bowl inhabited by Mayo players. He acknowledged that he was not as humble as he could have been in that first year of playing, but the time in Cardiff matured him by five or six years, resulting in a different character coming home. Having seen the benefit of his time away, Tom became aware that without Mayo football in his life, he had found a sense of purpose. With this new-found freedom, he gave himself permission to express himself more vocally in the dressing-room, and on the pitch. Nicking his hamstring before the game against Roscommon in 2014, he missed the majority of the championship, only getting back at half-time in the semi-final against Kerry, when the side, with Keegan sent off, were feeling sorry for themselves in the dressing-room. A blast of energy was needed, and the new loud Tom Parsons was the man to bring it. He made an immediate impact with some clever fielding and passing.

He acknowledges too the impact his career has had, not only on the life he shared with Carol both in Ireland and in Cardiff, but on his parents and uncles, for whom his career was a major distraction, which when it ended so early created a void that was only filled when he was back in the side.

ANOTHER MOMENT HE will never forget is the pain he felt after his sickening injury against Galway in 2018. He didn't need to be told it was bad, as he saw some of the Galway players looking, and then looking away in shock.

He recalls Aidan O'Shea having the wherewithal to come over, take his hand and say, 'Look at me, don't look down… just keep looking at me'.

What kept him going during that recovery?

'I didn't have resilience at the front end of my life, because I was all-consumed by sport. Whereas at the stage after the injury, I was playing with freedom, I was in a strong relationship, was very connected with my family and my close friends, within and without sport. I was an engineer and loved these projects that were making a difference in people's lives. I've had an element of spirituality and searching for the reason behind things.

'The pain and the prospect of not playing again, I was able to balance that by still having so much reason and purpose in life. That gives you freedom to play along and analyse what had happened. To think also, that I wouldn't have had the opportunity to work on that project or meet that person, had that tough time in my life not come my way.

'With every obstacle, there are opportunities. I remember meeting Aidan Kilcoyne at a wedding and he had significant knee injuries and he said that if you come back from this injury, it will be the greatest sporting return ever because I know what you're dealing with. And in my mind, that was the *opportunity*.

'We had workshops with Mayo on a Saturday with Stephen Rochford and Donie Buckley and James Horan, and we would ask the question, 'Why are we doing this?' What's the purpose? To get a gold medal?

'In so many of those workshops, the answer purpose came back to 'inspire the people of Mayo'. To inspire young people and old people. For thousands of years, Mayo has been hammered by wind and rain and famine, and we are resilient and we bounce back. We need to reflect the people of Mayo.

'People associate their character to the team that they follow. So inspiring was a big part of our purpose and that's what drove us on as a team. So, when this obstacle came our way, I asked myself if our purpose is inspiring people, Jesus, wouldn't it inspire so many people if I came back and played.'

One thing Tom Parsons has in buckets is resilience. He got knocked down, but he got up again. So many times. He would have been forgiven if he walked away from the game. The way he had been treated; the way fate had treated him. He has been through the wringer – and so it is fitting that a man who has known the highs and the lows is perfectly placed to articulate the concerns of inter-county players who annually give of themselves so that a nation can be entertained.

BEING DUBLIN AND UK-based because of work commitments in his role as a civil engineer, Parsons was no stranger to airports, but it was the long road from Dublin to Mayo for county training that he felt took a massive toll on the Dublin-based players. 'Travel and its toll on the body is a big thing for a player, and it becomes more important, the older you get.'

Dublin-based players had to have flexibility in their studies or work, in order to travel west for training. Often, they had to work late the night before in order to get ready for lunchtime when they would travel together to training, often arriving just an hour beforehand and having to use that hour to walk the travel out of the limbs. Then they'd do the session, have a team chat afterwards, grab a bit to eat and head back to the capital, often arriving home not far off 2am. Then the next day would be spent catching up on the work missed the previous day. Some toll, and an obligation not forced on other counties, whose players could be based locally, where there were jobs and study opportunities.

Tom Parsons was an ideal candidate to head the Gaelic Players' Association as any conversation with him over the years had displayed his evolving relationship with the game; which has given him an oversight that is invaluable when it comes to representing the needs and wants of younger versions of himself. He has often spoken about how the younger him would have reacted to the horrendous injury he suffered in 2018. He feels that younger players need to have something else in their lives apart from the games, because he knows that the cyclical nature of fate and fortune from one game to the next, leaves them exposed to serious anxiety and mental health issues if the proper support structures are not there.

Tom Parsons is not a player who is defined by the presence or absence of success; he feels pride at the beauty of the battle; the battles of wit and limbs, and pride that goes into winning game after game after game. A life not defined by a series of losing finals, he believes that those big games were only possible if other big games were played and won. This is an important facet of his psyche because he heads an organisation that represents players, 97 percent of whom will never taste success as defined by the binary of winning or losing. Every year, 1,000 players start a season with the hope of winning an All-Ireland, yet only three percent of them will achieve it. This does not mean that the 97 percent have failed in the strictest sense, even though they may not have achieved their objective.

He has spoken about the satisfaction he gained from the 2017 final, when both Mayo and Dublin went at each other, and ceased only when the whistle blew. He said that, at that moment, which perhaps should have been one of devastation, he instead felt an immense pride at having participated in such a spectacle. It's not that he was categorising that lost final as one vast Go-Game, but that in the intensity of the battle, both the Mayo and Dublin players were mentally and physically exhausted.

'There's that famous phrase about being physically exhausted on the battlefield, having given everything in the pursuit of victory for your cause. And although we'd lost and I was absolutely gutted, at the same time, I felt so proud... so alive, and I'll never forget that moment.'

When he looks back on the series of epic games against The Dubs, the greatest side of all time, he thinks back to how far the Mayo team had come.

'I was one of the few players who were there on that day we were knocked out by Longford. It's far cry from that to almost winning an All-Ireland. We're in a very privileged position in sport to be competing at that level and to be part of a squad of special guys who brought something different. Sometimes, it's not the best 15 players. I certainly wasn't in the best 15 players, but I brought a menacing energy around the place, and so did Seamus O'Shea and Chris Barrett, who had an aggression on matchday.

'We all had our flaws, but the diversity of characters and of skill-sets made us a very formidable team. That Dublin team were more talented and had the systems and the basketball movements. They had many more control processes in their game, but they could not match the menacing behaviour and character of us, and what we brought to the game.

'That's what made us so competitive. After 20 minutes we'd be gassed because of our aggressive play. They wouldn't be, but we'd sustain it and keep going. This was good enough to beat most teams and brought Dublin to a replay and brought us into the final minutes of a game where the opportunity to win was in our hands.'

MAYO GAA HAS been hit particularly hard with tragedies over the decades. The passing of Ted Webb and John Morley, and for Tom and his Charlestown clubmates the death of their friend and teammate, Colm Horkan who died on duty in Castlerea in 2020.

'Colm was a symbol of everything that was good about the club, he had that philosophy of helping others. He would always see the most vulnerable person in the room and go for them. Maybe, as far back as the famine in Mayo, a lot of life is trying to square off and rationalise suffering. Maybe it's in that suffering that we rationalise what brings us joy and happiness.

'I often meet Mayo players who are asking themselves if they can keep going or should they retire? I see in them that the prize of winning an All-Ireland for

Mayo is a much bigger prize and more significant than for any other counties.'

He believes it is worth exploring that journey, as a symbol of something much more pure than success. 'This should be celebrated, this relentless goal by Mayo people for success. If our kids want to do something in life, let them not take No for an answer. Inspire them to be successful in their relationships and their endeavours in life.

'It's a noble cause, that's much bigger than the game.

'The players are contributing to something very special for Mayo people and they need to do that, but not lose sight what life is, and remember that sport should not be all-consuming.'

★ ★ ★ ★ ★

IT'S COLD. SO cold, that the tips of my fingers are numb and their touch on the keyboard of the laptop produces no sensation. I feel like I'm typing with boxing gloves; the Macbook perched on my lap in the absence of a desk here in the heart of the main stand at Pearse Stadium.

It is November 15, 2020.

The stewards are mad keen to shut down the ground and get home to the fires, because there's nowhere else to go. It's a year to the day since the first sign of a deadly virus was detected in Wuhan, China. Who would have thought that 12 months later, it would be impacting on the outcome of the Connacht final. We are waiting for Galway manager, Pádraic Joyce to come and talk to us, but he is taking his time.

Today is the championship end of the road for his side, because Mayo have come here, played well below their best, and walked away with a single point victory. There haven't been many games since the restart of sport, but two months earlier, the league encounter between the two sides at the famed old rundown stadium in Tuam was a barometer for where they were at. At the start of 2020, Galway were flying; inspired by the Joyce appointment. Fans were flowing back, hoping to see his team create some of the moments he himself executed. For Galway fans, the sight of Joyce rounding the Kildare 'keeper and scoring that goal in 1998 is ingrained on their memories. But when the time came to play Mayo in the league in Tuam, the visitors tore up the script and left the town of the Saw

Doctors with a 15-point victory, and a score total of 3-23.

Now that they were to meet again in the championship, would the tables be turned? Would that devastating defeat give Galway the incentive to knock Mayo out of the championship? This was a truncated competition; no backdoors, no qualifiers.

It was being held really to preserve the mental health of the nation, to give us something to get angry about as we strolled, masked-up within a 5km radius of our homes, salivating at the thought of a €9 meal eaten at a table on your own.

It was the most miserable of times, and while the general public missed access to these games, in truth, they did not miss much, because they were depressing encounters, with players arriving with Tupperware boxes containing all they would need to prevent them from spreading the virus or contaminating one another.

Mayo were particularly fastidious and arrived with their individual boxes pitch-side, bottles named and numbered, sanitisers at the ready, every precaution taken. The ground was closed to all but the press and the matchday players, coaches and officials. The space-constrained press-boxes were shut; media were deemed essential workers so we had a letter to show any gardai with checkpoints on the edge of the city. In hindsight, it is hard to believe that any of this actually happened. But it did.

The world's great cities felt the brunt of the confinement, so the teams from New York and London had to concede their games. In order for London's quarter-final to take place, their entire squad and backroom team would have had to self-isolate in Ireland for two weeks prior to the match. Galway, who were meant to travel to the Big Apple in May, got a walkover into the semi-final against Sligo. When Sligo reported Covid cases, they also had to concede, so we had the weird sight of Galway making it to the final on walkovers alone. This was the kind of scenario detailed earlier in this book when the country was in the War of Independence and the Civil War.

Now, we were at war again, with an invisible enemy.

Mayo, on the other hand, were busy getting game minutes into their boots, beating Leitrim 2-15 to 0-10, and Roscommon 1-16 to 0-13. When it came to the Connacht final, we did not know what stage Galway were at. But one thing was certain, it would not resemble anything like the mauling in Tuam.

At the end, Mayo escaped with the cup and a single-point win that felt like a larceny. Galway had been nothing like the side in Tuam, but while they coughed up scores that day, in the final they coughed up possession. In terms of losing the ball, they did it 32 times in the game, enabling Mayo to build almost all of their match winning total. Aidan O'Shea came up to the impromptu press-box to collect the JJ Nestor Cup, said a few words and was gone. No celebrations, no showers, no team bus.

James Horan did likewise, but we waited for Joyce for another 30 minutes; when he turned up, changed out of his gear and angry at how his side had thrown away the game. What they had also thrown away was the possibility of advancement to a semi-final where the Connacht winners would play the winners of Tipperary or Cork. Cork had nicked a last-gasp win against Kerry, so a gateway of opportunity was open to the Connacht winners – but Galway had fluffed their lines.

WITH THE GAA hosting celebrations to mark the centenary of Bloody Sunday in 1920, a remarkable day of gaelic football shocks and landmark victories ended with the 2020 All-Ireland senior football semi-final line-up quite incredibly replicating that of the 1920 championship.

A day after the GAA staged their emotional and fitting Bloody Sunday commemorations at Croke Park, it was an afternoon of celebrations on the pitch as Tipperary and Cavan won the Munster and Ulster finals respectively. Tipperary defeated Cork by 0-17 to 0-13 for a first Munster crown since 1935, while Cavan ended their Ulster wait for glory that had stretched back to 1997, when they defeated Donegal by 1-13 to 0-12.

That set up semi-final ties with Cavan taking on Dublin and Tipperary playing Mayo. Once again, a window opened up for the Connacht champions to get into their first final since that narrow defeat to that late *late* Dean Rock free.

A lot had happened since that date. In 2018, after losing to Galway in Castlebar, they beat Limerick and Tipperary before they went out to Kildare in a controversially-staged match in Newbridge. Although tens of thousands of fans from both sides were unable to see the third round qualifier, the game was played at the small capacity St Conleth's Park in a saga which spawned the #newbridgeornowhere hashtag. In 2019, Mayo won the National League, their first national trophy for 18 years with a convincing 3-11 to 2-10 victory over Kerry involving a starring performance from Diarmuid O'Connor.

It sparked off an interesting summer and once again, some great road-trips for the fans, but they were caught napping in the Connacht semi-final when Roscommon stunned the Castlebar crowd with a 2-12 to 0-17 victory. Back on the road we went, beating Down, Armagh (in Castlebar) and Galway in Limerick – a game that will be remembered for James Carr's wonder bullet-goal that hit over a million views on YouTube in the days afterwards. They emerged from the quarter-final series with wins over Meath and Donegal, and a loss to Kerry; with the magical mystery tour coming to an end with a 10-point loss at the hands of The Dubs.

THERE WAS A new opportunity for advancement in 2020. The world had changed; the atmosphere in each ground was muted; the calls of every player audible; the whack of boot upon leather adding to the authenticity of it all. On the evening that Mayo played Tipperary in the semi-final, a heavy fog enveloped North Dublin and added to the already ghostly atmosphere. But it was not ghouls who emerged out of the mist to terrify Tipperary, but Cillian O'Connor who hit 4-9 and illustrated that he was operating at the peak of his game. Tipp had started quite well and should have had two goals in the first eight minutes but a disastrous second quarter saw them lost in the fog, as wave after wave of Mayo attack battered them into submission.

Tipp got three goals of their own in this heavy defeat and should have had two or three more. No matter the margin, Mayo were not convincing in the number of goal chances they were coughing up to teams. They also knew that Dublin would not be as profligate in the final.

Traditionally, the final of the minor championship takes place before the senior game. However, due to the pandemic, that competition was still in its preliminary stages as December arrived. Instead, the final of the 2020 under-20 All Ireland contested by Dublin and Galway, originally due to have been played in October before a further suspension of play occurred for underage teams, took place before the senior decider. The Tribesmen produced a wonderful display to beat Dublin, with several of that team forming part of Joyce's squad that reached the senior final in 2022. After we had done our match report and social media interviews, there was time to kill, so I decided to ring an old friend of mine from Ballinrobe, with whom I had travelled to that final in 1975. Anthony Jennings, known affectionately as Snook (everyone in my town had a nickname – FYI, mine was the Cat), grew up a few hundred yards from my house.

Although we were inseparable in the 80s and had made a few bob flogging 'Mayo Are Magic' t-shirts in the hype of 1985, we had gone our separate ways and had not met for decades. He took the decision to emigrate to London, while I stayed on at home. Nevertheless, he never missed a Mayo game and every summer made his way home for the championship. This year, with restrictions, there was no travel… and no tickets. I had asked his sister for his number in the days beforehand and vowed to ring him on the evening of the match. He was shocked to hear me after so long; and especially when I told him where I was and what the atmosphere (or lack of) was like in Dublin.

London was ridden with Covid, and pubs were shut, but he had an arrangement made to get in a back door somewhere where a group of Irish lads would watch the game. It felt sad chatting at this distance; but also because his enjoyment of the match seemed so much more fun than mine actually in the stadium. Strict numbers were imposed on the attendance. Media representation was kept to a standstill – my own media ticket granted almost certainly because Galway, where I work, were playing in the curtain-raiser. Many of the older Mayo hacks who would normally have been there, were not. We were told that the media room deep in the bowels of the stadium would not be available for post-match interviews.

All would be done at the side of the pitch.

Even the idea of a fantasy homecoming for Mayo would be stilted as the Sam Maguire Cup was withheld over concerns about the possibility of 'crowds gathering' around the victorious county. Sam would pop out for a few hours and then be retired for the year to the trophy room. On the day, it seemed that Mayo were going to have a shot to nothing at winning an All-Ireland. The goal chances they coughed up in the semi-final did not bode well, but they had won National League silverware at this ground a year earlier, and that might have added to their resilience.

To be fair, our record of generosity in the early stages of a decider knows no equal, and although The Dubs had scored inside two minutes the last time we met in a final, this time, they needed only 12 seconds before Dean Rock punched to the net. But, full credit to Mayo's resilience again; they did not let such a start faze them and within three minutes, they were level, with Oisin Mullin instrumental in creation and execution. By the 22nd minute, Mayo were 0-8 to 1-3 ahead and full of running, each call and mark audible in the vast empty bowl of a stadium.

It had all the feel and sound of a good training session, and then Con O'Callaghan did a little shimmy, a pass and a finish to net Dublin's second goal. To concede two goals in the first-half was again a killer for this Mayo side and they trailed by two at the break. Dublin got bodies back to make sure Mayo never got that elusive goal and the fact that Mayo scored just one point after the second water break was frustrating, and the champs were rolling to their six-in-a row without much bother by the end.

In the end, the gap was pushed to five points, and we experienced a tenth defeat in a final since 1951. Afterwards, the press duties were carried out on the steps of the Hogan and James Horan was keen to get out of the stadium and home through the night, across a dark deserted city. He bemoaned the fact that Mayo ran out of juice in the last quarter, as the Dublin energy rose the closer they got to that sixth Sam. For Horan, there was consolation in the performance of the young players, and the realisation that as it was now almost Christmas… the start of the new season would not be as far away as it normally would.

The message from the stewards at Croke Park was mostly the 'Have ye no homes to go to?' variety as we finished recording the after-match chats with the managers and players. Nobody felt like staying on to write it up. Nor was there an option of there being any hostelry open on the way down home to find a corner.

I HAD PARKED behind the Davin Stand and as I left afterwards, with Tommy Devane of Galway Bay FM and Colm 'Woolly' Parkinson, we bemoaned the state of the world that had forced us to have such an occasion in the manner in which it had been held.

Tall, dark and 99 percent empty, Croke Park was lacking the soul it gets from a full house; the packed streets, the frenetic atmosphere of people going this way and that, bellowing into mobile phones afterwards. There was none of that. We got into our cars and headed back through the city streets, the dark and silent centre of town akin to Gotham City rather than Dublin.

I had never seen any city, never mind Dublin look as quiet as this. There was something quite eerie about it all, indeed it had an *End of Days* feel about it.

The roads west were quiet too.

As I drove, I thought of Snook in London and what he had made of it all; I thought of the many who would normally make early morning starts to travel east. But tonight, there was none of that, and then the realisation hit me.

That of all the hundreds of thousands who had watched Mayo matches since 1951, the number of those who had actually seen every losing final was down to maybe a couple of dozen. Because the game was effectively played behind closed doors, it would be just a few local journalists or coaches who had been at every losing final from 1951 – from 1989 onwards, and I was one of those.

The term accumulated baggage came to me, and of how I felt that every sporting experience stays with you and adds or detracts from your being. Maybe the players do not accumulate the negative detritus of continued defeat, but there is an undoubted impact on the supporters.

But rather than see it as a negative attribute, I felt that there was a tremendous pride and privilege in seeing my county team compete at the top level in some many deciders. Their achievements went beyond finals; they brought pride to us all from all corners of the country. They had given a meaning to us that been absent in the lean years of the 60s and 70s.

Now, Mayo were being consistently consistent.

Mayo mattered. As one of the elite sporting set-ups in the country, they had played their part in distracting us from the boredom of lockdown. Even when the world had changed and everything had come to a standstill, Mayo had given us something to roar about in a depressing week before Christmas.

★ ★ ★ ★ ★

THE SUN WAS going down behind the church as the faithful gathered for Saturday evening Mass at Lavally; not the Lavally in Ballinrobe from where hailed Seamus O'Malley and his family, but the Lavally in Galway which is well steeped in Galway football. It's on the road towards Kilkerrin-Clonberne, the home area of county star Shane Walsh.

That evening's Mass at Church of Our Lady and St Jarlath did not suit Mayo supporters. The semi-final against Dublin had kicked off at teatime… for the past six years they had played 45 championship games undefeated and this evening, in the late summer of 2021, Dublin were hoping to make it 46. By the first sós uisce, everything was going to plan as they led by four points with Dean Rock and Ciarán Kilkenny leading the way on the scoring front, hitting five of the six points. Dublin continued their dominance in the second quarter, retaining possession at their ease as Mayo sunk back into a defensive pattern, and picked off scores when the chance finally came.

Rock kicked frees in the 23rd and 26th minutes to extend their lead to six, and two minutes later Paddy Small put seven between the teams after another long period of keep ball.

Seven points down, the faithful in Lavally felt they could go to Mass with ease. The game in Dublin was only going one way. Dublin would be creating 'Magnificent Seven' headlines over the next few weeks, having seen off Mayo.

The priest saying the Lavally Mass was Fr Pat Farragher, a native of The Neale and a member of a family I had long known as being decent stock. Fr Pat's brother, Stephen is also a priest in the diocese. Two nicer lads you could not meet.

The Farraghers are a wonderful family, steeped in Mayoness and goodness. A family that has also known tragedy with the death of their sister, Maura in a traffic accident in the past few years. Both Fr Pat and Fr Stephen have made an enormous contribution to education and spiritual life in North Galway, never eschewing their Mayoness. There are an amazing number of Mayo-native priests serving in county Galway, because the Archdiocese of Tuam spreads across the two counties, even taking in some of the island community.

When I remarked upon this to Fr Stephen a few years ago, he said, 'Well, it suited both counties. Galway needed the faith... and we needed the jobs', he laughed.

By half-time, as Fr Pat readied his vestments for Mass, the Dubs led by six points. When our team is behind like this, the optimist in us says this is the sort of chaos that we thrive on, but this was against them. The third quarter was a slow-moving affair with both sides keeping the ball for lengthy plays, probing and prodding looking for gaps. Dublin were kept scoreless by Mayo, who were starting to slowly pull in Dublin. Ryan O'Donoghue pointed after a long run.

Hennelly nailed a free and, right on the second water break whistle, Lee Keegan popped up to put the ball over the bar and leave just three between them. Dublin looked to have weathered the storm with quick points from Paddy Small and Rock to go five clear again, with just over 12 minutes left in normal time.

We then exploded. Exploded good.

We pushed up, clawed our way back, and…

Diarmuid made that memorable saving stretch to keep the ball in play, Conor O'Shea forced a turnover on the end-line and Mayo got a last chance '45' to level it up. Hennelly had a first effort that was sailing wide, but was given a second shot at it by the referee and he made no mistake sending it right over the bar and the game into extra time, just as Mass was starting in Lavally.

Covid restrictions were still in place, so masked stewards at the door showed the faithful 50 to their seats. Fr Pat was resigned to the fact that no matter how fast the Mass would be, the game would be over by the time they got out. He sermonised about the need for some refurbishment around the altar area, with new carpet needed, but all the time his mind was on the carpet of Croke Park. He said that as was customary during Covid times, that Communion would be served to the congregation as they exited the front door.

Then, with his eyes lifted to Heaven, he said, 'And, if any of ye have any spare prayers left unused, could I ask ye to think of a neighbouring county who are trying to win in Dublin at this moment'. There was a titter of laughter, and then a roar from the back of the church. 'Mayo have won, Father…'

The church lifted with the roars of the congregation… fists were pumped, yahoos roared out…

'Well, that's the power of prayer. The best news I could receive this evening, and on that happy note… I will hand out the communion.'

TWO HUNDRED AND fifty kilometres away, the Mayo players were collapsing on the turf in disbelief at what they had just achieved. When the game had gone into extra time, Sean Bugler got the scoring going after everyone got their breath back, but that was it for Dublin as Mayo took control of the game. Tommy Conroy drove through to shoot over two minutes in, three minutes later he landed another, and then Darren Coen curled one over from under the Cusack Stand. O'Donoghue hit another to put Mayo four clear.

In the end, they won 0-17 to 0-14 in a gamed that perfectly summed up Mayo's long journey from 2012. It had everything… mistakes, classic scores, controversial refereeing decisions… chaos, bravery and resilience. Diarmuid's stretch on the end-line to prevent the ball going out for that last vital push is an iconic image that only Mayo fans will appreciate.

When all is said and done, it is moments like these that warm the hearts of Mayo fans, to realise how fitting it was that it was ourselves who put a stop, temporarily, to the runaway train that was Dublin. The sight in Dublin that night was a world away from the previous winter, when they were a footnote in a game in a world where everything had changed.

At the end of that night, when Fr Pat locked the doors in the church in Lavally and went home, he did so with a warmth in his heart; a beating pride that sustains the soul of every Mayo supporter.

Again, Mayo were just 70 minutes away from their first title since 1951. Surely, with the greatest team ever having been vanquished in the manner they were, this had to be the year.

Tyrone.

Only Tyrone remained in our way.

2-14 to 0-15 was the final scoreline on the screen when Mayo lost that winter final of 2020.

Fast forward nine months.

2-14 to 0-15 was the final scoreline on the screen when Mayo lost the autumn final of 2021 to Tyrone.

It was our eleventh consecutive final loss since 1989.

Our sixth final loss in nine years.

IT IS ALWAYS felt that on the day a long awaited and much coveted All-Ireland is won, that it will be snatched; that there might not be much style to it, but that at the end, the victory will be secured by hook or by crook.

Just weeks before this final, Tyrone announced that they might have no option but to pull out of the Championship on Covid grounds – a stance that created quite an amount of controversy and cynicism.

Mayo started brightly. Indeed, we broke the habit of a lifetime by scoring first, after just 13 seconds when Tommy Conroy lashed over from O'Shea's pass. Ryan O'Donoghue nailed a second a short while later, and we were flying. It was the time to push on; not to sit back and enjoy the view. Niall Morgan pointed a free and when McNamee and McCurry scored, the Ulster champions were in the lead and never fell behind again.

Conor Loftus, with the goal at his mercy, snatched at it and Sludden saved the day for Tyrone. There were goal chances and penalty shouts at the end of which Tyrone had a two-point interval break. It is the third quarter that will give the players nightmares. Conroy turned Hamsey inside out, but dragged his shot wide. Another scramble resulted in a penalty. Was this the moment we had been waiting for?

Ryan O'Donoghue's shot was high and lashed against that sweet spot where the crossbar meets the upright. It was the 45th minute before Mayo opened their account for the second-half. We needed a goal... and one did come, but down the other end when Cathal McShane flicked it home. O'Donoghue replied with a free, but Walsh blasted wide when squaring it would have reaped more rewards. Loftus missed three chances – it was a masterclass in misfiring.

If it was frustrating for us all, it was contagious, because the players started to panic when there was no need to. We were still well in this and cool heads might have seen us prevail. This panic led to the breakaway by McKenna, who slotted the ball into McCurry, who tapped home. Tyrone had scored just twice in the second-half, but both were goals.

Mayo were visibly fading.

The wasted chances taking their toll on their renowned resilience.

0-15 to 2-14.

Again.

THE LOSS TO Tyrone was perhaps the most disappointing of them all.

Since then, many fans have become disillusioned. Tyrone won the final scoring the sort of goals that Mayo had spent all year trying to get. In the two years since, none of the excuses offered up were accepted. Four goal chances came and went, a penalty was missed, and minute by minute, Tyrone grew in stature to win an unlikely All-Ireland; the sort we have been trying to secure for more than 70 years.

Tyrone's Brian Dooher, standing as an All-Ireland winner as a player and as a manager, stated bluntly, 'The way we look at it with the players is... don't wait until tomorrow, do what you can today and the boys did that. It's very fortunate and very lucky that you get to an All-Ireland final... and you have to give everything you can when you get there.'

He could have been talking to us.

★ ★ ★ ★ ★

THE SUN IS belting down over the stand in Salthill, but even on this scorcher, there's the famous Pearse Stadium wind. A fella near me said that both sides needed 'a kick in the hole' for putting themselves into this position. Both sides had contested the league final a month or so earlier with Mayo emerging with the honours.

Man-mountains Aidan O'Shea and Paul Conroy have been knocking lumps out of each other for a decade, and continue to chase a dream in the awkwardly titled preliminary quarter-final. One of these two stalwarts is going to go home this evening out of the title race, when both should have been eying a semi-final at least.

Mayo had been chasing the game in the first-half, but now in the third quarter, a smacker of a goal has everyone seeing the bright lights again… a quick pass to O'Shea… smart hands and full-back David McBrien has it and… in the flash of an eye, the ball is nestled in the Galway net.

The dream is on again. In a year in which the National League title has been plundered after a patchy final in which we dominated Galway early on and built up enough of a lead to hold onto, we also coughed up five good goal chances which on any other day would prove costly.

Galway, on this occasion, almost goal twice in the dying seconds, but fate and fortune keeps it out. They exit the championship and Mayo, buoyed by another win, march on to face… Dublin.

A week after McBrien's wonder-goal, the year's odyssey is all over. Another summer gone. Back to 'next game is FBD' territory. Year one of the Kevin McStay era ends with silverware and loads of 'What ifs'… and a fair dollop of 'What happened?'

McStay gives a 65-minute interview to the *Mayo Football Podcast* and doesn't shy away from what happened. Even though we haven't made the last four, there is talk of hope and learnings and experiments.

★ ★ ★ ★ ★

ANOTHER SUMMER'S DAY, on that hot day in MacHale Park in 1975, I was just past my tenth birthday. Full head of hair… full head of hope.

Back to the present and in a year or two, I will be in my sixties.

If you had told me then that the odyssey would occupy this vast tract of my life, I would scarcely have believed it. Now, there is no guarantee that I will ever see them winning it. Nor do I feel there is any obligation on that bunch of players to deliver.

I think of the players I have spoken to for this book, and beyond, and of how they grew up pursuing this, and then when the time dictated, they let it go and filled their days with other pursuits… love, life, family, work.

But for the fans, there is no retirement, no hanging up of the scarves.

Til death us do part.

It goes on and on and will, regardless of success or otherwise.

What is the alternative?

We can't change county allegiance.

We won't be taking up following cricket. There is no doubt that a win is worth more to us than all the other counties. The Mayo journey is one of the last great sporting challenges left in the country. There have been learnings from all the final losses, but not all of them have been heeded. In fact, the most learnings should have come from the most recent final loss in which we were given a masterclass in how to win.

A death by a thousand cuts. I don't believe in the theory of the accumulated baggage either, that a final performance is impacted by one that went before. Every loss we have had can be traced back to a malfunction of the system, a lesson not heeded, a decision not taken. I do not believe that there is anything that has happened in the past that will prevent us from winning in the future, apart from identifying the mistakes that cost us.

The win will come because eventually all eras of greatness pass, and opportunities will arise. What is instructive is the need for Mayo to take advantage of such years by ensuring the scarce funds are there to develop smart intuitive players, as well as athletic and strong ones. Perhaps not enough commercial benefit was made of the expansion of the Mayo brand in the last decade. What is instructive too, is the need for Mayo coaches to transfer the knowledge of being game-wise, to be able to react to circumstances, to see out matches.

When that happens, the victory will come.

It might come out of the blue, a falling over the line, like Limerick had in 2018 when they looked like they had blown it against Galway. What Mayo need to pursue is a 'One-in-a-Row' triumph. A sneaky messy win in a game where they are able to counteract the blanket defence.

There are no curses to hinder us, nor fears.

All that remains is for us to be smarter than our opponents in the next final.

AFTER THE PERIOD of writing this book, I feel I have a better understanding of where we came from, of the efforts expended. We are not defined by the finals lost, but by the games won to get to that stage; culturally, the footballers have helped the brand of Mayo.

The eras of 'Mayo God Help Us' are shattered.

The 'Mayo of Death of An Irish Town' and 'No One Shouted Stop' are consigned to the past. Our towns are progressive and commuter hubs; they house remote working and enable fulfilled lives. Our students no longer have to travel far to study; from Mayo, we can reach the far ends of Europe without a car crossing the county border.

The footballers have shaped this identity, this new confidence, well against the odds, and in doing so have mirrored the Mayo spirit, hewn from centuries of battling against the elements on the most westerly side of the continent.

The pride that enables our fans to wear the Mayo shirt all over the world is a kiss to the badge of a club of which we are all proud to be members.

The brilliant odyssey continues.

Mayo parade before the 2021 All-Ireland final against Tyrone, as an 11th agonising defeat in the decider since 1951, cruelly awaits. And James Horan, who brilliantly managed magnificent Mayo teams, as well as the hopes and prayers of a whole county.

★ EPILOGUE ★

THAT BLOODY CURSE?

THERE IS A stillness masked by a hushed hum that surrounds half-time in a major stadium. The 35 minutes of to and fro are distracted by the need to eat, to pee, to drink, to vent, not particularly in that order. Simultaneously, they create a tension, of people going this way and that. In our childhood soundtrack, the half-time whistle was invariably followed seconds later by the drums of the Artane Boys Band, and the retreat to the dressing-rooms would see players departing as the music arrived. But on this day, there was something different.

The sunny days of All-Ireland finals have been replaced by a greyness developed with the shape and structure of the modern Croke Park. Above you, the stands soar, cathedrals of grey and noise, claustrophobically containing the tensions within the ground, for fear of letting any escape out onto Jones' Road.

I cannot have been the only one on that day in 2016 to feel the chill, that something was happening, something strange had just happened. In recent years, we have seen things we thought we never would; the world shutting down, war in Europe again, the Twin Towers collapsing. Nothing shocks us anymore.

If ET were to walk among us, would we be that surprised? Momentarily, perhaps and then we would convince ourselves that it was probably inevitable.

AS WE REPAIRED from our seats in the press box to the central press area where they serve a sort of cauliflower soup and a variety of chicken stuffing sandwiches, there was a stunned silence at what had just transpired. It was as if we had all just been witness to the physical representation of what an evil curse would look like, if one ever existed.

At that one moment, grown men and women looked at each other and wondered if, after all, there was some truth in this; or whether the sheer imagining of it had manifested itself into terrible bad luck. At the same moment, the skies darken ominously above the stadium and the floodlights came on; the pitch looked a dark green.

Mayo are playing Dublin and despite having outplayed the champions and denied them any opportunity to score from play, they are still losing, courtesy of two goals scored against us by members of the Mayo team. An own goal is a rarity in gaelic football; two own goals in the one half, never mind the one game was unprecedented.

For it to happen in the showpiece game of the year at Croke Park meant that not only the 82,000 in the ground were stunned by it, so were the millions watching on TV around the world.

A MONTH LATER.

A grey afternoon in Manchester on that Tuesday. The crew busied themselves around the purpose-built studios at Dock 10, Greater Manchester in MediaCityUK. On that day they were busy recording the new series of the popular game show *Countdown*. On TV, the show might be snappy and fast paced, but when you are on a crew that has to record five episodes in one day, there is no time to be lost. Shots are taken and retaken, links are re-recorded if there is any perceived imperfection. Guests and hosts have to change their costumes for every show. The host, Nick Skewer, half hidden behind the desk just changed his top; the presenters standing on the floor, like Rachel Riley, had to have a complete change as she is seen in full shot. Each show is shot three months in advance, so there is a stringent effort to not timestamp an episode with any topical reference.

Guest Colin Murray lowered his voice into the style of a parent telling a ghost story on Halloween night. The other guests listened, enthralled. At home, on the other side of the screen sat six million UK viewers. Murray, although a young man, is a veteran of UK TV presenting, having been behind the desk on shows such as *Match of the Day 2*, the Sunday night Premier League highlights show. A native of Dundoland in Belfast, he was originally born Luke Wright, but when a relative pointed out that this name sounded more like a direction, he took his father's surname. Tonight, he was the Dictionary Corner guest on *Countdown*.

'What I'm going to give you is an eerie curse, the ultimately unpalatable curse, but even if you support this team, you want to break that curse, but you kinda don't want it to end. But I'll get to that in a second. It's 1951 and Mayo were playing in the Gaelic football All-Ireland final... and win. They are buoyant and are on the way home... they've won the big one, the Sam Maguire, they're having drinks and they're celebrating boisterously.

'They go through a tiny town called Foxford, a town of very few residents and there is a funeral cortege. Oblivious to this, they party through the cortege, upsetting the family.

'The priest put a curse on them... and I'll get to the specifics of it at the end, but from then, there has been the most remarkable run of bad luck for Mayo since 1951. They have been to the All-Ireland final eight times... and they have never won it. They have had some amazing misfortune.

'What the priest said that day as they goaded him from the bus was that, 'You will not win another All-Ireland trophy until every member of this team has passed away. That's why I say this curse is a completely different kettle of fish.

'If you are a fan of Mayo, you might want to break it, but you don't want the curse to end.'

Host Nick Skewer responded by saying, 'Quite chilling, that one. To think that a Catholic priest would say that'.

IT WAS STIRRING television and the clip went viral. The story of the Mayo curse had gone international. To the outside world, it was a chilling and humorous subtext to the Mayo story. But to Mayo people, it was deadly serious and more often than not, viewed with contempt for the manner in which it was lionised.

As with any urban or in this case, rural myth, there are many variations of it. Some versions have it that it was not the priest who uttered it, but the widow of the deceased man at the alleged funeral. Other versions have it that it was a Traveller woman who set the curse on the future of Mayo football. Another says that it was a local witch. With each telling, the story gets more fantastical.

When the facts do not suit the narrative of the curse, they are moved around and there are reports that the curse was uttered as they passed a funeral as they left Dublin. In another, it was a funeral on the banks of the Shannon in Roscommon, where the Mayo team crossed the river with Sam Maguire in their hands.

It is a narrative that has followed the Mayo cause for the past few decades and was practically unheard of until the team started to lose finals with a mixture of misfortune and underperformance.

Most Mayo fans dismiss the curse, but fate has often fallen on the side of the myth-makers, not least in the drawn final of 2016 when a dominant Mayo first half performance saw them concede not one own goal (itself a rarity in gaelic football), but two. In the moments after that concession, the skies darkened over Croke Park and what had been a bright day turned dark. Even the most sceptical souls in the arena turned to one another and said, 'What's going on here?'

Journalist, Diarmaid Fleming who researched the curse for BBC News in 2016, said at that moment, as he sat beside renowned commentator Micheál Ó Muircheartaigh, that even the man who had seen everything in the GAA turned to him and said, 'There's something strange happening here'.

But it is time to put the curse to bed and to also acknowledge that talk of it defamed the heroes of 1951, whose great achievements in those years were now being reduced to an afterthought in the quest for that fourth All-Ireland.

SO, WHERE DID the Mayo curse come from? My research has indicated that it did not emanate from any perceived slight on a mourning family in the early 1950s, but instead emerged in the early 90s, having been conceived and given legs in the aftermath of the loss in the 1989 All-Ireland final, and then later in the next decade after the three finals in '96 and '97.

Amazingly, that 1989 game represented Mayo's first final appearance for 38 years, and the county's fear of finals was not an issue. In a remarkably open game, Mayo held sway and almost made it over the line, but missed opportunities and a late sucker-punch swung the game the way of Cork. Two further finals in the 90s suggested that luck was in short supply. There was grave disappointment at the way those finals turned out, with many feeling it was a golden chance to have rolled back the years. In that aftermath of disappointment, someone conceived the notion of the Mayo curse.

Much research has been done into the existence of the curse, and although 99 percent of the evidence suggests it is just a fiction, there is a still a one percent doubt.

Let us look at the evidence. Firstly, on the Monday night of the homecoming, the Mayo team did not even go to Foxford at all. The *Sligo Champion* reported that it was already dark by the time the team arrived in Ballaghaderreen, where a torch light procession met the players and guided them into the town's square. From there, the progress was slow as the team was celebrated in each town and village along the road from Ballaghaderreen to Castlebar.

The players had returned in a selection of cars, and at the junction of the Swinford and Ballina roads on the edge of town, they boarded a lorry which carried them into the town centre for the major celebration, led by the Castlebar Brass Band. They arrived there at 9.45pm and were feted by about 6,000 people who thronged into the town. Celebrations went on late into the night and into the early hours of the next day, so it was the next evening before the players were prepared for the next stage of their homecoming; the trip to Ballina. It was on this trip that they passed through Foxford after dark on the Monday night, so the idea that a funeral would be held at that hour of the night seems very fanciful.

But to that funeral…

There is no doubt that the returning Mayo team were followed wherever they went by devoted fans, yet there is not a single person who lay witness to the events, the supposed indiscretion by the team or heard the words of the priest. At the time, the priest in Foxford was Canon Thomas Curneen, a man who was held with great affection in the town – a situation that would be an unlikely scenario if he had cursed the county team at any stage during the stationing in the East Mayo town. A native of Sligo, Canon Curneen was a teacher and then president of his alma mater, St Nathy's College, Ballaghaderreen, before being appointed to Foxford. St Nathy's was a hot-bed of gaelic football in Mayo and the west – setting a curse on a Mayo team would be most out of character with his devotion to the game. He died four years after the Mayo All-Ireland victory and at the time of his passing, there was not any mention of him having uttered any curse on the county team.

In addition, the notion of a curse is a very Pagan tradition, and a step unlikely for a Catholic priest in the darkest days of early 1950s Ireland.

MAYO A BIOGRAPHY IN NINE LIVES

SO, THE FUNERAL. One man who was there said that it was impossible for the Mayo team to have come upon a funeral as it was almost midnight when they got into the town, and well dark. Even researching with the church records shows that there was not any funeral in that area on that day, or the day before, or the day after. So, there was no chance that the returning heroes would have ignored the pleas of mourners. Local journalist, Michael Gallagher did more in-depth research some years back in which he discovered that a local person had died in the area on the previous Saturday and was not buried until the following Wednesday. If the remains of this person had been in the church, and the team passed by at night, there was no way they could have known that, given that they were preoccupied with the events of the previous two days.

However jovial the response to the curse may be, in fact, it was a cruel sleight on a band of men who brought honour to the county. The media depiction of the origins of the curse also suggest that the team were boisterous and inebriated, when the reality was that almost two thirds of the team were members of the Pioneer Total Abstinence Association and so did not touch a drop.

One of these heroes, Paddy Prendergast told of the upset and sadness felt upon receiving calls nights before a final that someone wished him to be dead. He said in 2017 that the team were on the back of a truck in 1951 and that the cribs on either side were up to the top. 'I think we got on the bus in Ballaghaderreen and then we travelled through Swinford, and then to Foxford. All I recall about Foxford is that we didn't get off the truck because the sides were up and we were unable to get off the bloody truck. I remember Sean Flanagan saying a few words in Foxford. He said that there was only one thing warmer than a Foxford blanket, and that was a Foxford welcome.

'I have no idea if there was a funeral on that night in Foxford. I saw people standing near the church, but that was it. We had no idea if there was a funeral.' So too with Dr Padraig Carney. 'On the way home from that match, we all went our different ways,' he explained. 'Some of us went by train and some by cars, but there was no talk or mention of a curse at the time. I have no idea how it started, but I certainly don't believe in curses.'

THE DAUGHTER OF the Mayo player who scored the winning goal in that 1951 final was very vocal in her condemnation of the curse, saying it insulted the memory of her father and the rest of the team. Ailbhe Gilvarry from Killala is the daughter of Joe 'Joko' Gilvarry who scored one of two goals during that fateful All Ireland final against Meath. She had never heard mention of the curse until about 2004, after her father died.

'It has been a source of massive discomfort within the family. I actually get quite insulted by it. The idea that any of those men would have been disrespectful at a funeral. These were God fearing people. There was a priest on the team and my father always had a miraculous medal in his boot. In all my years growing up, I never heard a word about it until after dad died. It's annoying. I don't think it would be said if enough of the team were alive to sue them for defamation,' she added.

While she puts no stock in curses, she added that it caused hurt because it is based on an underlying untruth that is disrespectful to the team.

In reality, the only curse was one of misfortune brought on by sub-optimum performance. Mistakes were those caused by pressure, poor performances and in some cases, sheer bad luck. In hindsight, Mayo lost all those finals because in almost all cases, they were not the better team on the day; and on the occasions that they were close, failure to counteract the finer details proved costly.

The curse crumbles under cross examination. Like the one in Clare. Biddy Early was born in Faha, east Clare in 1798 to a poor farming family. A well-known clairvoyant, she was said to have cured people and animals from all over the country, including those cursed by the fairies.

She was tried for witchcraft in 1865, but witnesses were reluctant to testify against her. Biddy is reputed to have placed a curse on the Clare hurlers, which resulted in them not winning an All-Ireland for over eight decades, until the curse was lifted in 1995. All very stirring stuff, until you realise that Biddy died in 1874, 10 years before the GAA was even founded and 40 years before Clare won their first All-Ireland in 1914. She must have been a remarkable woman to condemn Clare from ever winning something that did not even exist when she was alive.

When Clare's 81-year All-Ireland famine ended in 1995, it was seen to have put paid to Biddy Early's curse. That she happened to come from Feakle, the homeplace of Ger Loughnane, added some interest to the notion of this nefarious old biddy casting her spell on the tormented and greatly afflicted stickmen of Clare. It was fiction. But many Clare followers assumed she had some axe to grind.

Like Mayo, they endured so much heartbreak and soul-destroying loss that it was tempting to believe some malevolent force was at work.

FORMER OASIS SINGER, and Man City fan, Liam Gallagher, whose mother Peggy hails from outside Charlestown and who spent many of his childhood summers with his brother, Noel in Mayo, is very forthright about it

'I've heard about it. I don't believe in all that b****cks. Listen it is what it is, mate, if you get beat by the better team, you get beat by the better team. It's one of them f***ing things, isn't it? It'll happen one day, mate.

'City were shit for years and look at us now,' he said.

FOR ANYONE WHO dismisses the actual evidence of there being *no evidence* the curse existed, there was broad agreement that only a Pope could overrule an alleged curse set by a parish priest. No doubt bishops had been implored and had batted away requests. Pope John Paul had come to Ireland in 1979, had celebrated Mass in Galway and prayed in Knock. The visit had come at the end of a decade when Mayo had not once made it out of Connacht and they got well beaten the next year. On the other hand, the 1979 visit did Galway the world of good because the following year, they won their first All-Ireland hurling title since 1923. So, what about Mayo?

In 2018 when Pope Francis announced that he would be visiting the country, there were hopes in Mayo that the long-time sports fan would make some gesture towards wishing the county well in the saga of their hunt for glory. Remember, if Mayo were not to win an All-Ireland in his papacy, the affable Argentinean would become the seventh successive Pope to have presided over this barren territory.

However, it took a Sligo woman to come up with the most recent attempt to exorcise the mí-adh that had befallen Mayo. Audrey Elliott told me of her plan to try to bring solace to her Mayo work colleagues at Ireland West Airport by getting Pope Francis to make some welcome gesture to Mayo football. At the time, Audrey worked in Ireland West Airport in the Marketing Department. Part of her job was managing social media, especially Facebook and Instagram.

'I was always trying to increase engagement on the channels and looking for new ways to gain followers. We had many celebrities pass through the airport and I was always eager to get a picture of them for social media. If I got wind of a celebrity in the airport, I would grab my phone or camera and run down to get them before they departed. I met many celebrities, and most times coaxed them into getting a picture… and getting a picture with me. Celebrities included Tom Jones, Sarah Jessica Parker, Ruby Wax, Alex Ferguson, Sergio Garcia, Jamie Dornan, Michael Flatley, Liam Gallagher, and Emily Blunt and many more. All of this helped create the narrative of the success of the airport as a venue of choice for discerning travellers.

'However, when it was football season, I would grab a t-shirt that we had hanging around that said, 'Keep calm – Mayo for Sam' on it. So instead of just taking a photo, I would ask or cajole them into holding the t-shirt. When she heard the Pope was coming, she came up with the idea.

'It wasn't until a few days before his arrival that I got the idea of doing something, but never thought I would be able to pull it off. As a Sligowoman, I didn't personally own any Mayo merchandise, so I went down to Linda in our Shop West Departures shop and told her of my idea and said that I needed to borrow a real Mayo jersey.

'I remember telling her the plan I had but not to say it to anyone. I really didn't want to raise expectations and I wasn't sure if security would allow me to take a 'top' in with me.' When the big day arrived, Audrey's role was to take pictures and videos for the airport social media channels. 'This meant I could get close as I had an 'access all areas' badge and hi-vis. However, as I didn't want to attract attention with a green and red jersey in my hand, I bundled it inside my hi-vis jacket. I was nervous… but I knew I had to seize the opportunity at the right time.'

This right time occurred just before the Pope's return to the aircraft after saying Mass in Knock, and after all the official greetings. It was his final goodbye, and it was wet and overcast. Audrey was hidden with her hood up, under a sea of umbrellas.

'Pope Francis was surrounded by a sea of people but still shaking hands as he approached the aircraft steps. It was now or never. I pulled out the jersey a few seconds before I approached him (this was also calculated as I didn't want anyone thinking I was pulling out something from under my jacket right beside him).

'So those few seconds as I approached him, I had the jersey in my hand and a marker at the ready. I then signalled to him and asked him to sign the jersey. He smiled at me, and took the marker from my hand and, without saying anything, motioned to me to hold and stretch the jersey so he could write on it more easily.

'Obviously, as a soccer-mad Argentinean living in Italy, he was well used to signing jerseys. I knew at this time, it was going to be a success and he was going to write on it. I didn't know what he was going to write… but he simply wrote… 'Francis'.

'As he was doing this, I pulled down my hood from my head and only then spotted all the attention and the cameras around me. I was so delighted… I thanked him, bundled the jersey back up inside my jacket and slid away back to the airport hangar.

'I would say most of the people all around did not know what was happening, as I was covered by umbrellas during the signing and not very visible. When I was back in the hanger on my own, I was wondering if anyone knew what I had done. Then slowly but surely, word was getting out. My phone started hopping and I was asked to pose for pics with the jersey in the hanger by various media personnel. They were all asking to look at the jersey and take pictures, but I was so worried someone would take it. I just wanted to get it back safely to my office and finish for the day.

'One text I got was from Linda in the shop, saying she had seen me on TV and what had happened the Mayo jersey I had borrowed? I was like OMG, What! I didn't realise that it was live and that it was all caught on TV, even though I had seen the cameras.

'I won't lie, our security officer did have a word with me; in fairness, I hadn't really breached any security, but I probably should not have approached the Pope like that. It was too late; I had done it and was prepared for any consequences. However, the reaction was way more than she expected.

'My phone did not stop. I finally got home and watched the video on my feed and the comments. I was getting a lot of praise, but I was expecting getting negative feedback too. This will always be the case and I know this working in marketing, that no-one will ever be totally happy. If you give it, you got to get it.

'Even years later, when Mayo are doing well, I still get calls asking me my reaction to the match and about the curse. One radio station introduces me live on air about being Mayo's No 1 fan — and sure, I go along with it,' she laughs.

The jersey signed by the Pope now occupies pride of place on a wall at Ireland

West Airport, but whatever of its provenance, it was unable to save Mayo from another final defeat when they fell to Dublin in 2020 and Tyrone in 2021, or when they were knocked out of the championship in succeeding years by Kerry and Dublin again, each of whom went on to the win the title.

PERHAPS THE REAL curse on this Mayo team is being alive in the same time as perhaps the greatest team to play the game, the all-conquering Dubs and also to be the next best team to their Connacht rivals Galway during the 1960s. Any other losses can be explained by sub-optimum performances and bad luck. Most of us regard good luck as our right, and bad luck as a betrayal of that right.

Perhaps, the only good luck many great men ever had, was being born with the ability and determination to overcome bad luck.